'Incredible . . . beautifully put together, with a wide array of photos, this unique book takes us right inside Davis's creative mindset. One of the most inspirational volumes on music' *The Times*

'The bestselling, most influential jazz record ever, put under the microscope in a beautifully written volume' *Observer*

'Creating a book around a collection of just five instrumental tracks takes great skill, but to his credit Ashley Kahn has achieved this with great insight and an ability to explore the music rather than just deliver an academic thesis' *Uncut Magazine*

'Essential reading for anyone even vaguely interested in jazz' *Jazz Rag*

'Beautifully produced. Kahn's great contribution is to provide the background to the album, carefully recreating the atmosphere inside the abandoned Greek Orthodox Church in New York's East 30th Street where it was recorded' *Independent on Sunday*

'An erudite but accessible study . . . the best compliment you could give any music book is that it fires you to hear more of the subject and this is certainly true with Ashley Kahn's writing' *The List*

Ashley Kahn   Foreword by Jimmy Cobb

Kind of Blue

Granta Books

London

Granta Publications, 2/3 Hanover Yard, London N1 8BE

First published in Great Britain by Granta Books 2001
This edition published by Granta Books 2002
First published in the US by Da Capo Press, a member of the Perseus Books Group
2000

A CIP catalogue record for this book is available from the British Library.

1 3 5 7 9 10 8 6 4 2

Printed and bound in Great Britain

WHEN ASHLEY KAHN asked me to write a foreword for the book he was writing on *Kind of Blue* I was surprised and flattered. Not being a writer, just being a musician, I wondered what I could say. But reading this book has reminded me of how I felt on that spring day in March of 1959. I remember getting up in the morning—kind of excited, because I knew I had a record date with Miles Davis—putting on my clothes and getting my instrument together. I went to Columbia's 30th Street Studio, took my drums inside and set them up, and waited for the guys to trickle in and see what we were going to do. I always liked that big church because it had such a beautiful sound. We started looking through some of the tunes and then, when we got into it, it started to be really beautiful and smooth sounding. I mean no effort— there was no tension—it was just relaxed. The band always sounded good! How could it sound bad? All of those beautiful musicians there: you've got Bill Evans, piano player, Wynton Kelly, piano player, you've got Paul Chambers, the greatest young bass player at that time, and John Coltrane and Cannonball Adderley.

As I listened to these guys on the playbacks of the tracks, I started thinking about how well they played, and the origin of their sound, technique, and ideas. When I think of Bill, I think of a guy whose mother made him practice all his life, went to a few music schools and conservatories, played a lot of classical music, but he never found his own style until he got out on his own. Wynton, he loved Erroll Garner for the way he played, felt things, and the way he could swing (sometimes Garner could sound like two players). Wynton

Foreword by Jimmy Cobb

got his spirit and flavor from his West Indian background. Paul, I know, came from the school of Jimmy Blanton and Oscar Pettiford—I could hear them in Paul's playing. Cannonball, I know for sure, came from Benny Carter, Charlie Parker, maybe a little Earl Bostic in there too for technique and Johnny Hodges for tone. Coltrane came from Don Byas, Coleman Hawkins, Lester Young, and in the later part of his development Sonny Rollins—and he learned something from Earl Bostic too. Miles came from . . . well, all trumpet players come from Louis Armstrong. He always wanted to play like Dizzy. He listened to Howard McGhee and Harry "Sweets" Edison sometimes too. Miles lived with Clark Terry; I'm sure he learned a lot there, and he always revered Clark throughout his life. I was brought up listening to Billy Eckstein's band with Art Blakey; I also heard Gene Krupa, Buddy Rich, Shadow Wilson, Max Roach and Philly Joe Jones. To improvise as well as they did, these guys had to have learned a lot from the jazz giants. You get to hear the spirit of all of those players in the recording of *Kind of Blue*.

Kind of Blue was also a different kind of music from what Miles had been playing. He was going into a "modal" thing. I think the whole jazz music business looked to Miles Davis's innovations to see what direction jazz music was headed. *The Birth of the Cool* was the first major change since Parker and Gillespie. It started the music in another direction—in my opinion, a musical direction related to music that Gil Evans orchestrated for Claude Thornhill's band in the forties. The instrumentation on *The Birth of the Cool* was directly connected to that sound, as was, ultimately, *Kind of Blue,* and the great collaborations to follow between Gil Evans and Miles Davis.

In no way, shape or form could we think that *Kind of Blue* could get to be what it got to be: one of the most famous jazz albums in the history of this music. That's hard to believe . . . and it's even harder to believe that I'm the only one still here to talk about it. I wish some of the other guys were here to make their comments about it—but—they're not, so it's left to me. Viva Miles Davis! Viva *Kind of Blue*! I'm very proud to be a part of it.

Jimmy Cobb (as told to Eleana Tee)
July 3, 2000

Acknowledgments

THE JOURNEY OF book-writing can be long and lonely. This particular ride was shorter, smoother and much more enjoyable thanks to the subject of Miles and his music, and to the passion and guidance of many people involved with the book. Andrea Schulz, my editor at Da Capo Press, proved the driving wheel on this project and embraced this undertaking from the very outset, lending a clear, navigational eye and unflagging support. Fletcher Roberts of the *New York Times*, Dave Dunton of Harvey Klinger Associates, Peter Shukat of Miles Davis Properties and Jeff Jones of Sony Legacy helped get the wheels turning at the start, while Seth Rothstein, Randy Haecker, Tom Cording, John Jackson, Adam Block and Steve Berkowitz (the Sony Legacy All-stars) kept the diesels humming, providing valuable contacts and access. Throughout the trip, Jimmy Cobb, George Avakian, Bob Belden, Orrin Keepnews, Nat Hentoff, Lewis Porter, Howard Mandel and Frank Laico (a rare, modest soul in an ego-driven industry) all provided necessary details and direction, with positive spirit and encouragement. Deadlines could not have been met without my own research, transcription and editing team: Aaron Prado (a budding jazz musician in his own right), Susan Neeley, Andrew Caploe, Mitch Goldman, Debby Patz Clarke and Martin Johnson.

For taking the time to speak at length on a much-discussed topic while generously sharing their first-hand memories and unjaded energy (after so many years in studios and on stages), I salute: Herbie Hancock, Quincy Jones, Joe Zawinul, Jimmy Heath, George Russell, David Amram, John Lewis, Gary Burton and Dick Katz.

For the privilege of hearing a masterpiece in the making, gratitude is due Sony Music Studios' engineers of excellence: Mark Kirkeby, Mark Wilder, Matt Kelly and Matt Cavaluzo. For providing valuable historical insights too numerous to mention, I stand indebted to that troika of jazz archivists: Dan Morgenstern at the Institute of Jazz Studies, Michael Cuscuna at Mosaic Records, and my old cohort from WKCR, Phil Schaap. And for sharing their respective journalistic perspective, I thank: Quincy Troupe, Bob Blumenthal, Stanley Crouch, Gene Lees, Jack Tracy and Barry Ulanov.

Making this book look as good as it does was a labor of love made infinitely less laborious by the supportive efforts of a number of professionals: Eric and David at Eric Baker Design Associates; veteran photographers Don Hunstein, Beuford Smith, Jack Vartoogian, Chuck Stewart and Lee Tanner; Loanne Rios Kong, Nat Brewster, Liz Reilly and Howard Fritzson at Sony Music; Valentina Morales and Michael Roberson at Sony Music Business Affairs; my brother-with-the-scanner, Peter Kahn; Frank Driggs; Judy Bell at the Richmond Organization; Miles Evans; Fred and Mike at the Jazz Record Center; George Boziwick, head of the American Music Collection at the New York Public Library; and Suzanne Eggleston at Yale University's Irving S. Gilmore Music Library.

Speaking of libraries: a sincere doff of the researcher's brim to the entire crew at Rutgers University's Institute of Jazz Studies, including Ed Berger, Don Luck and Esther Smith. The Institute is a singular and estimable resource deserving all the recognition it receives and more. Equally important and valuable is New York Public Library's Schomburg Center for Research in Black Culture; much thanks to the Schomburg's assistant director James Briggs Murray for his personal and professional support.

Other individuals who assisted beyond the call of their respective duties: Michael Buening at the Museum of Television and Radio; Terry Hinte and Tara Lochen at Fantasy Records; Bruce Lundvall and Cem Kurosman at Blue Note Records; John McCarthy at the Author's Guild; Cathy Williams at Rhino Entertainment; Chris Wheat at Verve Records; Holly George-Warren at Rolling Stone Press; Jane Snyder, Jennifer Charat and Amy Warner at Da Capo Press; and finally, a good attorney and great friend, George Gilbert, Esq.

Finally, I wish to dedicate this effort to the one man who truly made this book possible, whose life and legacy continue to resonate, inspire, and . . . breathe: Miles Davis.

Introduction

ON A DECEMBER MORNING in 1999, millennium mania and snowflakes swirled about me as I entered a squat, near-windowless building on Tenth Avenue. The awning outside read "Sony Music Studios." Inside, down a dimly lit corridor lined with posters of rock and rap artists, thick doors with porthole windows led into fully furnished studios, where large consoles with matrices of red and white lights stood next to racks full of the latest sound equipment. People lost in concentration scurried past me.

The few times I had visited the place before, I had felt the same way: This hi-tech beehive, a monument to Sony's global technological superiority, seemed somehow transitory. I felt that a careless flip of a switch could plunge the entire place into darkness. Maybe it was the signs of constant renovations—plastic sheeting covering doorways—that created the feeling of impermanence, or perhaps it was the rotation of posters from one visit to the next. It didn't surprise me to learn that Sony Music had built their recording center in the remains of the old Twentieth Century–Fox Movietone repository. Where dusty film canisters had once stored a week-by-week chronicle of the world's troubles and triumphs, four stories of state-of-the art studios now operated: new technology rising phoenix-like from the vestiges of old.

Four months earlier, for *The New York Times*, I had written an appreciation of Miles Davis's melancholy masterpiece *Kind of Blue* on the fortieth anniversary of its release. Now I had been granted a rare opportunity to hear the complete master tapes of the two sessions that produced the album. Sony Music—the parent company of Columbia Records, which released *Kind of Blue* and remained Miles's record label for the majority of his career— did not often send to their subterranean archives in upstate New York and allow the reel-to-reel tapes to be auditioned. When dealing with priceless and irreplaceable forty-year-old recordings, even the wear on the tape is a consideration. For a jazz fan like me, the occasion had the rarified, historic air of, say, the unearthing of an Egyptian tomb.

The receptionist directed me to room 305. Equipment dedicated to sound reproduction, including a turntable in a stone base with a speed lever reading "78 rpm," filled the room. Sitting amid the machines, scattered tape reels, vinyl records of varying formats, and general clutter was an engineer trained in audio formats new, old and ancient. In this room, I was convinced, whatever means of capturing audio information have ever existed—wax cylinders to the latest computer-driven, digital discs—all came back to life.

Delicately, the engineer placed a reel of reddish-brown, half-inch ribbon onto a tape machine, manufactured expressly to play back archival three-track tapes. He paused, asked if I was ready. (Ready? I had been giddy with anticipation for weeks.) He hit the "play" button.

The tape threaded its way across the playback heads and I heard the voices of Miles Davis and his producer, Irving Townsend, the instantly recognizable sound of Miles's trumpet, John Coltrane's tenor, Cannonball Adderley's alto and the other musicians. I listened to their harmonized riffs start and stop and grew acclimated to the rhythm of the recording process. A few engineers who had heard that the masters were being played that day dropped by and quietly pulled up chairs or stood in the corner to listen.

What could I hear or intuit that would reveal the secret of that spring day when Davis assembled his famed sextet (Coltrane, Adderley, Bill Evans, Paul Chambers and Jimmy Cobb with pianist Wynton Kelly taking over from Evans on one number) in a converted church in downtown Manhattan? I was flooded with questions, hungry for details. How did this band talk while creating music for the ages? Was that Coltrane's voice or Adderley's? How— if at all—did they prepare? What was Miles like in the studio? Why did that take end? I had learned that the three master reels, the few rolls of black-and-white film, and the less-than-distinct memories of the drummer, a photographer, and a tape operator who were in the East Thirtieth Street studio on that day back in 1959 were about all the evidence there was of the making of the album. The dearth of related material only heightened the album's mystique and intensified my desire to uncover anything that might throw light on what seemed such a shadowy, skeletal moment.

As the first full take of "Freddie Freeloader" began playing, I put down my pen and focused on the music. By the time Coltrane began soloing, I was transported to an austere twilight world that requested silence and contemplation. I was familiar with the album from years of dedicated listening but the music's seductive spell had not lessened—it still held the power to quiet all around it.

Still acknowledged as the height of hip four decades after it was recorded, *Kind of Blue* is the premier album of its era, jazz or otherwise. Its vapory piano-and-bass introduction is universally recognized. Classical buffs and rage rockers alike praise its subtlety, simplicity and emotional depth. Copies of the album are passed to friends and given to lovers. The album has sold millions of copies around the world, making it the best-selling recording in Miles Davis's catalog and the best-selling classic jazz album ever. Significantly, a large number of those copies were purchased in the past five years, and undoubtedly not just by old-timers replacing worn vinyl: *Kind of Blue* is self-perpetuating, continuing to cast its spell on a younger audience more accustomed to the loud-and-fast esthetic of rock and rap.

The album's appeal was certainly enhanced by Miles's personal mystique. Cool, well-dressed, endlessly inspired, and uncompromising in art and life,

Davis was and still is a hero to jazz fans, African Americans and an international musical community. "Miles Davis is my definition of cool," Bob Dylan has said. "I loved to see him in the small clubs playing his solo, turn his back on the crowd, put down his horn and walk off the stage, let the band keep playing, and then come back and play a few notes at the end."

Since his death in 1991, Davis's legend has only grown larger. But even before his passing, *Kind of Blue* was the recording that a vast majority called his defining masterwork. If someone has only one Miles album—or even only one jazz recording—more often than not, *Kind of Blue* is it. Even twenty-five years ago, as jazz guitarist John Scofield relates, the album had already become as common as a cup of sugar:

> I remember at Berklee School [of Music in Boston] in the early seventies, hanging out at this bass player's apartment and they didn't have *Kind of Blue*. So at two in the morning he said he'd just go to the neighbor's and ask for their copy, not knowing the people, assuming that they'd have it! And they did. It was like *Sergeant Pepper*.

In the church of jazz, *Kind of Blue* is one of the holy relics. Critics revere it as a stylistic milestone, one of a very few in the long tradition of jazz performance, on equal footing with seminal recordings by Louis Armstrong's Hot Fives and Charlie Parker's bebop quintets. Musicians acknowledge its influence and have recorded hundreds of versions of the music on the album. Record producer, composer, and Davis confidant Quincy Jones hails it as the one album (if that were the limit) that would explain jazz.

Yet, *Kind of Blue* lives and prospers outside the confines of the jazz community. No longer the exclusive possession of a musical subculture, the album is simply great music, one of a very, very few musical recordings our culture allows into the category marked "masterpiece." Many of its admirers are forced to reach back before the modern era to find its measure. Drummer Elvin Jones hears the same timeless sublimity and depth of feeling "in some of the movements of Beethoven's *Ninth Symphony*, or when I hear Pablo Casals play unaccompanied cello." "It's like listening to *Tosca*," says pianist/singer Shirley Horn. "You know, you always cry, or at least I do."

In the fin-de-siecle frenzy, *Kind of Blue* proved its evergreen appeal, becoming a fixture in the first tier of countless "Best of the Century" surveys and "Top 100" polls. Hollywood film in the nineties employed the album as an instant signifier of hip. *In the Line of Fire* shows secret serviceman Clint Eastwood, the cool loner at home, listening to "All Blues." In *Pleasantville*, a group of fifties high-schoolers are intellectually awakened to the tune of "So What." In *Runaway Bride*, Julia Roberts's character bestows an original vinyl copy of *Kind of Blue* on Richard Gere.

As I began the research for this book, Sony Music was in the midst of producing high-quality repackagings of Miles's recordings and of jazz in general, a fortunate change from the offhand reissue strategy of previous decades. They graciously provided me complete access to all information, photographs and recordings in their archives, and facilitated contact with former employees. I located session and tape logs that disclosed the identity of the recording staff who worked on *Kind of Blue*, most of whom—like the members of the sextet save for drummer Jimmy Cobb—are no longer with us. My conversations with Columbia engineers of that era painted a picture of what it was like to work in the 30th Street Studio, the former church where the album was born. Sifting through company files, I glimpsed the inner workings of the marketing and promotion departments which first brought *Kind of Blue* to market.

To bring the reader as near as possible to the actual creation of the album, I have placed the transcription and discussion of the record sessions at the heart of the book. The unedited studio dialogue, false starts and break-downs—herein reproduced for the first time—offer a rare glimpse of the inner workings of those two days in the studio. The transcribed chatter alone, revealing Cannonball Adderley's irrepressible sense of humor and Miles's constant ribbing of his producer, will delight those who love the music that occasioned it.

I stumbled on a number of surprises in my research. There were Bill Evans's original liner notes, neatly handwritten and hardly edited. Engineer Fred Plaut's photographs, never published before now, showing the sheet music for a tune's modal infrastructure. Proof that the famously dark and intense cover shot of Miles was taken during a live performance at the Apollo Theater. Never-before-published radio conversations with Adderley and Evans in which they spoke of Miles and the album in detail, conveying a personal dimension lacking from previously published interviews.

Beyond the new information my research yielded about *Kind of Blue*, I was equally drawn by the more mystical aspects of the album. The legend of its pure, one-take creation. The alchemic blending of classical and folk music influences. The interplay of Miles's less-is-more philosophy with the styles of the equally spare Bill Evans and his other, more voluble sidemen. The drama of Davis driven by an endless search for new styles creating a masterwork, then leaving it behind for his next endeavor. I was challenged to examine what is true in the mythology of the recording. Was the album really impromptu and unplanned? Did Miles really compose all the music? Did it change the jazz terrain forever, and if so, how?

To do the album justice, I needed to transport myself back to the place and time that brought it forth. I spoke with as many musicians, producers, and critics as possible—those who were involved in making the album, were influenced by the music, or who analyzed its effects. Eventually I conducted more than fifty interviews for this book, including talks with veteran jazzmen who knew or worked with Miles, newer arrivals who grew up with his music, producers, music industry executives, deejays, writers, and witnesses of the jazz scene of the 1950s. Priority was given to the people still alive who were present at the two *Kind of Blue* recording sessions: drummer Jimmy Cobb, photographer Don Hunstein, and tape operator Bob Waller. I found that though a few musicians and producers were reluctant to speak, burned out on the subject of Miles or simply burned by the trumpeter in uncomplimentary portrayals in interviews or in his autobiography, many were eager to share their memories and insights. I gave special attention to those who worked with Miles in and around 1959, or soon after: Jimmy Heath, Dave Brubeck, George Russell, John Lewis, Joe Zawinul and Herbie Hancock; producers George Avakian and Teo Macero; and engineer Frank Laico.

Some saw *Kind of Blue* as the sound of 1950s New York; some as a high point in Miles's career trajectory; others as one more successful product of a record label at the height of its dominance. As the anecdotes coalesced, the structure for the book that suggested itself was a reverse telescopic path—beginning with Miles's arrival in New York, then following his career course before closing in, take-by-take, on the album's two recording sessions. From there, the book moves outward again to trace the album's influence. Sidebars add further context: Columbia Records' rise to prominence and its role in the success of *Kind of Blue*; the unique acoustical properties that made music recorded at the 30th Street Studio distinctive; the eponymous Freddie Freeloader.

When I spoke of writing this celebration of *Kind of Blue*, whether to music professionals or to fans, reaction was uniformly positive: "You know, that's a good idea"; "Let's hear more about that album"; "It's about time." Then after a pause, with little or no solicitation, a testimonial would follow.

QUINCY JONES: "That will always be my music, man.
I play *Kind of Blue* every day—it's my orange juice.
It still sounds like it was made yesterday."

CHICK COREA: "It's one thing to just play a tune, or play a program of music, but it's another thing to practically create a new language of music, which is what *Kind of Blue* did."

GEORGE RUSSELL: "*Kind of Blue* is just one of those amazing
albums that emerged from that period of time. Miles's solo
on 'So What' is one of the most beautiful solos ever."

With the clarity of memory usually reserved for national disasters, personal traumas, or first romantic encounters, many I interviewed recalled their first hearing of *Kind of Blue*. Some encountered the music when it first appeared in 1959: on a late-night radio station in Cleveland; in a Wisconsin furniture store selling records; live in a New York nightclub or at an outdoor festival in Toronto; on a jukebox in a Harlem watering hole. Others came across it in the sixties: among the mono LPs a friendly salesclerk with a flowered tie was selling off at a dollar a disc; playing at a late-night party down in Greenwich Village. One acquaintance admitted hearing *Kind of Blue* in a college class on Zen.

Kind of Blue's aphrodisiac properties were mentioned frequently in reminiscences of listeners male and female, young and not-so-young. Jazz veteran Ben Sidran recalls that "clearly it was just a great seduction record. I can close my eyes and remember situations with long forgotten girls." Anthony Kiedis of the Red Hot Chili Peppers, when asked for his favorite make-out music, answered, "For slow action, I put on *Kind of Blue*." Because of "the trance-like atmosphere that it created, it's like sexual wallpaper. It was sort of the Barry White of its time," remembers Steely Dan's Donald Fagen. Essayist/playwright Pearl Cleage was turned on to the album in the late seventies: "I will confess that I spent many memorable evenings sending messages of great personal passion through the intricate improvisations of *Kind of Blue* when blue was the furthest thing from my mind. . . ."

My own discovery of the music came in the mid-seventies, when a high-school buddy yanked a dogeared album out of my father's record collection and explained: "This is a classic." Between the scratches and pops (Dad must play this one a lot, I recall thinking) a stark, moody world unveiled itself. Though the sound was far simpler and sadder than any of the peppy, big band music I then thought of as jazz, it was somehow immediately familiar.

If you are already a fan of the album, perhaps a "first time" story of your own comes to mind. Or ask the friend who turned you on to *Kind of Blue*. Bring that memory with you to the world we're about to enter. Use this book as a primer, a listening guide, a way to understand that there is even more to these forty minutes of great jazz performance than meets the ear. Allow this book to show you that occasionally that which is the least outspoken has the most to say.

COLUMBIA
MILES DAVIS
Kind of Blue
with Julian "Cannonball" Adderly
Paul Chambers
James Cobb
John Coltrane
Bill Evans
Wynton Kelly

Birth of

the Tone:

Miles 1949–1955

I prefer a round sound with no attitude in it, like a round voice with not too much tremolo and not too much bass. Just right in the middle. If I can't get that sound I can't play anything. Those old trumpet players used to tell me "Little Davis! Play with a straight tone."
— Miles Davis, 1989

SOME CONTEND THAT they can hear *Kind of Blue* in a solo Miles recorded fifteen years earlier on "Now's the Time," a Charlie Parker 78 from 1946. It is indeed possible in those mere forty-five seconds to discern the kernel of the trumpeter's mature, late fifties sound: the nineteen-year-old trumpeter solos with halting, economical phrasing free of flourish or embellishment, staying close to a blues scale as he invents a lyrical line. Most noticeable is his tone. In his other recordings of that era, Davis strains to copy the brash intensity of contemporaries like Dizzy Gillespie, Howard McGhee and Fats Navarro. But in a sign of things to come Davis delivers a firm sound, clearly stated, remaining within the trumpet's middle range.

Barely out of his teens, Miles blows alongside jazz giant Charlie Parker in 1948 at the Three Deuces nightclub, 52nd Street, New York City

An examination of Miles's work reveals a musical visionary balancing personal limitations with an expansive, intrepid spirit. Miles could not launch into the virtuosic, high-register fury of a Dizzy Gillespie, but he could plumb the emotional depths of a melody with economy and intensity. He was an autodidact and could not call on a background of formal musical theory or extensive conservatory training like that of jazz composer George Russell and pianist Bill Evans, but he learned from them and from many others. He lacked the compositional talent of Duke Ellington, but he knew how to assemble a great band, how to play one outstanding sideman off another. (And he had Gil Evans.) While others opted for the security and comfort of playing the same old same old Davis plowed ahead, cocksure that inspiration, value and musical discovery lay somewhere ahead.

Miles opens his autobiography with his earliest memory: concentrating on a steady, blue gas flame and experiencing fear for the first time. The feeling evoked in him was not flight, but "almost like an invitation, a challenge to go forward into something I knew nothing about." Long after the recording of *Kind of Blue*, Bill Evans would express the inspiration he found in that same tenacious, fear-defying spirit:

> Miles is . . . more or less a late arriver. You could hear him building his abilities from the beginning, very consciously, very aware of every note he played, theoretically, motifically and everything. I know Miles has spoken about how he didn't have the kind of facility that a lot of other trumpet players had for fast tempos and all this stuff and Bird would tell him, "Just get out there and do it!" There are always a lot of early-arrivers who have great facility. [Miles] had to go through a longer, laborious, digging, analytical process, finally arriving at something which is far more precious.

Miles Davis was the second son of a well-to-do dentist in East St. Louis. He was seduced by jazz at an early age:

> I was in the sixth grade and before we went to school there was a program on the radio called "Harlem Rhythm" and I listened to it for fifteen minutes—that's all it was. So I said, "I want to play music like that."

Duke Ellington, Jimmie Lunceford, Count Basie and other swing-era luminaries led the big bands that caught the ear of the precocious youngster, who soon started playing on a surprise gift from his uncle: a used trumpet. Several years later, music lessons at his high school provided him enough training and confidence to call a local bandleader needing a trumpet player. By fifteen, Miles was holding down the third-trumpet position in Eddie Randle's Rhumboogie Orchestra.

Miles discovered that his hometown had a vibrant and fertile jazz scene— "St. Louis then was like a conservatory," he recalled—filled with talented musicians like trumpeter Clark Terry, under whose spell Miles fell. His trumpet playing improved as fellow musicians taught him the value of a vibrato-less tone and stressed the need for sight-reading.

But when, in 1944, a big band led by vocalist Billy Eckstine and featuring alto saxophonist Charlie Parker and trumpeter Dizzy Gillespie hit town, Miles was awestruck. The sounds he heard from Bird and Diz were the earliest rumblings of the bebop revolution—intense, unbridled solos rife with harmonic invention. Miles's future was sealed. Before the year was out he headed for New York City, ostensibly to get a musical education at Juilliard. But when he arrived, he made a beeline for the bebop scene on 52nd Street and uptown in Harlem; that world had been his destination from the start. "I spent my first week in New York looking for Bird and Dizzy," Davis recalled.

The brashness was typical of Miles. He forged the shield of a tough, outer persona to pursue the extremely public and financially insecure profession of a musician. "Miles talks rough—you hear him use all kinds of rough words," Dizzy Gillespie told jazz historian Dan Morgenstern years after meeting Davis. "[But] his music reflects his true character . . . Miles is shy. He is super-shy. A lot of people don't believe that, but I have known him for a long, long time." Miles maintained the front throughout his life. Quincy Jones recalls, "He had that little cold exterior, you know. But he was the sweetest dude in the world."

Another trait that came to identify Davis, even in these early years, was his contradictory nature. In conversation—at times, in the same conversation—he might emphatically argue two entirely opposite viewpoints. Davis's autobiography provides a characteristic example from his first few months in New York. He had located his bebop heroes and begun to perform with them regularly. At the start of his second year at Juilliard he had also decided to drop out, complaining of the school's limited, classical approach to music education: "The shit they was talking about was too white for me." Yet, Miles thought less of his idols for ignoring the same music.

> I couldn't believe that all them guys like Bird, Prez [Lester Young], Bean [Coleman Hawkins], all them cats wouldn't go to museums or libraries and borrow those musical scores so they could check out what was happening. I would go to the library and borrow scores by all those great composers, like Stravinsky, Alban Berg, Prokofiev.

Miles arrived in New York with one other distinctive attribute: a truly cosmopolitan sense of art and style. In his music, his attire, his women, and his automobiles, "his taste was just world-class, innate," remembers Quincy Jones. "The way he carried himself—he had a thing going on," McCoy Tyner recalls. Early photos reveal a well-attired, smartly posed Miles, serious and a little self-conscious but confident.

He may have been on his own at first as he combed through classical music scores, but Miles was not alone for long. He soon had company in the person of a young drummer-turned-composer who arrived in 1945 from Cincinnati, George Russell. They met that year and shared a passion for modern European music: "Composers Alban Berg, Bela Bartok, Igor Stravinsky and Stefan Wolpe are just a few . . . who shaped my thinking," Russell recalled. Russell would eventually influence Davis's musical approach through a theory of musical scales and modes he would title the *Lydian Chromatic Concept of Tonal Organization* when it was published in book form in 1953. It was an approach that sought freedom of musical expression through a deep understanding of scales and their interrelationships. Russell's own compositions were among the first, noteworthy steps toward "modal jazz."

Russell began writing his *Chromatic Concept* during a year-and-a-half-long convalescence from tuberculosis. He recuperated first with Max Roach, then later roomed with Gillespie Big Band pianist (and future leader of the Modern Jazz Quartet) John Lewis. Lewis had been a neighbor of Davis's. "We were very close friends when he first came to New York, we lived close by to each other," Lewis recalled. "Then George and I were roommates together and then all of us got busy."

Like Russell and Davis, Lewis was a devotee of classical music, though it would be a few years before he would seek to fuse jazz and classical influences in what he and French horn player Gunther Schuller termed the "Third Stream." But during the 1940s, Davis, Lewis and Russell were still the students, woodshedding, crossing paths and sharing influences, performing and working with their chosen instructors, soaking up a wide range of sounds.

Meanwhile, Davis's career was taking off. He went from new kid sitting in with the giants to trusted bandmember touring and recording with Bird, sharing the spotlight and reaping the honors it brought. But his personal sound was still imitative of his bebop fathers. Lacking the technical prowess of soloists like trumpeter Fats Navarro, Miles kept up as best he could but his recorded performances from that period reveal a sometimes wavering, still developing tone.

Miles constantly questioned his ability. "It was so bad I thought I'll go study dentistry," he recalled. Onstage, he would often be so intimidated that he would half-seriously inform Max Roach that his next solo would not last long:

> I wanted to quit every night because Bird would leave me on stage. So Max would get done with his solo and I'd say "Give me one bar and two beats"... but Bird would make you play—I mean you would have to play or else die up there. Every night I'd be saying "Goddam!"

Years later, Miles would relate to composer David Amram some advice from Parker that helped him through the worst moments. Amram recalls:

> He said, "Bird told me, when I was real young, and just getting out of Juilliard, that if you play something that seems to be wrong, play it again, then play the same thing a third time. Then Bird gave a great smile and said, 'Then they'll think that you meant it.'"

Parker's sink-or-swim strategy meshed well with Miles's philosophy of fear-as-challenge. Amram adds:

> Miles was quoted later on as saying, "There are no wrong notes in jazz." What he obviously meant was that you could take one particular thing that might sound incorrect or jarring, and build something beautiful. He felt that that was a way of improvising: to get out of what seems to be a terrible situation was a challenge. "To me, it's all like a high-wire act," he said and moved his arms like a bird, just for a minute.

If Miles was on a tightrope, at least he had the advantage of a cheering crowd below. But the glory wasn't only because Parker's band and bebop in general had a devoted following. In 1947, Davis tied with Gillespie as top trumpeter in *Down Beat*'s critics' poll. Night after night of pushing himself, and he began proving himself in the studio as well. Drummer Roy Porter recalls a moment from Bird's historic 1946 recording of Gillespie's "Night in Tunisia":

Now on that break that Bird made, man, it was so hard for us to count it because we weren't used to listening and everybody wasn't coming in right. So Miles said "I tell you what, I'll go over here by the piano, I'll put my finger in my ear and on the first beat of the seventeenth bar when you're supposed to come in, I'll bring my hand down." That's how it was made.

But there was trouble in bebop paradise. Parker's penchant for the high life in general—and his heroin addiction in particular—led to a series of irksome problems. Insufficient rehearsals, miscues and general foolish behavior onstage, and having to chase after his pay were Miles's biggest complaints. By the end of 1948, as Parker's drug habit deepened and his mid-performance antics increased, Miles had quit Bird's band.

Davis was resolved never to play the attention-grabbing entertainer, even in the more professional manner of Louis Armstrong, Cab Calloway or Dizzy Gillespie. He would not allow himself to descend to that level. "I love Dizzy, but I hated that clowning shit he did for them white folks . . . I decided . . . when people came to hear me, they were going to be coming to hear my music, only."

Davis's outlook—fierce, determined, proud—was becoming common in the jazz world. A wave of jazz musicians were striving not just to be listened to attentively, but to receive the respect and rewards appropriate to the highest forms of artistic expression. In the clubs, they demanded attention and silence from their fans. "For the younger musicians," John Lewis told critic Nat Hentoff, "this was the way to react against the attitude that Negroes were supposed to entertain people. The new attitude was . . . 'Either you listen to me on the basis of what I actually do or forget it.'"

Miles was at the forefront of this group, and with the advantage of his tenure with Charlie Parker earned the respect of jazz fans and fellow musicians alike for his stance. Quincy Jones was a young trumpeter from Seattle who first worshipped the members of the bebop vanguard from afar and eventually became an integral part of the jazz scene during the fifties. But even before moving to New York in 1951, he was acutely aware of the mentality of the new breed of jazz musicians and Miles's stature within that pack:

There was something about the times then where it was so unhip to be accepted. [TV comedian and former jazz musician] Sid Caesar used to do this parody of a bebop band—"We got a nine-piece band where the ninth member plays radar to let us know if we get too close to the melody." That's where we were. . . . You just wanted to know the tunes that Miles knew and Bird knew. That's all you cared about.

When Miles departed Parker's band, he already had other projects cooking. He, George Russell and John Lewis had intersected again, and were hanging with a circle of like-minded musicians and composers. A small basement apartment on Fifty-Fifth Street belonging to Gil Evans, the former arranger for big band leader Claude Thornhill, became their meeting place. Miles and Gil had already run across each other:

> I first met Gil when I was with Bird, and he was asking for a release on my tune "Donna Lee" . . . I told him he could have it and asked him to teach me some chords and let me study some of the scores he was doing for Claude Thornhill.

The quid pro quo arrangement again revealed Davis's singular focus on his musical education, and his early interest in Thornhill's music. Thornhill was a pianist and arranger who worked with a number of major swing orchestras during the thirties, including Paul Whiteman and Benny Goodman. In 1940 Thornhill pulled together his own band, nurturing a distinct sound that relied on slower tempos, long tones and subdued energy. Of Thornhill's music, Gil Evans, who arranged for the band leader in the early and mid-forties, once commented: "The sound hung like a cloud." In the industry parlance of the day, Thornhill was pigeonholed in the "sweet" (versus "swing") band category; in addition to Evans, his orchestra later included such future jazz legends as saxophonist Gerry Mulligan, trumpeter Red Rodney, and alto saxophonist Lee Konitz.

Thornhill's spirit and influence certainly hung cloud-like in Gil Evans's basement as the musicians explored a more arranged, contemplative jazz sound that they had been hearing in their heads. Experimenting with different instrumental groupings, Gerry Mulligan, Gil Evans, and Davis started coaxing forth a consistent sound. The nine-man group they finally settled on was a reduced version of the jazz-band-cum-orchestra-brass Thornhill model: trumpet, trombone, French horn, tuba, alto saxophone, baritone saxophone, piano, bass and drums. "We wanted that sound but . . . as small as possible," Davis noted, adding: "I looked at the group like it was a choir . . . I wanted the instruments to sound like human voices."

The restrained, understated music Davis sought to create reflected an oncoming change in the jazzman's code of behavior and way of being. Whereas bebop had defined a particular esthetic—zoot-suited, extroverted, rapid-fire—Davis's new style heralded the coming of "cool." Trombonist Mike Zwerin—recruited to join the Fifty-Fifth Street cadre by Davis himself—offers a snapshot of that time:

> When I noticed Miles Davis standing in a dark corner, I tried [playing] harder because Miles was playing with Bird. Miles always seemed to be standing in dark corners. He came over as I packed up around three. I slunk into a cool slouch. I used to practice cool slouches. We were both wearing shades. No eyes to be seen. "You got eyes to

make a rehearsal tomorrow?" Miles asked me. "I guess so." I acted as though I didn't give a shit for his stupid rehearsal. "Nola's [Studio]. Four." Miles made it absolutely clear that he could not care less if I showed up or not.

The musicians who popped in and out of that band during its rehearsal period represented the cream of the next generation of jazz modernists. Besides Davis's old friends George Russell and John Lewis, they included Lee Konitz, trombonist Kai Winding, pianist Al Haig, Max Roach, French hornist Gunther Schuller, and bassist Al McKibbon.

The Fifty-Fifth Street project saw Davis taking on a leader's chores: making the calls, arranging rehearsals, landing the gigs, even dealing with the scorn he received from fellow black jazzmen for hiring Lee Konitz and other white musicians. At first, Davis was "unsure of how to be boss," recalls trombonist/writer Mike Zwerin. "He relied quite a bit on Gil Evans to give musical instructions to the players." But soon he had "cracked the whip" and "dominated the band completely," according to Mulligan.

In September 1948, the marquee at the Royal Roost at Broadway and Forty-Seventh Street announced the band's first engagement, alternating with Count Basie. The sign's wording, which Davis pushed for, accurately reflected the inner dynamics of the band: "Miles Davis's Nonet; Arrangements by Gerry Mulligan, Gil Evans and John Lewis."

The nonet's residency lasted two weeks. It played only one other gig, but by the time it disbanded a year later it had made twelve recordings for Capitol Records. With Miles credited as leader on the record label, the music was released over the next few years as a series of influential—if not best-selling—78s. In 1950, *Down Beat* was impressed enough to devote four columns to analysis of the nonet sides. But their lasting impact would not be accurately gauged until after 1954, when the sides were collected and released as a single LP dubbed *The Birth of the Cool*. By decade's end, the critical consensus was that *The Birth of the Cool* sessions constituted a seismic shift in jazz.

Davis had earned the right to have the music released under his name. "Left to our own devices, Gil, [trumpeter and composer] John Carisi, and I would probably have procrastinated and maybe never gotten the rehearsals together—Miles was the prime mover," Mulligan admitted. Leading one loose-knit group through a dozen recordings, Miles had effectively introduced the first major movement in jazz since the bebop revolution.

The young trumpeter's bold effort came with a price. While planning the nonet recordings, Davis had received the call of a lifetime: the invitation to join the Duke Ellington Orchestra, arguably the jazz world's most established and respected outfit. Years later, Miles recalled his reaction: "[Duke] tells me I'm in his plans for the fall [of 1948], musically speaking, and he wants me in his band. Man that knocked me right out . . . But I had to tell him that I couldn't make it, because I was finishing up *The Birth of the Cool*." Even at twenty-two, Davis had the presence of mind and sense of commitment to turn down the security and boost in stature of a seat in Duke's band.

To his chagrin, Miles would also miss the rewards that followed the nonet recordings. In 1951, Mulligan moved to Los Angeles, where he and a

Miles takes charge: *The Birth of the Cool* recording session, 1949. From left: Junior Collins (French horn), Bill Barber (tuba), Kai Winding (trombone), Max Roach (drums, obscured), Gerry Mulligan (baritone saxophone), Miles, Al Haig (piano), Lee Konitz (alto saxophone) and Joe Shulman (bass)

number of inheritors (mostly white) of this new restrained sound—Chet Baker, Stan Getz, Shorty Rogers, and to a degree, Dave Brubeck—found themselves at the forefront of jazz fashion, enjoying a popularity and fortune that had eluded the nonet two years before. The advent and success of cool jazz was a compliment of sorts to Miles's visionary spirit; his role as progenitor of this new jazz wave was implied in the very title of *The Birth of the Cool*. However, by the time the LP appeared it was far too late for Davis to share in the dividends of cool. He had long since abandoned that style and, along with fellow New York jazzmen (mostly black), moved toward a new one—hard bop, which reinstilled the driving blues and gospel feel that bebop, with its fire and precision, had sacrificed. The cool/hard-bop schism, a split with strong racial overtones, developed between the coasts and was only exacerbated by the commercial success of the sound Miles had pioneered. "It was the same old story, black shit was being ripped off all over again," Miles maintained forty years later, still bitter, even though he was aware that much of *The Birth of the Cool* was written, arranged and performed by white musicians.

It is no surprise that Miles looked back on 1950 with bitterness: that year was the start of a period full of personal pressures and professional upheaval. In 1949, he had traveled to France for the first Paris Jazz Festival and had been granted star-like status. He had also fallen in love with a young actress named Juliette Greco. By the summer of 1950, he was back in New York, dealing with racism, a broken heart (Greco had remained in Paris), a wife and two children he needed to feed, and a lack of work. The nonet's dissolution (they had hardly been bound together long enough to warrant the term "breakup") left Davis a struggling free agent.

Like many jazz musicians around him, Miles had experimented with various drugs. But in 1950 he began using heroin more and more. "I was never into that trip that if you shot heroin you might be able to play like Bird . . . what got me strung out was the depression I felt when I got back to America." As Davis added, "That was the beginning of a four-year horror show."

Drug addiction exacerbated Miles's problems, but strangely also cemented his relationship to the jazz community. Whether or not Davis bought into it, the myth that heroin or other drugs enhanced creativity pervaded the jazz world. Charlie Parker's simultaneous genius and heroin habit was the classic example. "I couldn't wait to tell Bird, to let him know that I had become a member of the club," saxophonist Frank Morgan related to *People* magazine in 1987, recalling the first time he shot up heroin.

The long list of intermittent or consistent junkies in the fifties included Thelonious Monk, Bud Powell, Jackie McLean, Tadd Dameron, Chet Baker, Billie Holiday, Sonny Rollins, Gerry Mulligan, Stan Getz, Sonny Stitt, Jimmy

Heath, Philly Joe Jones, and almost all the members of the group that would record *Kind of Blue*: John Coltrane, Bill Evans, Paul Chambers, Miles Davis. At the decade's midpoint, it was more difficult to figure out who was not shooting than who was.

The pairing of jazz and junk reinforced the romantic, "outsider" aura of the music, but it marginalized the musicians even further. It killed some (Freddie Webster), hastened the passing of others (Fats Navarro, Billie Holiday), and severely curtailed many musicians' ability to secure gigs and earn a living in the long run. Police captains and other civic leaders targeted jazz clubs, sometimes patrons but most of all musicians. Throughout the fifties, narcotic cops in Philadelphia and Los Angeles were notorious for the inspections with which they greeted every band that came to town. And when Davis's addiction was made public in *Down Beat* and *Ebony* magazines, he "couldn't buy a job anywhere."

Though he remained a leader, touring when he could, Miles could not fuse a steady unit. He began recording for small, independent record labels like Prestige and Blue Note with a rotating crew of musicians.

Despite the turmoil, Davis's recordings from this period—"Tune Up," "Four," (from the album *Blue Haze*) and "Solar" (from *Walkin'*)—laid the groundwork for the new hard bop sound. It was a time of struggle and of searching, but it also brought Davis in contact with the musicians and institutions that would lead to his comeback in 1954, to the formation of his renowned quintet in 1955 and his sextet in 1958, and eventually to *Kind of Blue*.

Sonny Rollins was an eighteen-year-old tenor player from Harlem when he first jammed with Davis in 1949. They became partners on stage and off, sharing gigs, recording sessions (it was through Davis that Rollins first recorded as a leader for Prestige in 1951), and a heroin habit both would later kick. Davis was smitten by Rollins's sound from the start. "Some thought he was playing saxophone on the level of Bird. I know one thing—he was *close*," Miles would later recall.

A 1950 date as sideman with Sarah Vaughan found Miles in the recording studios of Columbia Records, exposed for the first time to the production values of a major label. Columbia was also the pioneer of the twelve-inch long-playing record, and Prestige had been one of the first jazz labels to embrace it. Before 1948, the 78 format relegated all recorded performances to no more than three minutes. A 1951 Miles session, featuring Sonny Rollins as well as the debut of fellow Harlem-based reedman Jackie McLean, yielded an almost ten-minute original titled "Bluing" that showed Miles's abilities in an extended format and was featured on the album *Dig*.

1952 marked the introduction of a new tenor to Miles's circle. John Coltrane was playing in Gillespie's band when Davis first met him in person. But Davis had been aware of the North Carolina-born tenor man as early as 1946. It was then that a private recording made by the nineteen-year-old Coltrane, arranged by a drummer named Joe Theimer, found its way to Davis. As Theimer wrote in a letter to a colleague:

> Miles was knocked out by Coltrane's playing. Isn't that mad. Trane would flip if he knew that *the* Miles said that about him—too much.

A few months after meeting him face-to-face, Davis decided to use Coltrane on a one-night stand at the Audobon Ballroom in Harlem. Miles's arrangement of the gig was a developing trademark: suddenly throwing together musicians of different styles and resources, challenging his sidemen and at times leaving them bent out of shape.

> I wanted to use two tenors and an alto but I couldn't pay three horns. So I used Sonny Rollins and Coltrane on tenors . . . I remember Jackie [McLean, his regular alto player at the time] getting nervous when I told him I was using Trane instead of him: he thought I was firing him. . . . Sonny was awesome that night, scared the shit out of Trane, just the way Trane would do to him a few years later.

As Cobb put it, "He's a trickster, he would like to try to do things to people just to see how they would work out, you know?"

That same year, Davis began hanging with a drummer named Joe Jones from Philadelphia, who soon adopted the sobriquet "Philly" to distinguish himself from Count Basie's renowned timekeeper Jo Jones. As with Rollins, their partnership was built on music and drugs: both were full-fledged junkies at this point.

In 1952, Davis also toured with an all-star band assembled by noted jazz deejay "Symphony" Sid Torin. A young drummer from Washington, D.C. named Jimmy Cobb ended up playing behind Miles. Cobb remembers being impressed by Miles's lyricism: "He played nice ballads, like maybe he might [have] wanted to have been a singer, if he hadn't picked up the trumpet."

By 1953, having tried and failed to kick his heroin addiction, Miles returned to his primary moneymaker: the road. But his appearances, pitting him with local pickup bands of varying talent, were not presenting the trumpeter in the best light. Philly Joe Jones acted as both drummer and advance man:

> Miles and I had been barnstorming around the country. When we got in a city where we had a gig, I'd get there first and find another horn player and a bass player . . .
> it got to be a drag because every town we'd play, I'd try to find the musicians that were the cream of the crop, but they wouldn't be worth shit.

In Chicago that year, a phone call from his sister Dorothy brought Miles down to the Persian Lounge to hear a twenty-three-year-old pianist named Ahmad Jamal. Jamal's sound would have a profound and lasting effect on Davis. Playing exclusively in a trio format, the pianist had developed a delicate sound that some critics dismissed as pretty cocktail music. Miles, however, was immediately charmed by the same refinement he had found attractive in Thornhill's recordings. "He knocked me out with his concept of space, his lightness of touch, his understatement." Jamal's nightly song lists, a mix of originals and lesser-known show tunes, also inspired Davis's own, which soon developed a reputation for including unlikely but compelling jazz material. "A Gal in Calico" and "Surrey with the Fringe on Top," as well as Jamal's own "Ahmad's Blues" and "New Rhumba," were among the new and unlikely songs Miles covered during this period.

Miles's recordings were becoming so influential that when he began introducing new material into the jazz lexicon, and reinterpreting older compositions, other jazz musicians followed. "Everybody bought his records to see what tunes he did and what how he played them," recalls jazz bassist/journalist Bill Crow, a regular player on the New York scene during the fifties. "Every time he recorded a tune it became a standard."

Taking a cue from Jamal, Miles was allowing himself creative license to reinterpret standards by simplifying a song's musical structure. An unfamiliarity with the material may have been one motivating factor; but more often he was simply willing to sacrifice form for feeling.

As an example, Crow mentions a Prestige record from 1953. "When [Miles] did 'When Lights Are Low' [from the album *Blue Haze*], a tune that hadn't been very popular, he didn't know the bridge. Instead he repeated the first eight [bar] figure in a higher key and went back to the original." Davis's streamlined way became *the* way to play it. What had been a tune that veterans might have known through Benny Carter's original from the thirties, was repopularized through the fifties by many musicians who adopted Miles's version.

Nonetheless, everything that Miles valued and held dear—his music, his public stature, even his appearance and self-regard—was suffering from his drug habit. Seeing Davis nodding out in front of Birdland in the summer of 1953, Max Roach had stuffed a couple of hundred dollar bills in his pocket;

the unexpected charity pierced his pride and gave the trumpeter a wake-up call. "People started looking at me like I was dirty or something . . . with pity and horror," Miles noticed. By the end of that year, he reached a personal and professional turning point. In two short months he restored his health, his music, and his career to solid ground. He returned home to East St. Louis, locked himself in his family's guest house, and kicked his heroin addiction cold turkey. To reestablish both physical and musical prowess, and to avoid his drug connections in New York, he relocated to Detroit, home to a fertile jazz scene. Playing regularly alongside a list of stellar players, including Elvin Jones, Tommy Flanagan and Curtis Fuller, Miles made Detroit's Bluebird Inn his temporary home. By remaining in one place, he began to replace his frenetic, one-night stand style of performing with a more consistent, set-building approach.

At long last, Davis felt he was on to something.

> I came back to New York in February 1954 . . . I really felt good for the first time in a long time. My chops were together because I had been playing every night and I had finally kicked heroin. I felt strong, musically and physically. I felt ready for anything.

"Anything" included a looser, more independent musical exploration. Color, timbre and even atmosphere began to play a more prominent role in Miles's musical palette. In March of 1954, having trouble recording an original track, "Blue Haze," Davis turned out the studio lights and found the right ambience to nail the take. His trumpet sound was becoming noticeably more pinched and withdrawn. He relied more and more on devices to accent that restrained quality. In April, he recorded an entire session for Prestige with a cup mute. By June, as Davis biographer Ian Carr notes, Miles had discovered the accessory with which he would be associated throughout the rest of his career:

> The metallic Harmon mute with its stem removed. The mute has to be placed very close to the microphone, and the resulting sound is full and breathy in the lower register and thin and piercing in the upper. The two registers can therefore be played off against each other in a dramatic way. . . .

The proof of Miles's sea change in 1954 is his musical output, which became steady in both its quality and its influence. His April cup-mute session in particular brought together a well-chosen group of fellow bebop refugees, plus one relative newcomer destined for hard-bop greatness (the young Horace Silver). That session also brought forth Davis's first personally satisfying success since *The Birth of the Cool*.

"Walkin'" is credited to Richard Carpenter, a Harlem running buddy of

Davis's who at one time or another managed both Chet Baker and Dizzy Gillespie. But other, more schematic, less polished recordings of the same tune predate the version titled "Walkin'." It would seem that Carpenter—not a performing musician himself—took the simple outline from the 1950 single "Gravy" by Gene Ammons (another member of Miles's narcotic-fueled circle) and structured a neat, easy-flowing blues number around it. Miles first recorded the arrangement as "Weirdo" for Blue Note in 1952, crediting himself as composer. But hearing the tune's more sophisticated possibilities, he decided to re-record it for Prestige, with Carpenter receiving composer credit.

"Walkin'" incorporated most of the elements that would define many of Miles's later fifties' recordings. It was an extended (13:54), mid-tempo blues structure balancing a simple melody line with soulful solos that swung insistently in a relaxed mood. It resulted from a "head arrangement"—an opening musical theme—Miles threw together in the studio (it had been Thompson's responsibility but his arrangement was not up to snuff). Davis's own solo was a standout of economy and hushed feeling. Critic Martin Williams would later hail the recording as a watershed for Miles's trumpet playing: "Beginning now, one passionate note from Miles Davis seemed to imply a whole complex of expressive sound, and three notes a ravishing melody."

It was also a showcase for Davis the maturing jazz bandleader. His talent in hearing and combining disparate instrumental voices comes to the fore on "Walkin'":

> I got J.J. Johnson and Lucky Thompson for that session because I wanted that big sound that both of them could give me. You know, Lucky for that Ben Webster thing, but a bebop thing too . . . Kenny Clarke replaced Art Blakey on drums because I wanted that brush stroke thing. When it came to playing soft brush strokes on the drums, nobody could do it better than Klook [Kenny Clarke]. I was using a mute on that date and I wanted a soft thing behind me, but a swing soft thing.

For the first time in Miles's career, personal artistic satisfaction matched popular—if not critical—reception. "That record was a motherfucker man . . . the critics' heads were still someplace else, but a few people were starting to buy my albums." In one fell swoop, "Walkin'" became the anthem of hard bop and revitalized Davis's career. Not coincidentally, it was also a rough blueprint for his culminating performance of the decade: *Kind of Blue*.

In a few short years, Miles had transformed not just his career but his whole sound. In 1949, when he had been plucked to perform at the Paris Jazz Festival, Miles had blown hard and high, still under a tangible Fats

Miles in the studio with Horace Silver in 1954, at the Blue Note session that yielded "Weirdo," the precursor to his hit "Walkin'"

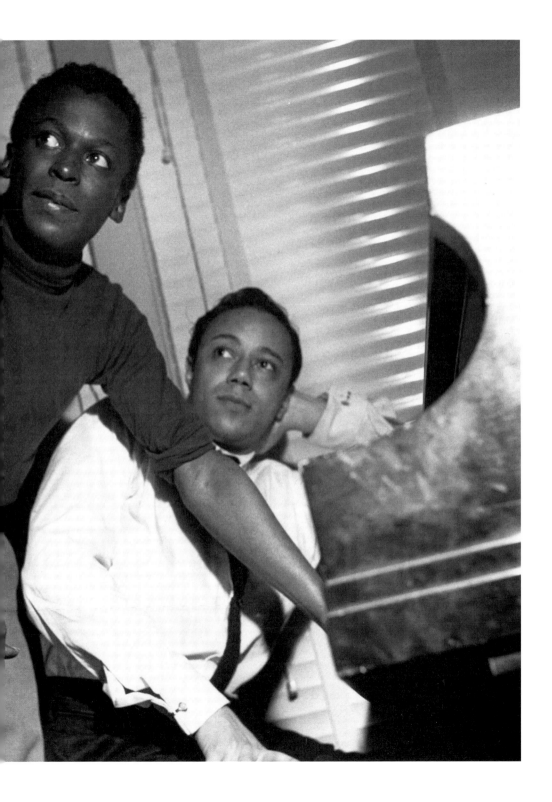

Navarro influence. But Davis had realized he would never be the technician Gillespie was. As he often related, Miles once queried the bebopper. "I asked Dizzy 'Why can't I play like you?' because I tried to play like him but I just couldn't. He said, 'You don't hear high notes, you hear middle register. You play the same chords I play, only you play in a lower register.'"

What he was hearing, first and foremost, was melody. Fellow trumpeter Art Farmer commented on Davis: "When you're not technically a virtuoso, you *have* to say something. You have no place to hide." Cannonball Adderley said, after they had played together: "Listening to Miles—who is not a good trumpet player but a great soloist—all of a sudden the fundamentals don't mean that much to me because he's so brilliant otherwise. A solo is the way he thinks about the composition and the solo becomes the thing."

Near the end of 1954 a moment occurred that revealed Miles's secure confidence inside the studio. For Prestige, he had assembled an all-star group that included Thelonious Monk, Milt Jackson, and the same bass/drums combination as on *Walkin'*: Percy Heath and Kenny Clarke. Things were not going smoothly at that Christmas Eve recording session. Monk was perturbed that Davis had asked him not to play behind his solos, and an uncomplicated take on "The Man I Love" seemed to be generating more trouble than it should. The overlapping studio chatter and general chaos that followed a false start were preserved on the master session tapes. With one stern aside to the engineer Rudy Van Gelder, Miles cut through the hubbub and got the proceedings back on track.

MILT JACKSON: (plays introduction)
MONK: When am I supposed to come in?
VARIOUS: Ohh . . . No, no . . .
UNKNOWN: Man, the cat's cutting his thing . . .
MONK: Man, I want to know when to come in. Can I start . . . to it . . .
DAVIS: Hey Rudy, put this on the record, all of it . . .

A masterful take of the tune followed immediately without a hitch. Miles the bandleader, unafraid to crack the whip now and then, was more than ready. The only thing he lacked was a band.

By 1955, Davis possessed an instantly recognizable voice on the trumpet, intense, lyrical, and generous in its use of space and laconic, mid-range phrasing. With a maturing grace and economy, he was assimilating a wide variety of experiences and influences, and channeling them into a sound that was his own. With the twin critical successes of "Walkin'" and *The Birth of the Cool* reissue behind him and with his reputation and remuneration on the rise, Miles was able to turn his attention to the one component of professional success that had eluded him: his own steady group. In April of that year, only weeks after the stunned silence that followed the death of Charlie Parker, Davis debuted a new band comprised of virtual unknowns at New York's premier jazz club, on Broadway near Fifty-Second Street: Birdland.

Little at that time suggested the impact this group would ultimately have, but Miles's 1955–57 band has since become renowned as his first classic quintet (as distinguished from his mid-sixties combo with Herbie Hancock, Wayne Shorter, Ron Carter and Tony Williams), and the rhythm section is hailed definitively as The Rhythm Section. The original lineup, besides Miles, was Sonny Rollins on tenor sax (soon to be replaced by John Coltrane, who became an integral part of the quintet's sound), Red Garland on piano, Paul Chambers on bass, and Philly Joe Jones on drums.

Why a quintet? After *The Birth of the Cool*, Davis had worked in groups that numbered from quartets to septets and featured a wide range of instruments. But playing in Bird's mid-forties band had left a seminal and indelible impression. Miles knew he wanted a five-piece, with a saxophone by his side.

Rollins had always been on Miles's A-list. "He was an aggressive, innovative player who always had fresh musical ideas," Davis later said. Until he disappeared later that year, ostensibly to move to more lucrative opportunities in Chicago but in reality to end his own drug habit, Rollins was Davis's horn apparent.

Having partnered with Davis off and on since 1953, Philly Joe Jones provided the initial spark for the band. Jones's and Davis's shared road experience had honed a musical telepathy between them. Miles did not hesitate to credit his input.

> Philly Joe was the fire that was making a lot of shit happen. See he knew everything I was going to do, everything I was going to play; he anticipated me, felt what I was thinking. Sometimes I used to tell him not to do that lick of his with me, but after me. And so that lick he used to do after I played something—that rim shot—became known as the "Philly lick," and it made him famous, took him right to the top.

Jones's rate of progress matched Miles's; he had developed into one of the most propulsive, sensitive timekeepers in jazz.

Red Garland was a Texas-born, Philadelphia-based pianist whom Philly Joe had introduced to Miles back in 1953. Garland had attended the 1953 Prestige session on which Philly Joe Jones and Davis first recorded together (memorable for featuring one very drunk Charlie Parker on tenor). Miles liked Garland's playing, more for his ability to emulate than create. "Red knew I liked Ahmad Jamal, that that was the type I was looking for, and so I asked

The Rhythm Section: Paul Chambers, Red Garland and Philly Joe Jones, Los Angeles, 1956

him to give me Ahmad's sound, because Red played best when he played like that." Garland's pronounced, rhythmically driving left-hand work behind the soloists would become an inherent part of the quintet's sound.

On Jackie McLean's recommendation, Davis had lured Paul Chambers—only a few months on the New York jazz circuit—away from the George Wallington Quintet. Miles had been impressed with the Detroit native during his stay in 1953. Chambers had proved his mettle after moving to New York, with Wallington as well as with a group led by J.J. Johnson and Kai Winding.

The band worked on and off into the summer of 1955, solidifying a strong, collective sound and an impressive stage show that contrasted with Davis's inconsistent live performances of the past. Miles himself was playing stronger than ever before, and the word was spreading. At the second annual Newport Jazz Festival that summer, producer George Wein had arranged an all-star group led by Miles's former *The Birth of the Cool* colleague Gerry Mulligan to fill in the gap between Count Basie and Dave Brubeck. As an afterthought—the programs and posters were already printed—Miles was invited to join the lineup. He walked on unannounced, proceeded to blow low and cool on three tunes, including the Monk standard "'Round Midnight," and received a standing ovation. It proved a pivotal moment in his career.

Whatever glory critics had failed to shower on "Walkin'" was bestowed on those brief minutes onstage. Miles's performance on Sunday, July 17, 1955 became the public return of a confident jazz master, at least to the jazz pundits. *Down Beat* editor Jack Tracy, in the audience that night, wrote: "Miles played thrillingly and indicated his comeback was in full stride . . . it was

Miles . . . who captured most ears." As Tracy recalls, Davis was unmoved by the praise. "The next time I saw him, he said, 'What the fuck do you mean comeback? I didn't go anywhere.' Typical of Miles."

But the evening proved most consequential not so much for the reception of Miles as one person's witness of it. George Avakian was a longtime jazz fan and also director of Columbia Records' Popular Album Department (there was no separate jazz division at the label in those days). He had known Davis for years, having first met him in Los Angeles just after World War II. And for years, each time they met, Miles had sung Avakian the same song: "Hey, George, sign me up!"

Avakian had always been intrigued by the idea, but until now had dismissed the notion because of Davis's heroin addiction, his recording contract with Prestige (exclusive since 1954), and his lack of a permanent band. But by summer 1955, Miles was clean, boasted a cohesive working group, and, even before his Newport triumph, had brainstormed a win-win solution to his contractual obligation.

> Miles got a crazy idea and it worked. He said, "Tell Bob Weinstock [president of Prestige Records] you'd like to record me, and you won't put the masters out until the end of my [Prestige] contract, which would be about two years hence. Meanwhile they can stockpile albums, and when Columbia comes out with my first album, you're going to advertise it and promote it, right?" I said, "Sure we will." "So Prestige will get the benefit of that. . . ."

In the 1950s, a jazzman could set his sights no higher than Columbia Records. It was a transitory time for jazz at the label. Label stalwarts like Duke Ellington had exited, and while newer signings like Erroll Garner and Dave Brubeck had begun to re-establish Columbia's reputation as a home to younger jazz artists, the company needed to secure the next generation to maintain its supremacy in the jazz realm. Riding on the succcess of Brubeck's LP *Jazz Goes to College*, Avakian had license from his higher-ups at the label to gamble on a former junkie who looked like a rising star.

With Miles's voice urging him in one ear, and his brother Aram—a fellow jazz fan and photographer—warning him in the other to "sign him up because somebody else will do it if you don't," Avakian heard the unexpected walk-on solo at Newport as a sign. He made a qualified offer. He would sign Miles if Miles went on the road supporting his future releases on Columbia, backed by a steady band.

> I said, "If you can get a group together and keep a group together, I will record you. If you're still together when the record comes out, we can really do something with it. The guy who can really help you is Jack Whittemore, with Shaw Artists."

Miles, in stellar company, makes his comeback at the second Newport Jazz Festival, July 17, 1955. From left: Percy Heath, Thelonious Monk, Zoot Sims, Miles, Gerry Mulligan and Connie Kay

Shaw Artists was one of the top booking agencies representing jazz groups in 1955, and, "Jack had more faith in Miles than anyone at that time," according to Avakian. The effect of Columbia's offer on Davis's travel itinerary was immediate. "Jack said, 'Look, if Miles can hold a group together, I will knock myself out booking it and keeping it working so that it's still going a year-and-a-half from now.'"

That eighteen-month projection turned into a career-long commitment on the part of Whittemore and Shaw Artists. But before 1955 drew to a close and their deal could be sealed, the stability of the band was thrown into doubt. Avakian recalls:

I have this poster of Columbia's jazz artists right here in my house, I can see it from here. I'm sitting at the piano with Count Basie, and Miles is stand-ing next to Louis Armstrong, Benny Goodman is there, and Charlie Mingus, Billie Holiday and Cab [Calloway] are there. When I look at that, which I do every day, it's a reminder of a lot of things. You've got the whole culture of the U.S. there. In that period, Columbia was very, very strong. Columbia was the dominant company as far as being able to get the music to the pub-lic. Worldwide, you know, it wasn't just the U.S.

The roster of influence Dave Brubeck describes above gives a sense of the overwhelming talent commanded by Columbia Records during the forties, fifties, and well into the sixties. A contract with the label conferred unparalleled status, a place in the company of music legends. Even the distinctive red-and-black label exuded worldliness and elegance. Columbia's catalog offered not just the leading jazz artists, but "Master-works," as its classical label was called (featuring such luminaries as Leonard Bernstein and the New York Philharmonic), international stars (such as Edith Piaf), important historical documents (such as Edward R. Murrow broadcasts), and Broadway's latest successes (such as *South Pacific*, one of the first best-selling 33 1/3 rpm, long-playing recordings—

In 1948, Columbia Records introduced the LP, the first new recorded sound format in 40 years, and changed the course of the music industry. From left: Columbia Records president Edward Wallerstein, future label head Goddard Lieberson and conductor Fritz Reiner

a marketable format Columbia engineers had invented). The creation of the LP was only one aspect of Columbia's decade-long preeminence through the fifties. The gamble on a format designed to increase the duration and quality of music playback, had repaid the label in spades. As *Billboard* noted in 1959 on the format's tenth anniversary, the LP had expanded not only the label's suc-cess, but the music business in general: *The long-playing record . . . today accounts for 61 percent of the total industry volume. Album sales in fact now represent two-thirds of all popular music sales.*

If there was one LP that symbolized Columbia's dominance over its competitors during that period, it would not be *Kind of Blue*, but *My Fair Lady*. In 1957, the cast recording of the Broadway smash, personally produced at 30th Street Studios by Columbia's president, Goddard Lieberson, sold an unprecedented 5 million copies, making it the *Thriller* of its generation. Lieberson had also convinced Columbia's parent company, CBS, to buy into the musical itself; a $500,000 investment returned an additional $32 million to the company.

A year later, Lieberson indulged in a moment of corporate braggadocio: "With its development of the world's largest LP catalog, phonograph line, and record club, Columbia has become the dominant force in the billion-dollar sound industry."

Lieberson was British-born and, to the delight of many of Columbia's artists, was musically trained as well. As Dave Brubeck recalls: "When you have the president of a company in the control booth, and he can read a score and he's a composer himself, that's a great feeling." Originally recruited in 1940 to assist the head of Masterworks, he had worked his way up the corporate ladder, and by the mid-fifties was positioned to take charge of the label.

Columbia had not always been top dog in the record business. As late as 1950—two years after bringing the LP to market—the label was still trailing behind the music industry pack. All the best-known pop artists recorded for other labels. Columbia was on the lookout for fresh talent, and for a fresh talent scout. Mitch Miller, an oboist and the musical director at Mercury Records (he had been involved with the renowned *Charlie Parker with Strings* project there), was recruited for the job. As he tells it:

> Before 1950 when I came on board, [Columbia] was number four, behind RCA, Decca and Capitol. My title was Head of the Popular Division. I came in with nobody—no stars—Sinatra we couldn't give away even though he made good records. I was given a budget and told to go find people.

In his pied piper role at Columbia, Miller attracted a whole generation of Columbia stars, including Rosemary Clooney, Percy Faith, Tony Bennett, Johnny Ray, and later, Johnny Mathis (originally signed by Avakian as a jazz rather than a popular singer). Miller himself even

made it onto the charts in 1950 with his take on the folk tune "Tzena, Tzena, Tzena," portending his hugely successful *Sing Along with Mitch* album series. By 1952, Columbia exploded with a slew of number one pop hits, and profits were up a staggering 60 percent. Miller gives credit to Columbia for filling its top positions with people who were musicians or who had been musically trained. "It was the first time a musician was in control of a record company," he says, speaking of himself.

Miller's greatest success was in creating pop singles, which translated to creative freedom: "We're not going to second-guess you. Just stay within the budget,"

"Mind if I get in this ad, too?" said FRANK SINATRA

Columbia Records

were his marching orders from Lieberson. As the chart-topping songs rolled out, it became apparent that a hit single would propel sales of the album on which it was featured. By that token, Miller's license to experiment was shared by others, including jazz enthusiast George Avakian. Columbia had originally hired the young Avakian in 1940 to take charge of jazz singles. With the advent of LPs, his responsibility shifted to albums in general—new recordings and reissues. In Avakian's words: "The catalog was doing incredibly well at the cash register. So I could risk new ideas without undue panic in the counting house. Hysteria maybe, but not undue panic."

Avakian's—and Columbia's—ongoing success in the jazz marketplace was part of a general trend throughout the fifties. Spurred by technological advances and the booming post-war economy, the music industry enjoyed unprecedented growth. Jazz shared in the wealth, enjoying a newfound, mainstream popularity far more widespread than it had in its swing or bebop past. The expansion of jazz was so rapid and pronounced during the decade that by 1959, jazz journals like *Metronome* even warned: "A widening public for jazz may result in a dilution of the music itself [and] too many of the hundreds of albums that are continually being released aren't very good."

Well, the magazine was at least on the money about the widening of the music: as the jazz scene expanded, there was significantly more to choose from, and older, established styles rubbed shoulders with newer forms. By the end of the decade, a jazz lover's collection might have included traditional jazz and swing-style soloists (Louis Armstrong, Jonah Jones), big bands (Stan Kenton, Duke Ellington, Woody Herman), bebop stalwarts (Dizzy Gillespie, Sonny Stitt) and bebop transmuters (Thelonious Monk, George Russell), new and veteran vocalists (Sarah Vaughan, Ella Fitzgerald), purveyors of cool (Gerry Mulligan, Chet Baker), classically inspired conceptualizers (John Lewis, Dave Brubeck, Miles Davis), gospel-fueled hard boppers (Art Blakey, Horace Silver), and avant-garde visionaries (Ornette Coleman, Cecil Taylor).

It was a more accepting jazz scene. "These styles weren't vying with each other," says former *Metronome* editor Barry Ulanov. It was also a healthier one. A decade prior, bebop had had to muscle its way in past hostile reception. The music had been relegated to (sometimes very)

A star is a star is a . . .: A Columbia advertisement from the late '40s makes no distinction between jazz and pop stars of the day

Opposite: Mitch Miller (top) and Tony Bennett in the studio

Jazz for the masses: In 1955, Columbia Records' highly successful "I Like Jazz" campaign targeted middle America with a $1 sampler LP featuring artists from Bessie Smith to Dave Brubeck

late-night broadcasts and badly distributed, independent-label 78s. Quincy Jones recalls Seattle in the forties: "You have to imagine the setting. There was nothing but radio, man. One jazz radio station from San Francisco and *Down Beat* magazine."

In contrast, jazz was well documented and well distributed by the end of the fifties. *Metronome* joined *Down Beat* in focusing on the national jazz circuit; by the late fifties, *Jazz Review* and *Jazz: A Quarterly* added to the coverage. The back pages of these magazines listed regular jazz radio shows in metropolitan areas. In the young medium of television, a variety of programs broadcast jazz of a wide variety. There were cop shows with jazz soundtracks like *Peter Gunn* and jazz specials sponsored by Texaco and Timex. With Columbia in the lead, record labels with strong national distribution ensured that recordings by *all* their artists—jazz, pop, classical or whatever—were affordable and on retail shelves coast-to-coast.

Columbia assigned its classical efforts to its Masterworks department, but there was no such segregation between jazz and pop during the fifties. One department handled both; the same engineering, marketing, and publicity team that reaped success with such popular songbirds as Dinah Shore, Jo Stafford, and Doris Day was doing the same for Brubeck, Goodman, and Garner. In those days, the two musical genres were a lot closer: they were recorded in the same studios, working with the same producers, arrangers, and often the same musicians. Pop crooners like Frank Sinatra and Tony Bennett ably handled jazz arrangements; Sarah Vaughan and Billie Holiday recorded with string sections; and cross-pollination of pop stars performing with jazz luminaries—Rosemary Clooney with Duke Ellington; Frankie Laine with Buck Clayton—was not at all uncommon at Columbia.

Columbia's genre-blind attitude caught many jazz stalwarts of the day off guard. Avakian remembers being visited in the fifties by a European jazz record distributor who was befuddled to find the word "Popular" on his office door: "He said, 'I thought you were in charge of jazz.' He was very upset—in his mind, popular albums were nothing."

But to Avakian, Columbia's equal-opportunity approach guaranteed jazz's ultimate success on the label.

Jazz was never thought about as being something that, "Well, it's not going to sell a whole lot, we won't pay that much attention." We treated jazz as part of the entire album output, it got the same attention, the same kind of advertising and promotion that everyone else did.

Miles called to say, "Sonny had to quit because he's got so much work in Chicago, where they really know him. But I've got a good substitute—Cannonball Adderley."

Miles had been one of many New York musicians bowled over by the arrival of alto saxophonist Julian "Cannonball" Adderley from Tampa, Florida that year. Cannonball, accompanied by his brother, trumpeter Nat Adderley, had walked into Café Bohemia one night while bassist Oscar Pettiford was holding forth. As Cannonball sat in, Pettiford counted off an intentionally frenzied version of "I'll Remember April" in an attempt to blow off the uninvited altoist. With jaw-dropping dexterity and ebullience, Adderley blew a set of fluid, bebop changes that set the jazz community buzzing.

Miles began a subtle, long-running recruiting drive. "I could almost hear him playing in my band the first time I heard him," Miles recalled, though at the time he kept his outward cool. Where others saw the second coming of Bird, Davis perceived a more earthy stylist: "He had that blues thing and I love me some blues."

But, committed to a teaching position back home, Adderley thwarted Miles's plans by returning to Florida. An unsuccessful audition with Sun Ra tenor man John Gilmore gave Davis second thoughts. Columbia and Prestige were ready to begin recording, and Whittemore's first series of bookings were set to begin in late September of 1955. Almost as an afterthought, Jones—fulfilling his old role of talent scout and recruiter—traveled to his native Philadelphia to look up a journeyman tenor player who had once played with Miles: John Coltrane.

The relationship that ensued was one of the most intense and fruitful in jazz history. Over the next five years—with Davis's tight-lipped tutelage providing Coltrane creative license rather than explicit direction—the tenor saxophonist was cajoled and challenged into an individual direction that sired an entirely new school of jazz. Bill Evans later described the unswayable faith that Miles had in his new tenor man:

> I don't think we would've had Coltrane's great contributions without Miles's belief
> in his potential. Because at the beginning, most people wondered why Miles had
> Coltrane in the group—he was more or less a withdrawn presence on the bandstand,
> not fumbling exactly, but just sort of searching. But Miles really knew, somehow,
> the development that Coltrane had coming.

Coltrane arrived from Philadelphia unknown outside the New York scene, an R&B sideman still playing in a "standard bebop style." At his first audition, remembering how Rollins had "set [Coltrane's] ears and ass on fire" three years before at the Audobon Ballroom gig, Davis was prepared to be unimpressed. "I wasn't excited. But after a few rehearsals . . . I could hear how Trane had gotten a whole lot better." But the disparate styles of communication between the two almost lost Davis his most legendary sideman before he had even joined the band.

> I think the reason we didn't get along at first was because Trane liked to ask all these motherfucking questions back then about what he should or shouldn't play. Man, fuck that shit; to me he was a professional musician and I have always wanted whoever played with me to find their own place in the music. So my silence and evil looks probably turned him off.

The clash reveals much about Miles's developing, oblique method as a musical director, and the expectations he had of his sidemen. Years later, saxophonist Dave Liebman, who played with Davis in the early seventies, described Miles's fully matured approach: "He is . . . able to really control, manipulate a band by . . . not saying a word, just by nuance, by the way he plays." Irrespective of his sidemen's feelings, Davis demanded a musical communication bordering on telepathy.

Coltrane returned home, somewhat disgruntled, to a sideman gig with organist Jimmy Smith. But Miles had heard something in Coltrane, and was determined to have him in his band. Davis's ability to hear great talent in its developing stages would serve him well throughout his career as his groups became the proving ground for generations of jazz talent. "I recognized it in Wayne Shorter and Herbie [Hancock] and Chick [Corea], Keith Jarrett, Sonny Rollins . . . Philly Joe, Red Garland, George Duke," Miles told Ben Sidran in 1986.

Miles certainly was not going to let one confrontation stand in the way. A conciliatory call was made, Coltrane accepted, and on September 27 at the Club Las Vegas in Baltimore, Davis and his legendary quintet performed together for the first time.

After a week in Baltimore and then Detroit, Davis and the group returned to New York in mid-October for a two-week run at Birdland. Nat Hentoff, reviewing the quintet for *Down Beat*, reported that "Miles himself had not played as consistently and strongly in a New York club in some time, but the band as a whole is not cohesive yet."

But the band did not take long to gel. The speed with which they fell together surprised even Davis. "Faster than I could have imagined, the music that we were playing together was just unbelievable. It was so bad that it used send chills through me at night." He called George Avakian, who recalls:

> [Miles] said, "Come on down Saturday night and listen to the group, because Coltrane's working out real well." Sure enough, it was really first-rate. I went down

there, never having heard Coltrane play before as far as I knew. He didn't have the flash of Sonny or Cannon, although he ripped off a searing solo on the last set.

Avakian was happy, and Miles could not have been happier. "In 1955, Columbia represented for me a doorway my music could go through to reach more listeners." He was prepared and more than ready to take on the task of being a jazz sensation. He had a powerful booking agent leading him forward, an awe-inspiring band playing with him, and an experienced label that knew how to record and market great talent—especially jazz—to a vast national audience. Soon his recordings would be heard by an ever-expanding sphere of music fans. His name would become familiar to even more. In one manner or another, from 1956 on, Miles's music would influence all jazz that followed.

He and his quintet were just one step away from the band that would father the apex of small group jazz statements: *Kind of Blue.*

The Quintet,

the Sextet,

and the Rise of Modal Jazz

When I first joined Miles in 1955, I had a lot to learn. I felt I was lacking in general musicianship . . . I am quite ashamed of those early records I made with Miles. Why he picked me, I don't know. Maybe he saw something in my playing that he hoped would grow . . . But there were so many musical conclusions I hadn't arrived at, that I felt inadequate.

John Coltrane, 1961

JOHN COLTRANE's self-deprecating tone should sound familiar. Ten years earlier Miles had felt the same way sharing the spotlight with Charlie Parker. Now it was Coltrane's turn to question himself. And Miles? It had been two years since he had thrown away the needle and refocused on his career, and everything was just fine, thank you. As he put it, "I was playing my horn and leading the baddest band in the business, a band that was creative, imaginative, supremely tight and artistic."

At the end of 1955, buoyed by the artistic and financial freedom afforded him by a generous advance from Columbia Records and consistent roadwork arranged by Shaw Artists, Miles stood ready to climb atop the jazz world. The new quintet landed on the West Coast early in 1956 for a two-week stand at the Los Angeles nightclub Jazz City. Miles counted off the first tune, and the sound of New York—funky hard bop with a sophisticated lyrical edge—impinged on cool territory where Gerry Mulligan and Chet Baker had debuted their pianoless quartet a few years before. Jazz composer and arranger Sy Johnson, who was there every night, would later recall: "Nobody knew what to expect. It literally blew everybody out of the water. It destroyed West Coast jazz overnight."

A jazz frontline rarely — if ever—paralleled. From left: Miles, Cannonball and Coltrane

The quintet soon became a cross-country phenomenon. Booking agent Jack Whittemore made good on his promise, and through 1956 Miles's quintet played constantly in a series of gigs, in venues that varied from small, black clubs on the East Coast to more integrated showplaces in cities like St. Louis, Chicago and San Francisco. For the first time in his career, Miles was able to deliver performances of a consistent quality, night after night. At their exuberant, full-throttled best, the group simply had so much to offer: Coltrane's raw, edgy—at times endless—tenor improvisations. Red Garland's fiery, left-hand chording. Philly Joe's exciting cymbal work and propulsive rim shots. Miles's *misterioso,* muted trumpet. Chambers's adept and soulful bowed solos. Years after the quintet's debut, jazz writers were still exhilarated by their sound. "The intricacy of the linkage between the minds of these musicians has never been equaled in any group, in my opinion," wrote Ralph Gleason in 1972.

Both of Miles's record companies—Prestige, still his official label, and Columbia—were thrilled with the new group. Prestige president Bob Weinstock hailed them as "the Louis Armstrong Hot Five of the modern era." Both companies soon took the quintet into the studio. The recordings they made over the next eighteen months, ultimately released on six titles for the former label (*Miles, Cookin', Relaxin', Miles Davis and the Modern Jazz Giants, Workin',* and *Steamin'*) and one for the latter (*'Round About Midnight*), define a high-water mark for small group jazz improvisation.

Despite the disparity in the number of released albums, it was Columbia that sacrificed more recording tape and studio time on Miles. Four out of the six Prestige albums—*Cookin', Relaxin', Workin'* and *Steamin'*—were generated from two marathon sessions in which the quintet simply performed their well-rehearsed live set list with no retakes. On the other hand, Miles's debut on Columbia resulted from three long sessions, with multiple recordings of carefully selected material. The final release of each tune spliced together the better parts of two or more different takes.

Miles's flexibility in the recording studio—his assurance with meticulous crafting as well as with unbridled, one-take spontaneity—would serve him well during his years as a Columbia artist. By decade's end these two approaches would converge, shaping the process that would yield *Kind of Blue.*

In 1956, Miles's Prestige recordings with the quintet began rolling into the receptive hands of critics, who responded ecstatically. *Down Beat,* which had qualified its praise of the group's debut album *Miles,* offered an unconditional five-star review of *Cookin'* in 1957:

> All the tremendous cohesion, the wild, driving swing, and the all-out excitement and controlled emotion that was present at the best moments of the Davis quintet has been captured on this record. [Philly Joe] Jones has said these sessions . . . are the best Davis has made. I am inclined to agree.

The combination of universally acclaimed live performances and the Prestige albums secured the quintet's reputation, as they did Miles's. But the attention went beyond the music. Davis was evolving into a universal symbol of cool. What the trumpeter wore, what he said on stage (or did not say), whether or not he turned his back to audiences, received as much ink as his performances. When he walked offstage after finishing a solo, it was no matter that he was concentrating on the music or trying not to draw attention away from other soloists. Miles began to receive critical flak for his apparent distance and disdain.

The image Columbia chose for Miles's first album for the label, *'Round About Midnight,* was striking but intentionally or not, the photograph also served to bolster his aloof image. Taken by Marvin Koner at Café Bohemia, the shot captures a brooding, sunglassed Davis, protectively cradling his horn, with his hands around his ears. Could a portrait make him seem any more detached or withdrawn? In actuality—as many other live shots of Miles attest—Davis was simply and habitually doing what many singers do

when focusing on the music at hand: he cupped his ears to filter out extraneous noise.

The same silent manner and blunt attitude that Coltrane had found disconcerting became part of the rising Miles myth. The previous year, Miles's voice became as gruff as his manner: while healing after a throat operation, Davis got into a yelling match with a music businessman and permanently damaged his vocal chords. For the rest of his life, his hoarse rasp would be his vocal calling card.

What was controversial to white audiences carried positive significance in the black community. For a black man of Miles's stature to adopt an intransigent, uncompromising public posture was uncommon in the 1950s. His quiet but determined sense of self in a society bristling with racial

Left: Columbia introduces their new jazz hopeful: the album cover of 'Round About Midnight, featuring the portrait taken at the Café Bohemia, 1956

Below: Miles live in Los Angeles, 1956

tension offered fellow African Americans an example. To them, there was no mistaking the symbolism of his turning his back on his mostly white audiences.

In the mid-fifties, few of the other black heroes—Nat Cole, Jackie Robinson, Sugar Ray Robinson, Ralph Ellison, Sidney Poitier—seemed as strong, hip or (by 1957) as successful as Miles. McCoy Tyner remembers that to African American musicians and fans alike, "Miles was an icon . . . a real jazz star"; to Herbie Hancock, he was a "kind of guru for a lot of people."

As Bill Cosby recalled:

> In the fifties, the status symbol in North Philadelphia for certain groups of teenagers was to be into Miles Davis. I mean, if you said "Miles Davis" you were cool, if you had Miles Davis albums you were on top of things, so the man was more than just a musician.

Hugh Masekela, listening to his records in his native South Africa during the first years of apartheid, found a much-needed exemplar:

> Not only in music, but Miles influenced the way I dressed, influenced my attitude toward authority: his perspective on life, his disdain of authority that curtails people's freedom. He was just honest. If he didn't like something, he said, "Fuck you," instead of putting it in fancy language.

Miles's position as role model was an outgrowth of the respect he had earned in his earliest days as a bebop star. Jimmy Cobb recalls fellow musicians imitating Davis's attitude and stance in the late forties: "There were guys walking around trying to dress like Miles, holding and carrying their horn like him. It happened for the rest of his life, guys were trying to emulate him, you know?" Quincy Jones freely admits being one of those guys in the early fifties.

> I had to play a solo on a thing I wrote for [Lionel] Hampton called "Kingfish" [in 1951]. I had to play a one-chord solo on it. It was very influenced by Miles, you know that Gil Evans, [John] Carisi stuff. In those days everybody hung out, you know, and one night, standing behind me was Oscar Pettiford and Miles talking, and [Miles] said he had heard it on the radio: "some little motherfucker trying to play like me."

Miles officially and publicly became a Columbia artist with the release of 'Round About Midnight on March 18, 1957. The label and its staff had been chomping at the bit, publicist Deborah Ishlon perhaps more anxiously than anyone else. She had proven her mettle breaking jazz artists like Garner and Brubeck into the mainstream press, even getting the latter placed on the cover of Time magazine in 1954. Avakian remembered having to temper her enthusiasm when she first saw Miles in 1955: "'With the Italian suits and Cole Porter mute, we'll get a full page in both *Time* and *Newsweek*,' she said. 'Slow down, Debbie,' I said. 'We've got till 1957.'"

The delay ultimately worked in Miles's favor, gaining Columbia time to marshal its energy and strategize Davis's debut. The label had also grown significantly in profits and size in those two years (sales volume had more than doubled, as had the number of employees) and the careers of all Columbia artists benefited.

Miles's certainly did. "When *'Round About Midnight* came out, it soon outsold [Prestige's] five [albums] combined," Avakian recalls. The trumpeter celebrated his first royalty check by buying a gull-wing, two-seater Mercedes and taking his producer for a spin through Central Park.

Avakian already had a plan for their next project. Ravel, Debussy, and other French Impressionist composers had come to mind when he had first heard Miles's *The Birth of the Cool* recordings. He had also been a Claude Thornhill fan and was familiar with Gil Evans, the arranger behind the band's restrained sound.

Left: The creative trio behind *Miles Ahead*: Gil Evans, George Avakian and Miles

Right: Miles recalled, "My ambition has always been to write like Gil."

> I was very fond of the Miles Davis nonet recordings that he had made for Capitol Records. I said to Miles, "Let's expand the idea. Somebody of course has to write the arrangements and conduct, because we're going to go beyond nine pieces. There were only two people who could do it, and luckily they had been in the nonet recordings: Gunther Schuller and Gil Evans."

Davis chose Evans, and work on the album *Miles Ahead* began in earnest.

Columbia's willingness to allow and fund creative ideas like *Miles Ahead* was long established. Past projects had encouraged jazzmen of sufficient talent and interest to try their hand in cross-genre experiments. In 1940, the label recorded Benny Goodman with Bela Bartok in a piece for clarinet, violin, and piano commissioned by Goodman. Fifteen years later, while Miles was still signed to Prestige, Avakian used him as a featured soloist on two newly written pieces, John Lewis's "Three Little Feelings" and J.J. Johnson's "Poem for Brass," included on Columbia's landmark album *The Birth of the Third Stream*. The album also included Gunther Schuller's "Symphony for Brass and Percussion," directed by the New York Philharmonic's Dimitri Mitropoulos. Avakian recalls Davis's eagerness to work with the conductor.

> Miles came and listened [to a recording session for "Symphony"], entranced. "Hey George . . . ask [Mitropoulos] if I can play with his band sometime." Maestro nodded sagely and hummed an "Ahhhhh, perhaps." Miles beamed. (Yes, he used to beam now and then.)

Three decades later Columbia—by then a part of the Sony conglomerate—would pursue a similar "let's-see-what-the-kid-can-do" approach with the new trumpet sensation Wynton Marsalis, whose efforts landed him twin Grammies for jazz and classical recordings in both 1983 and '84.

The *Miles Ahead* sessions proved the most demanding and least improvisational effort of Davis's career to date. But even before it was released, Miles was uncharacteristically blown away by the album:

> I don't keep any of my records. I can't stand to hear them after I've made them. The only ones I really like are the one I just made with Gil Evans, *Miles Ahead,* the one I made with J.J. [Johnson] on my Blue Note date about four years ago and a date I did with Charlie Parker.

Miles Ahead also brought pianist Wynton Kelly into Miles's orbit. Not credited on the original liner notes or session logs, Kelly pops up during studio dialogue as the pianist on "Springsville," a John Carisi original chosen by Evans for the album.

The jazz world's positive reception to Miles's efforts on Prestige paled in comparison with the critical and popular hoopla that heralded his first two albums on Columbia. Employing typical pop promotion strategy—creating an easily identifiable title track, using the first album to boost sales of the second—Avakian ensured *Miles Ahead* breakout success.

> I had told [Miles and Gil], "Look, give me one more composition that's an original and it has to be called 'Miles Ahead' because that's going to be the title of the album. We will push the album by pushing the 'Miles Ahead' title." Everything worked out perfectly: the first album did extremely well, of course, and the second one just took off like a skyrocket and established Miles all over the world. From then on, he was home free.

Miles Ahead had the right level of sophistication for its time; wearing its classical influences on its sleeve, it satisfied intellectually. He had also chosen to record the whole album playing flueglehorn, further emphasizing his clearly stated, refined approach. *The New York Times*'s powerful critic John S. Wilson had for years berated Davis's "limp whimpering and fumbling uncertainty," but even he finally admitted that "within the guiding lines of an arrangement, he could be a clean-lined, soaringly lyrical soloist."

With two profitable albums behind him, Miles had become a *recording* artist, a true hit-maker. His personal income now derived as much from his studio efforts as from his live appearances. His sports car was proof of that, and there weren't many jazzmen driving the same make or model. "You have to keep in mind—for the jazz musician, nightclubs were work," states producer Orrin Keepnews. "The studio was where experimenting happened, but when you hit the stage that's where you made your money." Studio commitments had to be balanced with touring to provide income and steady work for his sidemen.

Miles had turned a large part of his time and attention to the studio in 1957, and his quintet was suffering. Long-simmering problems stemming from substance abuse by Jones and Coltrane were pushing Miles to his limit: "They were running up tabs at the bar, overdrawing money they had coming [and Trane was] playing in clothes that looked like he had slept in." On April 28, less than a week before the sessions had begun for *Miles Ahead,* the Miles Davis quintet finished an engagement at Café Bohemia. It was the last for that stellar lineup: Miles fired both his tenor man and his drummer. Sonny Rollins and Arthur Taylor were immediately brought in to cover the quintet's live commitments.

From late spring through the summer of 1957, the modern jazz community in New York City seemed like the NBA a week before trading deadline. In a series of musical round-robins, Coltrane ended up with Thelonious Monk, performing with the composer over a legendary long summer and fall at the Five Spot. (Miles himself was a frequent patron.) The new Miles Davis lineup returned intermittently to Café Bohemia, once playing opposite the Cannonball Adderley Quintet; Davis immediately renewed his courtship of the alto player.

All the while, Miles was yearning for the sound of his quintet. He found that "as much as I loved Sonny's playing in my band—and Art Taylor's, too—it still wasn't the same for me as when I played with Trane and Joe."

Rollins remained with the quintet until September, when he left to start his own band. At roughly the same time, Red Garland was fired, presumably for his habitual lateness. Tommy Flanagan—Davis's old acquaintance from Detroit—took over on piano.

The summer ended with Cannonball finally deciding to accept Davis's offer over a similar opportunity to join a small group led by Dizzy Gillespie. Adderley admitted his motivation was not purely esthetic. "I had two things in mind. I had the commercial thing in view, like I wanted to get the benefit of Miles's exposure." But, he added: "I figured I could learn more than with Dizzy. Not that Dizzy isn't a good teacher, but he played more commercially than Miles. Thank goodness I made the move I did." Cannonball added:

> Miles hired me essentially because he didn't dig any of the tenor players around and Trane had left. Plus he was always having problems with Red and Joe—not because they were bad guys but everybody had his own style and attitude about what he would do. So we went out on tour: Tommy Flanagan playing piano, Art Taylor playing drums, Paul Chambers playing bass and me.

Though this group was adequate musically, Davis returned to New York determined more than ever to reunite his classic quintet, with the addition of Cannonball. Miles had heard that Coltrane had kicked his habit and his stint with Monk was about to come to an end. "I had this idea in my head of expanding the group from a quintet to a sextet, with Trane and Cannonball on saxophones. Man I could just hear that music in my head and I knew that if I got it together, it would be a motherfucker." But Miles had to postpone acting on his latest vision; he was scheduled in late November to fly to Paris, where he was to perform as a guest soloist with a Paris-based quartet that included Kenny Clarke. An impromptu studio project there would have a lasting effect on his approach to recording.

Miles during the recording of the *Ascenseur pour L'Échafaud* soundtrack with saxophonist Barney Wilen (left) and director Louis Malle

Through his old Parisian girlfriend, actress Juliette Greco, Davis met the young film-maker Louis Malle, who was in the process of completing his first feature *Ascenseur pour L'Échafaud*. Malle needed a musical score for his dark and brooding film, a French take on the *Double Indemnity* story. Working with a limited budget, but also with the advantage of having Davis away from his coterie of lawyers and other representatives, the filmmaker proposed that the trumpeter write and perform the score. Miles accepted.

Relying on the same four local musicians he was performing with (only one of whom he had played with before), Davis recorded the entire score in one overnight session. As the group watched various scenes from the film, Miles, in an ad hoc tour de force, composed, arranged and played trumpet on almost an hour's worth of straight ahead blues themes and simple riffs.

Clarke recalled Davis's confident and hands-on method of musical direction:

> He said, "Wait a minute, right there! Stop! Right here." And he'd say, "We play this,
> and this right here." Because this seemed to go with the scene and it was really well
> thought out. And we did the music to the film right then and there. . . . Miles really
> put it together wonderfully. And, I mean, it all happened on the spur of the moment,
> you know. After about three hours it was over. . . .

Miles's directorial role is clearly audible on the complete recordings to
the *Ascenseur* session. Davis whistles to mark the end of each take as one
brief musical sequence follows another ("Assassinat," "Sequence Voiture").
The compositions hardly seem "composed"; little recognizable melodic
structure and few familiar blues patterns were employed.

This free-fall composing and recording was new and exciting territory for
Davis. Playing in a functional mode—creating sound background to
on-screen images—gave Miles the opportunity to break out of conventional
structures and experiment like never before. If he wished to solo over a
series of chords interminably—or over one chord, for that matter—he could,
as long as the music made sense within the film's narrative. In a manner
that anticipates the suspended effect of a composition like *Kind of Blue*'s
"Flamenco Sketches," "Le Petit Bal" on the *Ascenseur* soundtrack eschewed
any chordal movement at all, allowing Miles to project a mood by simply
playing off one scale, subtly implying a lyrical line.

In the late fifties, Hollywood was just beginning to explore the full
emotive possibilities of jazz musicians and composers on full-feature soundtracks. The list of examples is still awe-inspiring: Elmer Bernstein and
Shorty Rogers on 1955's *Man with the Golden Arm*, Chico Hamilton on
1957's *Sweet Smell of Success*, Duke Ellington on 1959's *Anatomy of a Murder*,
and Charles Mingus on 1960's *Shadows*. Even in comparison with these film
scores—the result of careful planning and generous budgets (or as low
budget as *Ascenseur*, in the case of Cassavetes's *Shadows*)—Miles's one-night,
improvised accomplishment holds up, and indeed stands out all the more.

Back in the New York jazz scene in December 1957, Miles resumed his
effort to reassemble his dream sextet. This time he was not disappointed.
Adderley, Garland, Chambers and Jones were ready and willing. Having
finished his stint with Monk, Coltrane was looking at an idle winter. When
the call came from Davis he jumped at the chance to return.

"By the time he came back, Coltrane had completely changed his image,"
recalled Cannonball in 1972, diplomatically avoiding direct mention of

Coltrane's drug abuse. "He used to drink and do other things. He no longer did anything. He was an instant Christian."

Coltrane was physically healthier and musically stronger. But suddenly, he was in a sextet with one more soloist than before. The musical effect was like turning the heat up on a pressure cooker: Coltrane would have less time to solo onstage, and there was an additional voice (and a very fluid, assertive one at that) to interact with, play off of, and factor into the band's total sound. His musical approach had also expanded dramatically during his time with Monk.

> I felt I learned from him in every way—through the senses, theoretically, technically. I would talk to Monk about musical problems, and he would sit at the piano and show me the answers just by playing them. I could watch him play and find out the things I wanted to know.

Whereas Miles was still distilling his trumpet sound, Coltrane had, with Monk's support, intensified his unbridled, rapid, "sheets of sound" approach (a term coined by producer Ira Gitler in 1958) over the summer and fall. The disparate styles of these two searching, intrepid spirits were about to mesh. The result was surprising and profound. Coltrane would explain it this way:

> On returning . . . I found Miles in the midst of another stage of his musical development. There was one time in his past that he devoted to multichorded structures. He was interested in chords for their own sake. But now it seemed that he was moving in the opposite direction to the use of fewer and fewer chord changes in songs. He used tunes with free-flowing lines and chordal direction. This allowed the soloist the choice of playing chordally (vertically) or melodically (horizontally) . . . due to the direct and free-flowing lines in his music, I found it easy to apply the harmonic ideas that I had.

Coltrane's words limning the departure from jazz tradition that Miles's sextet was about to take aren't particularly abstruse, but his terminology deserves clarification and discussion in the context of basic jazz vocabulary.

If there is one word that accurately describes the unique and defining feature of all jazz styles, it is improvisation. The spirit of jazz is spontaneous invention; the standard form is variations played off the melodies of well-known blues or songs. The melodies of tunes like "Wild Man Blues" would be interpreted, played with, and "jazzed" to the delight of the soloist and his or her audience. When pioneers like Louis Armstrong brought spirit and form together, the result was timeless jazz.

A melody is basically a line of notes, each a root to a matching chord, with the whole melodic line moving (in jazz, swinging) horizontally through time. This movement is referred to as "chord changes" or simply "changes." In the notes of these chords—the "chordal structure" that is often discussed in jazz theory—lies the harmony, or vertical component of jazz. In almost all jazz prior to 1960, harmony was the improviser's only compass. Without knowing which notes work with the chords being played, the soloist was lost. Then came bebop to make the harmony even more complex.

The genius of Charlie Parker and Dizzy Gillespie was to reinvent jazz's harmonic and rhythmic possibilities. Their solos broke through to new territory in jazz harmony, locating new notes to play in the chordal structure. At full throttle, they blew through the changes with phrasing that had become more elastic, bending over and across bar measures with a flurry of sixteenth notes never heard before.

With the advent of Bird and Diz's pioneering daredevilry—richly expanding the number of notes available to play within any given chordal structure—there came the need for an even more accurate harmonic compass. In Cannonball Adderley's words: "Bebop's discipline means that you have to have information to play bebop."

Despite bebop's innovations, improvisation and chord changes remained inextricably linked. Various alumni of bebop—and of the cool school that followed it—had tired of the same changes defining the same well-trodden improvisatory paths. It wasn't the material itself; jazz composers were still creating new, exciting tunes and melodies. It was the too familiar structure of changes-after-changes that bred dissatisfaction. By the fifties, signs were pointing players off the chordal thruway, into a new jazz style: modal.

"Modal" (or its synonym "scalar") literally means "of scales." By this definition, all music, or any sonic system that follows a pattern with one, central "tonic" note, is modal. "Modal jazz," in a late fifties context, qualifies that denotation somewhat. Here's how Miles Davis laid it out for Nat Hentoff in October of 1958:

> When Gil wrote the arrangement of "I Loves You, Porgy," he only wrote a scale for me. No chords. And that . . . gives you a lot more freedom and space to hear things.
>
> When you go this way, you can go on forever. You don't have to worry about changes and you can do more with the [melody] line. It becomes a challenge to see how melodically inventive you can be. When you're based on chords, you know at the end of 32 bars that the chords have run out and there's nothing to do but repeat what you've just done—with variations.
>
> I think a movement in jazz is beginning away from the conventional string of chords . . . there will be fewer chords but infinite possibilities as to what to do with them. Classical composers—some of them—have been writing this way for years, but jazz musicians seldom have.

When I want J.J. Johnson to hear something . . . we just play the music over the phone. I did that the other day with some of [Aram] Khachaturian's Armenian scales; they're different from the usual Western scales. Then we got to talking about letting the melodies and scales carry the tune. J.J. told me, "I'm not going to write any more chords." And look at George Russell. His writing is mostly scales. After all, you can feel the changes.

Call it *The Modal Manifesto*. Subtitle: *You Can Feel the Changes*. In one way, modal jazz was a step in re-simplifying the music, in that it created a structure over which to improvise that, unlike bebop, did not demand extensive knowledge of chords and harmonies. In another way, the use of modes implied a greater responsibility for the musician. Without an established chordal path, the soloist had to invent his own melodic pattern on the spot.

The idea of soloing extensively over one chord was not alien to jazz musicians. Jazz educator and pianist Dick Katz points out that since chords imply certain scales, and modal jazz is all about soloing on one scale for an extended period,

it's like a structured cadenza, where at the end of a piece you take one chord and run with it. Or like in Latin music, a lot of Latin bands will stay on one chord and these virtuoso trumpet players would really do their thing. Or you know there's that Duke Ellington tune, "Caravan." It has twelve bars on one chord (sings) until you land on that F minor chord.

Miles himself had touched upon modal ideas in the past. His "Swing Spring" from 1954 flirted with modal construction. In 1956, he approached a ubiquitous pop song modally as a made-to-order addition for Avakian, slowing down the rate of chord changes and quieting the harmonic activity of the song. Avakian recalls:

Leonard Bernstein wanted me to give him a version of "Sweet Sue" done in cool jazz style for the album that we did together called *What Is Jazz?* Instead of using house musicians to see how it would sound if Miles Davis were doing it, I said, "Let's have Miles Davis play it." I had Miles do two versions and what he did when he performed "Sweet Sue"—a very familiar, trite song deliberately chosen by Bernstein—was a formal introduction before it goes into total improvisation, very free. It was a sudden departure in which he streamlined the chordal structure of the melody—it sort of lost the harmony of the song. That could well have been a spark for his going into the floating quality of what he did on *Kind of Blue*.

Modal jazz was different because it was composed with that simpler approach as its primary goal. Relative to the complexities and intellectual heights jazz had attained, it was a step backward. It seemed to question the progress of jazz up to bebop and beyond. "Playing changes was the sign of elegance," commented keyboardist and jazz writer Ben Sidran. Miles himself had sought that elegance at one time. "When I asked him in the forties what music he was playing," recollected George Russell, "he said he wanted to learn *all* the changes. That sounded ridiculous to me. Miles *knew* how to play all the changes." Russell recognized in that comment the essence of the search that eventually led Davis to modes and modality.

> I felt that Miles was saying he wanted a new way to relate to chords, and the thought of how he might go about seeking this way was constantly dwelled on. Miles and I talked about modes in the late forties and I wondered what was taking him so long, but when I heard "So What" I knew he was using it.

It is worth noting that the brand of modal jazz brought forth in the latter half of the fifties was not pure modal music. When faced with strict modal guidelines, music scholar Barry Kernfeld explains, many jazz soloists would play off a prescribed scale—hitting the same bluesy notes that were an inherent part of chordal jazz. Even musicians like Miles and Coltrane, who adhered more closely to the modal path, suggested chordal patterns in their solos.

There were two immediate effects—and recognizable characteristics—of late fifties modal jazz. The first was that, reflecting the esthetic espoused by Davis and other modal pioneers at the time, it brought the tempos down to a slower, more deliberate pace. As a means of comparison, author Lewis Porter noted that "in most jazz pieces, the chords and their associated scales change about once a measure. But Davis's new music would stay on the same scale for as long as sixteen measures at a time."

Jazz writer Barry Ulanov recognizes that the structure of modal jazz elicited a welcome relaxation of tempo, further emphasizing the "linear," melodic aspect of the music.

> I think that was a happy development in jazz. As in Baroque music and the classical tradition, when you move into long [melodic] lines, there's a softness and slower speed that follows because you're concentrating on what you're trying to say and not surrounding yourself with overwhelming sound.

The second effect was that modal jazz compositions tended to extend the duration of solos. Loosed from the traditional thirty-two or twelve-bar song structure—the most common lengths of jazz compositions (ballads at thirty-two, blues at twelve)—the soloist was free to invent and reinvent as long as necessary to tell the story. In theory, with no chords to define a melody, the solo became the song and the improviser became the composer. The modal jazz soloist was indeed the master of the creative moment.

In the case of Miles's sextet, this elastic approach to solo length was particularly suited to Coltrane, whose penchant for long, tireless improvisations had become legendary. And sometimes, as Gil Evans remembered, an occasion for sarcasm:

> One day when Miles came back from a tour I said "Miles, how was the job?" and he said "It's fine. Coltrane played fifty choruses, Cannonball played forty-six and I played two."

Saxophonist Jimmy Heath, an old friend of Coltrane's from Philadelphia who would later sub for him in the sextet, recalls how the freedom offered by modal jazz pieces might have exacerbated Coltrane's long-windedness.

> Coltrane said the reason he played so long on [modal tunes like "So What"] was that he couldn't find nothing good to stop on. That statement really holds true, too. Because if you haven't played in the modal concept, you're looking for some final cadence to stop. I know musicians had the same problem I did, a lot of them because of the absence of the final cadence of II-V-I [the typical ending of a chorus] or some of the cadences that music, heretofore, had been affording.

It should be added that Heath may well be speaking more of his own trouble with modal structures than Coltrane's, since Trane's recordings from the late fifties and sixties certainly reveal other factors that motivated his verbosity, including an ability to hear and play extended statements and phrases.

What of the modes that gave modal jazz its name? Jazzmen of the fifties—in the spirit typified by Miles's music library visits—sought out new and unusual modal patterns beyond the usual major and minor scales. Those who attended music school could study the twelve modes of the Western musical tradition. All permutations of the basic major scale, the twelve scales were originally defined in the Middle Ages, some to classify Gregorian chants, and were arbitrarily named after ancient Greek cities and regions. Some, like the Ionian and Aeolian modes, are basically modern major and minor scales, respectively. Other modes correspond to folk music scales of various countries. For example, the Phrygian can be exploited to

A detail of a photograph taken by Columbia engineer Fred Plaut on April 22, 1959. Cannonball's music stand reveals the modal structure of "Flamenco Sketches," as written by Bill Evans. The five scales are C Ionian, A-flat Mixolydian, B-flat Major 7th, D Phrygian and G Aeolian. Note Evans's instructions to "play in the *sound* of the scales."

exude a Spanish sonority, as on *Sketches of Spain*. The Dorian mode—favored by classical composers like Ravel and Rachmaninoff—works well as a blues scale and was employed by Miles on "Milestones" off the album of the same name.

New scales would also be found in musical exercise books. "A lot of the scalar material Coltrane was playing was Nicolas Slonimsky's *Thesaurus of Scales and Melodic Patterns*," keyboardist Joe Zawinul remembers, and he adds: "Most of the reed and trumpet players played out of different violin books, and also scale books like [Carl] Czerny."

Other New York musicians discovered modal inspiration nearby, in local restaurants. David Amram recalls:

> I knew about some of those primary modes, because living in New York you could go to these belly-dancing restaurant-bars like the Egyptian Gardens and hear Egyptian, Lebanese and sometimes music from Morocco, all of which had in common a certain rhythmic pattern and a certain mode. Some of the jazz players were really into that. They'd say, "The baddest cats are Bela Bartok, Arnold Schoenberg, and the guys playing in those belly-dancing clubs."

During the fifties, exotic scales—particularly those of India and various Middle Eastern cultures—found their way into the jazz lexicon, and wound up under the "modal jazz" rubric as well. Miles writes of turning Dizzy on to the "Egyptian minor scales" he had learned at Juilliard. Coltrane shared his own fascination with foreign sounds when he wrote in 1960:

> I want [my solos] to cover as many forms of music as I can put into a jazz context and play on my instruments. I like Eastern music . . . and Ornette Coleman sometimes plays music with a Spanish content as well as other exotic-flavored music. In these approaches there's something I can draw on and use in the way I like to play.

The Austrian-born Zawinul, who would join forces with Miles in the late sixties, brought a native familiarity with ethnic modalities of eastern Europe when he arrived in New York in 1958.

> In the early fifties, we were doing modal stuff in Vienna, you know? We were getting into all these different scales from folk music. Where I come from there were all these different influences from Slavic music, Turkish, Rumanian and Hungarian. I was actually surprised when I came to the States that more people weren't doing this.

By the late fifties, that would change.

Davis—with Coltrane and the rest of the sextet—was at the vanguard of this new wave of experimentation that would lead to the prime statement of modal jazz: *Kind of Blue*. But Miles and his group were not alone. In a 1986 interview with Ben Sidran, Miles spoke of how the modal approach had taken hold in the late fifties jazz scene:

> We were just leaning toward—like Ravel, playing a sound with only the white [piano] keys [a common way of defining a mode]. . . . It was the thing to do. . . . Like all of a sudden *all* the architects of the world started making circles, you know, like Frank Lloyd Wright. All of his colleagues are leaning the *same* way at the same time.

McCoy Tyner felt the subtle change in the air in his native Philadelphia during that time. "We were trying to incorporate what was going on at the time, the modal thing. It was such an organic situation—it grew like a plant."

One other musician experimenting with modal structures was a relative newcomer on the New York jazz scene. Bassist Bill Crow remembers a young Bill Evans substituting for pianist Dick Katz in a gig with multi-instrumentalist Don Elliott in 1957.

> At that time, Bill sounded like Lennie Tristano but more up on the time [aggressive rhythmically]—Lennie liked to lay back. Every once in a while, Bill would shift gears and any bass note I'd play would sound wonderful and I'd say "What was that?" He was fooling around with modes then. It was probably some blues we were playing. That was the first time I had heard that "no-chord change" where the same chord would just kind of hang in the air through the tune.

Unlike Davis, Bill Evans had arrived at modal jazz more through his own conservatory studies (at Southeastern Louisiana University and later Mannes College of Music) than through the environment of clubs and studio dates. But both of these jazz artists would have profound influence on the future of the music. And it was their relationship that created the spark that resulted in *Kind of Blue*.

On the surface, it would be difficult to imagine two more contrasting musicians. One had grown into a charismatic performer, comfortable and serenely confident on center stage; the other, bookish and withdrawn by nature, held himself and his music in extremely modest regard. Whereas Miles had left the conservatory for a nightclub education, completing only a year at Juilliard, Bill had an extensive academic background in classical studies and general music theory. While Davis was riding the crest of modern jazz explorations through the mid-fifties, from bebop to cool to hard bop, Evans was performing with society bands and orchestras, taking Nat "King" Cole's swing-based piano playing as a model.

Despite their opposing characteristics, Davis and Evans proved to be two musical explorers bound by kindred passions and visions. Both were ardent fans of modern classical composers such as Rachmaninoff and the French impressionists. In their ears, jazz and classical were two streams feeding into the same river. Miles's live-in girlfriend (and future wife), the dancer Frances Taylor, recalls that "the music we heard at home was Khatchaturian, Ravel, Brahms, and all of that, constantly." As related in Peter Pettinger's biography of Evans, *How My Heart Sings*, an old girlfriend of the pianist's remembered his daily routine: "He would usually play classical music . . . Rachmaninoff . . . Beethoven and Bach. He would play that and then just drift into jazz in a very fluid kind of way."

Both Davis and Evans had also developed personal voices that, in strong contrast to the technique-driven jazz styles flowing around them, were all about pruning away excess and distilling emotion. They shared an obsessive lyricism and a melodic flow that suggested, rather than obviously defined, musical structure. Evans's rich, classical voicings on piano—uncommon in a jazz context—avoided playing the root note of a chord, thus opening up the music's harmonic possibilities. Miles's, by "playing one note and having it relate to several chords at the same time," accomplished something similar from another direction. Cannonball Adderley told Ira Gitler: "Coltrane and I call it the 'implied reference,' the things Miles does."

In 1955, an introduction to George Russell by a mutual friend brought the pianist and Miles to within one degree of separation. Russell's and Evans's relationship became one of teacher and pupil. The pianist caught Russell's enthusiasm regarding modal jazz as Davis had. In Evans, Russell found a talented pianist for his recording efforts who could follow his compositional instructions and still swing.

Through 1956, Evans was applying the modal lessons he had learned. During the year, Russell produced a number of sessions for his own Victor album *Jazz Workshop* including "Concerto for Billy the Kid," written especially for Evans. Evans also recorded that year with clarinetist Tony Scott, on the modally based tune "Aeolian Drinking Song." Six months later, Evans was called to work with Scott on a follow-up big band effort, arranging and performing on a number of tunes, including a distinctive version of Davis's "Walkin'."

In 1957, Russell was invited to contribute a piece to the Brandeis University Festival of the Arts organized by an alumnus of *The Birth of the Cool* get-togethers: the composer, conductor and French horn player Gunther Schuller. Russell offered "All About Rosie," a suite that featured Evans against a hard-driving, orchestrated backdrop. The piece was later recorded for the

Columbia album *Modern Jazz Concert*, in the same 30th Street Studio that would be the setting for Miles's own modal masterpiece, *Kind of Blue*.

30th Street Studio

was born out of necessity. In the late forties, Columbia Records' parent company CBS, expanding into TV, had commandeered Liederkranz Hall and unceremoniously sliced the company's only large recording venue into two separate TV studios (as John Hammond later put it, thus ruining "acoustically one of the finest recording spaces ever to exist in New York"). Columbia was forced to look elsewhere for a home in which to record their larger, orchestral efforts. The same year they launched their new LP format, the label found what they required in an abandoned Greek Orthodox church at 207 East 30th Street, just east of Third Avenue in the shadow of the Empire State Building. Columbia immediately began equipping it as a recording facility.

In 1946 Columbia had recruited Frank Laico, an electronic engineer by training, who, in his second year with the company, was transferred from their uptown Seventh Avenue offices to the new studios:

> *30th Street Studio was a hundred feet by a hundred feet and had very high ceilings; the room was just tremendous. We could record [anything] from solo [musicians] to full symphony orchestras, and Broadway cast albums with forty or fifty musicians. When Columbia got CBS to agree to buy the building, one of the stipulations was that CBS was not going to go in there and clean it up and make it look pretty. We didn't change a thing: for years we had drapes from the old church hanging askew and dust all over. We closed in the balcony upstairs and that became the control booth.*

30th Street began operating mostly as a studio for classical recordings. One of the earliest sessions dates back to December 1947, when pianist Robert Casadesus and the New York Philharmonic under the direction of Charles Munch recorded Mozart's Concerto #21. But soon, thanks in part to Mitch Miller, the studio began producing hit records for Rosemary Clooney, Tony Bennett, Jo Stafford, and Frankie Laine. One of the first producers to work mostly at 30th Street, Miller produced his first session there in February of 1950 with Rosemary Clooney.

> *30th Street was in operation when I got there, but most producers were still afraid to use it because they didn't know what to make of the reverberation. I started to use it immediately. Solo piano, orchestras, vocals with arrangements—my first hit, "Tzena, Tzena, Tzena."*

From left: The mixing board and tape machines in the engineers' booth upstairs at 30th Street; 30th Street Studio in the mid-fifties. Note the vintage cars; Fred Plaut at the controls

30th Street developed a reputation throughout the music industry, and began drawing outside business. When not in use by Columbia artists, the studio and its engineers were hired out to other labels happy to use the reverberant room for their own projects. At 30th Street, there was an implicit guarantee that the room would yield only the highest-quality audio recording.

"It had something you don't find in today's studios—it had an identifying sound," says Mike Berniker, a Sony Music vice president who produced Barbra Streisand in 30th Street during the sixties. "There was a grandeur to the sound—a size and a scope that you don't find from very close miking [the industry standard since the late sixties]." Photographs taken at 30th Street bear out Berniker's words: in countless pop, jazz, and classical sessions, microphones are suspended far above the musicians, apparently recording the room more than the instruments.

Boosted by the explosive success of *Miles Ahead,* Davis's reconstituted sextet had been performing into early 1958. With Coltrane and Cannonball blowing side by side, and The Rhythm Section intact, all should have been running smoothly. But the shadow of heroin addiction was still upon the band, particularly in the case of Garland and Jones. Problems with money, tardiness, and attitude persisted. Nonetheless, the first sextet album for Columbia was in the works: the aptly named *Milestones* was recorded at 30th Street in March and April. "This was the first record where I started to write in the modal form," Davis noted. "On the title track I really used the form."

With Cannonball's bluesy alto added to the mix, Davis's group conjured the glory of the quintet and took it to another level. But the balance shifted during the sessions. When it came time to record the slower blues-based "Sid's

Outside producers and musicians express a similar fondness and nostalgia when recalling 30th Street. Quincy Jones: "I used to record down at that studio with a band with J.J. [Johnson], Kai [Winding], and Sonny Stitt. It was pure *acoustic* sound. What was great about it was all the wood—for woodwinds and other acoustic instruments." Berniker echoes the importance of the room's being made of a natural material. "There wasn't any metal in there. There was a correspondence between the sound of strings and other instruments and the sound of the room because of the wooden surfaces."

Teo Macero, who was first hired by Columbia as a tape editor and later became Davis's producer, credits the engineers as well. "All the engineers were top-notch. They knew the room." That knowledge—where the right spots were for a small jazz combo, or a singer and orchestra—was crucial, and a matter of individual taste. "All of us [engineers] were a good bunch of guys, but we never worked the same way," recalls Laico. "Fred [Plaut] was an excellent engineer, but I could never set up the way he set up, because it was just wrong for me, audio-wise. But we'd get the same result."

30th Street was part of a family of well-known recording facilities in the New York area turning out the music of the 1950s and '60s. Today musicians, engineers and producers nostalgically recall 30th Street and other revered studios in and around the city, including Victor's Webster Hall on the Lower East Side, Vanguard Records' Masonic Temple in Brooklyn, and the less grand Regent Sound on Fifty-Seventh Street. They became the true shrines in the age of hi-fi, worshipped for their generous space, curved interiors and wooden walls, all offering a warm, natural reverb. In those hallowed halls, great musical performances were transubstantiated into timeless recordings.

Ahead" (an undisguised reworking of "Walkin'"), Davis leaned over Garland's shoulder to make a point regarding his playing. What was actually said will remain a mystery, but it was enough to push the pianist over a personal edge. In a huff, Red exited the studio, leaving Miles to play piano on the track.

The incident strained the already frayed relationship between Davis and his pianist. Cannonball recalled the breaking point.

We used to go to Philadelphia to play three times a year and it was an especially bad town for dope addicts and people who had any record for "utility"—narcotics and so forth. Red had a wife there and nonsupport lien on his wages, so he said, "What's the point?" Miles would say, "Man, you're playing in the band, you're supposed to go where the band goes." And Red said, "No man, I ain't gonna do that." Miles had this little Mercedes 190SL, and he said, "Cannon, I'd like you to take a ride with me." We were driving up [Manhattan's] West Side highway and he asked, "You ever heard of Bill Evans?" I said "Yeah," because Nat [Adderley] had been freelancing and he worked someplace in the Village with a drummer who had hired Bill Evans to play. I went down to see them and I heard this cat and said, "Wow, this is a beautiful piano player." So I said, "I think he's beautiful."

As Jimmy Cobb later noted, "When he had to fill a spot in the band, [Miles] used to take the consensus of opinion from everybody." But Miles had been out in the field as well. Evans remembers playing a series of solo gigs at the Village Vanguard. "One night I looked up, opened my eyes while I was playing and Miles's head was at the end of the piano listening."

Russell took it upon himself to bring Davis and Evans together.

We [Russell, Evans, and guitarist Barry Galbraith] got in my Volkswagen and went to a club in Bed-Stuyvesant, Brooklyn. After the intermission he asked Bill to come up and play and that night he hired him on the spot. He said, "You're goin' to Philadelphia with us next Saturday."

Finally, the two searchers were sharing the same stage as well as musical ideas and experiments. Evans brought a quiet strength to Davis's music that complemented his sense of space and subtlety. Describing the pianist's effect, the usually terse trumpeter waxed poetic: "Bill had this quiet fire that I loved on piano. The way he approached it, the sound he got was like crystal notes or sparkling water cascading down from some clear waterfall. Red's playing had carried the rhythm but Bill underplayed it. . . ."

Having settled on a pianist, Davis turned his attention to Philly Joe Jones. A problem had developed with the drummer that must have seemed all too familiar after Garland's issues with Philadelphia. As drummer Elvin Jones remembers, an opportunity to substitute for Jones turned sour once he discovered that Philly Joe had a history with the city's narcotics squad.

I played with [Miles] once, oddly enough. I subbed for Philly Joe one week and they had to go to Philadelphia and Joe didn't want to go so I took his place. Miles and I got arrested at the [Sunday] matinee. The cops came in and they thought I was Philly Joe and they swept us off to jail. But the fellow who owned that Blue Note in North Philly had an uncle who was a judge, so it didn't last very long.

Around the same time Evans entered the band, Jones left the band for the last time. Cannonball, the group's de facto tour manager, recalled:

Philly Joe had drawn up all of his money when we worked at Café Bohemia. At the end of the [week] he didn't have any money coming and he insisted that he hadn't drawn everything. I said, "Well, man all you get is what you're supposed to get and that's it." Philly said, "Well, you play in Boston without me." So we went to Boston and Miles said, "Joe ain't coming." I said, "Call Jimmy Cobb."

Cobb had already filled in the previous summer when Art Taylor had left the bandstand in mid-set under similar conditions to Garland's mid-session departure. He got the call, but without much warning.

> When I first got the call from Miles it was like six-thirty in the evening and he said, "We're working tonight." I said, "Great, where?" He said, "In Boston." I was in New York and we hit at nine! I said, "We hit at nine o'clock really?" I throw all my stuff together right quick, really frantically and go to the shuttle with all the drums and stuff. When I get up there I get a cab to Copley Square where the club is, another one of George Wein's clubs [Storyville], and they're on the stand playing without drums. So I start setting up and they're playing "'Round Midnight" and by the time I'm ready, they're right at the interlude and the horn line says Bah-bah-bah-bah-bah. That's where I started. I played that lick and from then on I was with the band.

Left: *Milestones* was the last Miles project Columbia Records producer George Avakian worked on before departing the label

Right: The first incarnation of the sextet. From left: Coltrane, Davis, Garland, Chambers and Adderley

Following: August 23, 1958: The sextet at the New York Jazz Festival, Randall's Island, New York City

The time was late May 1958. A more reliable and musically more subtle version of Miles's sextet was officially in place: Miles Davis, Bill Evans, John Coltrane, Cannonball Adderley, Paul Chambers, and Jimmy Cobb. It was a lineup that would remain intact for almost seven months—and it would reunite for an encore studio performance in early 1959 to make *Kind of Blue*.

Evans may have been ready to join Miles's group musically, but his New York-based career up to that point—random nightclub gigs and recording sessions—did not prepare him for the sextet's whirlwind touring schedule. From the late spring and through the summer, the band traveled from Washington, D.C. to Baltimore, back to New York, up to Newport, playing incessantly in nightclubs, theaters and various summer festivals. For Evans—

still slightly damp behind the ears—the stint was an eye-opening introduction to the rigors and demands of being a member of a popular jazz outfit.

On May 26, Miles's thirty-second birthday, the sextet stopped long enough at 30th Street to record for the first time with Evans and Cobb in the band. They recorded "Fran-Dance"—a tune based on a children's game and alternatively titled "Put Your Little Foot Right Out"—and two Jamal-inspired numbers, "On Green Dolphin Street" and "Stella by Starlight." Evans introduces both songs delicately and thoughtfully, the latter so sparsely and softly that the simple effect of the rhythm section kicking into high gear at the beginning of Coltrane's solo is startling. Evans's own solo is both lush and laconic, suggesting the bittersweet spell he would help cast over the *Kind of Blue* sessions the following year.

The session exposed Evans to Davis's spontaneous ability in the studio to simplify complicated musical structure. In 1979, Evans told New York City jazz radio station WKCR:

> Miles occasionally might say, "Right here, I want this sound," and it turns out to be a very key thing that changes the whole character of the [song]. For instance, on "On Green Dolphin Street," the original changes of the chorus aren't the way [we recorded it]: the vamp changes being a major seventh up a minor third, down a half tone. That was [one when] he leaned over and said, "I want this here."

But as Evans told jazz arranger and journalist Sy Johnson, the last track they recorded that day indicated that the band's new restrained approach—a direct consequence of Evans's arrival—did not totally satisfy all its members. "Paul Chambers and Jimmy Cobb were getting edgy having to hold back, and wanted to cook on something. Miles just turned and said, 'Love for Sale' and kicked it off." On record, the release is almost palpable as the band finally got their chance to swing.

Evans was caught in a dilemma from the outset. He had been hired for his rich precision, his ability to understate the piano's solo voice. Miles was happy; he was fascinated by the sound of the new band and the challenges it inspired. But the remainder of the group wanted a piano man with at least one foot firmly planted in the rhythm section. Cannonball, writing in a *Down Beat* column in 1960, noted: "Especially when he started to use Bill Evans, Miles changed his style from very hard to a softer approach. Bill was brilliant in other areas, but he couldn't make the real hard things come off."

Evans was no Garland, and Cannonball, for one, missed the drama Garland had created behind his solos. Whereas Davis happily explored new levels of musical nuance with Evans, Adderley told Ira Gitler:

> I like the piano player to stroll . . . Red Garland is a master of that. He'll stroll then he comes back in and he plays a little more and by the time you get through playing he's made a big production of it.

Despite Cannonball's preference for the dramatic, it should be noted that Adderley himself fell under the pianist's spell to a lasting degree. He used Evans on his own *Portrait of Cannonball* in July of 1958, a session attended

The sextet waits backstage in Chicago's Civic Opera House, February 14, 1959. From left: Chambers, Adderley, unidentified, Coltrane and Davis

by Miles (who contributed his tune "Nardis," which became a staple of Evans's repertoire). Three years later Cannonball called on Evans again, seeking to recreate the modal magic of *Kind of Blue*. Built around the Evans approach, *Know What I Mean?* featured the pianist's name on the cover, and a number of his compositions (as well as the Modern Jazz Quartet's bassist and drummer, Percy Heath and Connie Kay).

On certain recordings, Evans certainly proved he was up to the challenge of the band's more charged, rhythmic songs. One need only listen to the passion of the sextet's Newport set from 1958, and the light-fingered, Monk-inspired solo on "Straight, No Chaser." But there is also evidence that Evans may not have provided the rhythmic foil needed. In September of that year, the group was recorded as part of a star-studded concert at the Plaza Hotel in Manhattan, featuring Davis, Ellington, Billie Holiday, and Jimmy Rushing. It was another high-charged set, with some inventive and chance-taking solo work on Evans's part, especially on "Oleo" and "My Funny Valentine." (The latter tune is a rare and valuable example of direct interplay between Miles and Evans alone together as Coltrane and Cannonball sit out.) But Evans took a backseat rhythmic role on some numbers, laying out (not playing) rather than comping during solos by Cannonball and Coltrane.

Evans certainly discerned some resentment about his style from within the band. But the most difficult test he had to endure, as Evans's biographer Pettinger put it, was "his status as a racial minority of one." As Cannonball recalled: "Miles made him uncomfortable and used to mess with him—not about his music or anything—he just used to fool with him, call him 'whitey'." Davis himself admits putting Evans through the wringer from the outset, telling him: "You got to make it with everybody, you know what I mean? You got to fuck the band."

Evans diplomatically declined ("I'd like to please everyone . . . but I just can't do that"). But what he eventually could not ignore was a constant flow of "Crow Jim"—prejudice against white jazz musicians—from nightclub audiences. As he told *The New York Times* in 1977:

> It was more of an issue with the fans. The guys in the band defended me staunchly. We were playing black clubs, and guys would come up and say, "What's that white guy doing there?" They said, "Miles *wants* him there—he's *supposed* to be there!"

Nevertheless, by November 1958—with one studio session, two live sets, and a few nightclub radio broadcasts the only recorded evidence of his membership in the sextet—the various pressures of touring ("being on the road drained me in every respect") proved to be too much. "Bill put in his notice," according to Cannonball.

Miles rehired Red Garland, though as Cannonball would later recall, old habits die hard—and so did Garland's.

> Miles hired Red back. We went into Birdland and Red was the kind of cat who was notoriously late. We all *knew* we were going to start playing without a piano. One night before we were in Birdland we went down to Brooklyn to see Dizzy's band—it was fantastic. He had Sam Jones, Wynton Kelly, Candido and Sonny Stitt. Miles just spent all evening listening to Wynton. So we went into Birdland and we had been there about a week and Red was always late. One night Wynton was there when we started and Miles asked him to sit in. When Red came, Wynton was playing. Miles told Red, "Wynton's got the gig." Just like that.

Comparing the three pianists that overlapped his tour of duty with Miles, Adderley commented on their relative merits:

> Bill is a fine pianist, and his imagination is a little more vivid so that he tries more daring things. But Wynton plays with the soloist all the time . . . he even anticipates

your direction. Red is another excellent accompanist. He fits well with the drummer always and he doesn't leave you anything to do but go where you want to.

Cannonball's viewpoint brings to light another aspect of Evans's personality that may have limited his stint with Davis. Evans, like Davis, was meant to be a leader. Though he would not form his first permanent group until 1959 (initially with bassist Jimmy Garrison and drummer Kenny Dennis, both on Davis's recommendation), Evans came out of his seven-month experience a more assured, if slightly tired, musician: "It did a great deal for my confidence. I thought it was the greatest jazz band I had ever heard."

Onstage at the Civic Opera House with Wynton Kelly at the piano

After leaving the sextet, Evans returned to Louisiana to relax with his brother. Back in New York, the pianist's sound had left its mark on Davis. Saxophonist David Liebman recalls:

> He said Bill was really the guy who opened the doors for him musically . . . Bill was very special to him. He said to me, "I used to call Bill up and tell him to take the phone off the hook; just leave it off and play for me because I loved the way he played."

Miles had hired Evans because he needed a pianist who was "into the modal thing." But the band's performances and recordings of standards and a handful of originals to date had left the sextet's modal jazz possibilities largely untested.

The following spring Miles would change that.

Columbia Records'
1959 studio reservation
book

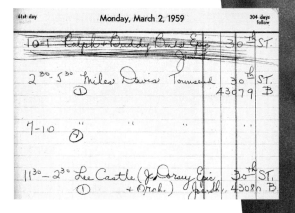

61st day	Monday, March 2, 1959	304 days follow

10=1 Ralph + Buddy Bass Epic   30ᵗʰ ST.

2³⁰–5³⁰ Miles Davis Townsend   30ᵗʰ ST.
                              43079 B

7–10

11³⁰–2³⁰ Lee Castle (Jy Dorsey Epic 30ᵗʰ ST.
            + Orch.)   43080 B

First Session

March 2, 1959
2:30 pm

"The machine's on . . .

here we go: co 62290, no title, take one . . .'

THE INITIAL SOUND heard on the master tape of the first *Kind of Blue* session is producer Irving Townsend's Massachusetts twang. Townsend had inherited the role of producer for Miles after the successive departures of George Avakian (to Warner Brothers Records) and Cal Lampley (to RCA Records) the year before. In a few months, he would take over West Coast production duties for Columbia Records, passing the baton to Teo Macero, the newcomer who would remain Davis's primary producer at Columbia for many years.

Townsend had been a jazz bandleader before World War II, and joined Columbia as an advertising copywriter after Benny Goodman introduced him to George Avakian. Townsend had sold Avakian on the idea of using him to assist on recording sessions. By the mid-fifties he was producing full-time, handling a number of Columbia's pop and jazz acts, including Rosemary Clooney; Lambert, Hendricks and Ross; Dave Brubeck; and Duke Ellington. It was Townsend who produced Billie Holiday's *Lady in Satin* album in 1958, granting her longstanding wish to record with strings. Over the years, Townsend had become Duke Ellington's primary producer: less than a week before the first *Kind of Blue* session, at the same commodious studio, he had produced a late-night session with Duke that would yield two tunes for the album *Jazz Party*. The previous September, he had overseen the recording of the press gala featuring Davis, Ellington, Holiday, and Jimmy Rushing.

Next to "Engineer" on the *Kind of Blue* tape logs are the initials "FP." By luck of the draw, Fred Plaut was working that day. The session was Plaut's

Irving Townsend producing Duke Ellington's 1958 classic *Black, Brown and Beige,* with Mahalia Jackson

Right: The *Kind of Blue* tape log, first session: note the initials "IT" on the line identifying the producer

Sheet No. 1								Job No. B 43079	
Date 3/2/59								Reel No. 1	
Program *Miles Davis*			Tape Identification Data			DEPT. OR CLIENT *Pop*		Studio 30	
Start No.	Start Time	SELECTION TITLE SPOT DATA			Take No.	F. S.	Master No.	OK	REMARKS
1		CO 62290			1/2	8/8			10/30/93 used
2		(FREDDIE FREELOADER)			3/4	8/	9:38		1" Sx Solo
3			Ins. 1		1				
4		CO 62291 N. 2			1/2	8/8			
5		(SO WHAT)			3/3	8/	9:30		
6		CO 62292 N. 3			1/2	8/8			
7					3/4	8/8			
8					5		5:30		
9									
10									
11									
12									
13									
14									
15									
SPLICING DATA									

| Producer *IT* | Engineer *FP - RW* |
| CR-588 | |

first with Davis. One of Columbia's top three studio engineers (along with Frank Laico and Harold "Chappie" Chapman), Plaut had a back-of-the-hand familiarity with the 30th Street Studio. Born in Germany, he had run his own studio in Paris before fleeing the Nazi takeover, coming to New York and eventually Columbia Records in the late forties.

Plaut was also an avid photographer who trained his lens on both his in-studio work and other, nonmusical subjects (his archive of images now resides in the Yale University Music Library). But he was without camera that day, and as no Columbia staff photographer was assigned, no photographic record of that first *Kind of Blue* session exists. (The images presented in this chapter were taken during the better-documented second session.)

One essential that the studio did provide that day was a tuned piano. "What stands out is that the piano was always in tune," remembers Dave Brubeck. "The tuner was usually there before the session, and sometimes he'd stick around for the session." The Steinway piano Brubeck normally used was the same one played by Bill Evans and Wynton Kelly for the *Kind of Blue* sessions. Tape engineer Bob Waller recalls one other distinguishing characteristic of that piano: "Brubeck beat the shit out of it so it had very little felt left on the upper register. It was quite metallic." (As of this writing, the piano is still in use in New York's Clinton Recording Studios on Tenth Avenue.)

Townsend had booked 30th Street that Monday for two consecutive sessions, from 2:30 to 5:30 P.M., and from 7:00 to 10:00 P.M. The studio had been empty since a Saturday afternoon session recording pop singer Jerry Vale, which Mitch Miller had produced. Now, on this cloudy, late-winter afternoon, Townsend, Plaut, and Waller awaited the musicians.

This was to be Miles's first small-group studio session since May of the previous year, when he had recorded "Stella by Starlight" and three other tracks. Following that date, Davis was recorded live at the Newport Jazz Festival in August and at the Jazz at the Plaza gala in September, and closed out 1958 by recording his second Gil Evans-arranged orchestral landmark, *Porgy & Bess.*

Miles and the sextet showed no signs of slowing down in 1959. They had opened the year at Birdland in New York City. A two-week run in Chicago from January 21 through February 2 had culminated in a sextet-minus-Miles recording session for Mercury Records (*Cannonball Adderley Quintet in Chicago*) and a concert appearance at the Civic Opera House (sharing the bill with Thelonious Monk, Gerry Mulligan, and Sarah Vaughan). A one-week engagement at San Francisco's Black Hawk had followed, and they returned home before the end of the month.

Getting Davis into the studio—though not yet the challenge it would

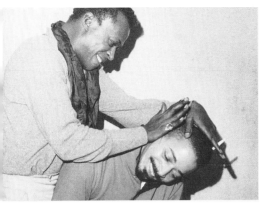

Miles clowns with Jimmy Cobb in the studio during the *Sketches of Spain* sessions. Cobb was never photographed during the recording of *Kind of Blue*

become during the sixties—was usually induced by an advance payment on his annual contract, and the *Kind of Blue* session was no exception. By now, the back-and-forth process was predictable: Miles would request an advance on his contract, or loan from his producer, and the label would counter by requesting another studio effort. The amount of the advance would be determined by Davis's recent sales history. (In an internal Columbia memo from November 1960, on the heels of *Kind of Blue* and *Sketches of Spain,* Townsend argues for a payment to Davis—who had asked for $15,000 but "would accept $10,000 with only a mild oath"—"if his current earning status has improved enough so that he can get another loan.")

With an eye to ensuring a minimum output from their exclusive artists, and providing sufficient time between releases so that consecutive albums would not compete with each other, standard Columbia contracts of the day called for at least two album releases a year. But since many artists proved unavailable or distracted when it came time for another recording effort, Columbia developed the habit of squirreling away extra tracks from one session to another. As it turned out—in a coincidence that reflected the unity of mood and feel of the album—the *Kind of Blue* sessions produced exactly what was needed for the album, no more, no less.

After Avakian's departure, Cal Lampley, in his brief stint as producer for Miles, had discovered that at times Davis needed to get comfortable with a concept. Inspired by the unusual arrangement of "Summertime" from the *Miles Ahead* sessions, Lampley had called Miles to ask him to consider making a *Porgy & Bess* album:

> He said, "Cal, I'm sitting here trying to think of doing something with my wife and you're calling me with this shit," and hung up! Uh-oh, I guess I blew that. Then ten days later he called me and said, "Cal, that *Porgy & Bess* idea's a good one—let's get started."

In Davis's own telling, "Frances [Taylor] was dancing in *Porgy & Bess* at City Center . . . that's where I got the idea." When it came time to book the studio for the *Kind of Blue* sessions, there was little discussion: Columbia was happy to have Miles back at 30th Street only three months after *Porgy & Bess*, and he was ready with an album idea that he was itching to record.

DAVIS SESSION: 4/22/59

3 1/2 hrs. worth of playing time on 3 h

One check was issued for $129.36 -- Miles has cashed this, is equivilent t
3 1/2hr. payment.

One check was issued for $392.00 --- to be broken down as follows:

SAX:

J. ADDERLEY _____
J. COLTRANE _____ $64.67
64.67

PIANO:

W. KELLY _____
W. Evans _____ 64.67
64.67

BASS:

P. CHAMBERS _____ 66.67 (cartage included)

DRUMS:

J. COBB _____ 66.67 (Cartage included)

4 Musicians @ $64.17
2 Musicians @ $66.17 _____ $258.68
133.34
$392.02

Jimmy Cobb arrived early, to give himself time to set up his drum kit and the engineers time to deal with its placement in the studio. Cobb had been with Miles for almost a full year at this point, and his tenure felt more and more secure. Though Philly Joe Jones's reputation was formidable, Cobb found comfort in the shift in the sextet's musical direction.

> You know, I was playing after Philly Joe and I didn't know how that was going to work out. Luckily, the music started to change where I really didn't have to play the way Joe played—it went to modes. I was relieved to know I wouldn't have to try to outplay Philly Joe, which was going to be impossible.

It was the drummer's third studio session with Miles Davis (after the "On Green Dolphin Street" and *Porgy & Bess* dates), and it was business as usual. "The call I got from Miles for that record was just like any other record. He'd say we've got a date, where it is and what time it is—I didn't know if it was *Kind of Blue* or *Kind of Green* at the time, you know?"

"43079" was the project number Columbia had assigned the as yet unnamed *Kind of Blue* sessions. Trumpeter Lee Castle and the Jimmy Dorsey Orchestra were scheduled to follow the Miles Davis Sextet from 11:30 to 2:30 that night with project 43080.

Miles was himself responsible for booking and contracting the members of his sextet. As was standard practice for the day, sidemen were paid union scale for a three-hour recording session, which in 1959 came to $48.50. As the day called for two consecutive sessions, Davis's sidemen were due double scale. How the band members took this allotment, knowing of the lucrative success of Davis's releases, is hard to say. But a series of memos from Columbia's files does reveal that for both *Kind of Blue* sessions, Miles requested—and with Townsend's help, succeeded in securing—an additional $100 for the more senior members of his group: Chambers, Coltrane, and Adderley.

For the first *Kind of Blue* session, Davis called in one significant former member of his sextet. As Davis later wrote, he "had already planned that album around the piano playing of Bill Evans." Intentionally or not, he had not bothered to apprise his current pianist and newest band member, Wynton Kelly, of his decision.

Kelly, whose own entry into the group had resulted from the unexpected, offhand firing of Red Garland, must been surprised to arrive at the studio and find one of his predecessors there. Cobb remembers that Kelly was a little out of sorts and out of pocket as well.

Wynton used to come to the gigs from Brooklyn by cab because he couldn't stand the subway. So he saw Bill sitting at the piano and was flabbergasted! He said, "Damn, I rushed all the way over here and someone else is sitting at the piano!" I said, "Hold it before you go off, you're on the date too."

Opposite: A Columbia memo recorded the union scale payments due Miles's sextet for the first session

Below: Mapping it out modally

As Cobb set up his kit, the others arrived, hung their coats on the rack near the door, and arranged themselves and their instruments on various stools and chairs in the studio. "I remember Miles and others milling about, running through the heads (arrangements), so by the time I was ready they were pretty well set [to start recording]."

Evans's liner notes famously assert that "Miles conceived these settings only hours before the recording dates," and *Kind of Blue* is still largely thought of as totally unrehearsed and totally written by Davis. However, if what the participants, including Evans himself, reported over the years can be trusted, the source of the music is not as clear-cut as the notes claim.

First, just how new were the five tunes? Despite the lack of any evidence (nightclub broadcast or other recording) from the preceding months, Cobb claimed that "we had played ['So What'] once or twice on gigs." A few months before the release of *Kind of Blue,* Miles himself admitted to jazz journalist Ralph Gleason that "All Blues" had originated as a live number and evolved over six months, benefiting at one point from a workover by Gil Evans. "I wrote it in 4/4," Gleason quoted Davis as saying. "But when we got to the studio it hit me that it should be 3/4. I hadn't thought of it before, but it was exactly right." Bill Evans had not been playing regularly with Davis's group for over three months; he would not have known any new material that had been introduced on the bandstand in that time, whether roughly conceived or fully arranged.

And what of the contention that all five of the tracks were Davis's creations? For whatever reason—perhaps a tight deadline—

in *Kind of Blue*'s well-read liners Evans wrote away his own role. As he recalled years later, the responsibility for providing material was a shared one.

> It was the first time Miles recorded an album which was *largely* his compositions. That morning before the date I went to his apartment. I sketched out "Blue in Green," which was my tune and I sketched out the melody and the changes to it for the guys. "Flamenco Sketches" was something Miles and I did together.

Miles's stand on the issue could be less than consistent. In his autobiography, Miles adamantly refused to share composer credit for the album as a whole: "Some people went around saying that Bill was co-composer of the music on *Kind of Blue*. That wasn't true; it's all mine. . . ." Yet Davis also told his biographer Quincy Troupe in 1986: "'Blue in Green'—we [Bill and Miles] wrote that together. . . ."

The authorship of "Blue in Green," and Evans's collaborative role on *Kind of Blue* in general, have long been a point of contention. Friends, band members, and critics close to Evans have spoken of the bitterness he showed when talking of his claim. In Pettinger's biography one colleague recalled being told by Evans of Miles's alleged response to the pianist's demand to share in the album's significant royalties: a single check for $25.

Decades after the album's completion, Miles's copyright seems to have solidified, less by his own assertion than by Evans's passivity. Despite his vitriolic complaints, the pianist never actively pursued the matter in his lifetime, and Miles—in many interviews—certainly made an effort to give the pianist credit for inspiration and sound, if not for specific songs. "Evans's approach to the piano brought that piece [*Kind of Blue*] out," Miles told Ben Sidran in 1986.

Jimmy Cobb is more definite about Evans's role. "Actually, a lot of that stuff [for *Kind of Blue*] was composed in conjunction with Bill Evans," he has stated. "The ideas and music were mostly where Bill was coming from."

One point remains uncontested: *Kind of Blue* is all original music, resulting from motivations musical and beyond. First, the new modal style required new standards. One could not just graft modality onto well-known jazz tunes. "You play 'Confirmation' and play a solo in modal form and it's funny," noted Adderley. It also, according to pianist Dick Katz, reflected a significant social change for Davis and the New York jazz scene in general. "I think, on the part of black musicians, they didn't want to play the standard songbook anymore. They didn't want to play any more Cole Porter. They wanted to come up with their own music, which was African American totally." In 1958, Miles himself noted that he "wanted the music this new group would play to be freer, more modal, more African or Eastern and less

Western." "Love for Sale" did not fit the bill anymore.

Teo Macero recollects pushing Davis on the subject of writing around the same time. On the 1955 recording of "Sweet Sue" they had achieved a level of comfortable intensity.

> He was prolific when he wanted to be but he was also very lazy. I told him that too. I'd say, "You're a lazy sonofabitch, why don't you go out and write some music?" "Oh fuck you," he'd say. So at that point I'd laugh. When you're going to talk to genius, you just have to [keep] talking, you know. . . . After *Porgy & Bess,* he finally started writing and kept writing and writing and writing.

If not entirely unrehearsed or of Davis's composition, *Kind of Blue* was still a bold step forward for the trumpeter. He was defining a self-reliant, studio-based approach that in 1959, for the first time in Columbia's studio, allowed him to direct a whole project from composing to bandleading and recording. "A composer-musician-performer" was the label Teo Macero applied to Miles when speaking with *Down Beat* in 1974. It was an approach that would last for the rest of Miles's career.

If Miles prepared any written directions for *Kind of Blue,* they would have been a few motifs sketched on staff paper. ("It could have been done on a napkin, the forms were so simple," notes bandleader and reissue producer Bob Belden.) Evans remembered that, "Like 'Freddie Freeloader,' 'So What,' and 'All Blues,' there was nothing written out." Davis later admitted: "I didn't write out the music for *Kind of Blue,* but brought in sketches for what everybody was supposed to play because I wanted a lot of spontaneity in the playing."

In addition, Miles gave each musician specific instructions at the last minute. Cobb recalls: "Mostly he would just say 'This is straight time' or 'This is three,' 'Latin flavored' or 'This is whatever you want.'" At times, as Evans remembered, Davis's spoken directions came when the tape was actually rolling:

> Miles ran over the charts a couple of times. You know, "Do this," "Do that" and then he laid out a structure, like "You solo first." Sometimes during a take we didn't even know that. He would walk around behind you and say "Take two choruses" or "You play next." That's all everybody hears and absorbs. Once we had the chart straight, the rest was up for grabs.

In the control room, Bob Waller had placed one reel of Scotch 190 tape on each of the two Ampex reel-to-reel tape machines, in order to record one master and a safety. Sony Music engineer Mark Wilder has worked on no less than seven reissues of *Kind of Blue* over the years, but notes that he is always surprised when calling for the session tapes.

Normally you get a cartload of tapes for an album, particularly with Miles. On Duke Ellington sessions, or *Miles Ahead* for example, the tape was rolling most of the time and you hear most of the conversations. With *Kind of Blue*, there's only three reels—the edited master and the two safety reels, one from each session. It was like they were trying to save tape—only turning on the machine for the music, so you don't hear much chatter.

The Scotch recording tape was a relatively new product made with a strong, reliable acetate and only one mil thick. This resulted in an uninterrupted forty-five minutes of recording as the tape passed over the tape heads at a rate of fifteen inches per second. For the first session, one reel proved to be all that was needed.

The tape box holding the master session reel

As it happened, the seemingly trivial choice of tape would bestow on the recordings a well-deserved durability. Four decades on, Scotch tape survives incredibly well; the master tapes can still be played on modern machines with little fear of tearing or stretching. Other tape brands that became standard in later years—such as Ampex in the late sixties and seventies—are notorious for becoming brittle and for flaking; many valuable masters have been ruined because of such tape deterioration.

In place in the studio, the group looked up to Townsend to signal their readiness. "Our control room at that point was above the studio floor, up a flight of stairs," noted Frank Laico. "They had closed in the balcony of the church and through the windows you could look out and give directions."

As the view was limited, the engineers would normally arrange the bands close to the wall under the window, surrounded by rolling audio baffles to control room echo and limit sound leakage from one microphone to another. Cobb recalls—and the photographs of the second session reveal—that the band was close enough "to see each other so we could communicate, but I was set up away from them."

In the days before multitracking and other devices that would allow for remixing, that musical communication was meant to be self-regulated. The "mix"—the relative volume and dynamics of the different voices in the band—was more a product of the musicians' placement in the studio, and of their own regulation of the volume of their playing, than a matter of knob-turning on the mixing console. "We would insist on a test before we started to get a balance," Laico says. "After that it was the musicians' responsibility to balance themselves. When it came to solos they had to slide it back a bit, play a little lower."

Close listening to the master tape reveals that Plaut provided each player a microphone, with Cobb's drums receiving two—one directed to the snare and an overhead to catch the cymbals. It was a straight-ahead arrangement for a first-generation recording engineer whose specialty was classical music and monaural (single-channel) mixes. Laico also recalled that Plaut then favored the new Telefunken U-49 microphones, a workhorse of the recording industry. Their warm, rounded response especially in the mid to lower range of the dynamic spectrum made them a favorite for jazz and other acoustic music sessions.

A total of seven microphones were used, mixed through the control-room board down to the then state-of-the-art three tracks. In 1959, with the phenomenon of stereo only beginning to establish itself among music consumers, the three-track master would then be used for both stereo and monaural versions of the album.

In addition to 30th Street's natural reverberation, a small amount of echo was added to the general mix. Traditionalists like jazz producer John Hammond were dismayed by such studio "trickery." "Ever since about 1948, when [Columbia] started playing tricks with sound—making those horrible echo-chamber recordings, for one thing—all the record companies have been knocking themselves out to achieve phony effects," Hammond complained to the *New Yorker* in 1953. "What's the good of having every instrument in a band sound like it were being played inside the Holland Tunnel?"

By 1959, thanks to years of trial and error, echo could be subtly controlled, and the effect on *Kind of Blue* was characterized by Frank Laico as "just a bit of sweetening. At 30th Street, a line was run from the mixing console down into a low-ceilinged, concrete basement room—about twelve by fifteen feet in size—where we set up a speaker and a good omnidirectional microphone." The sound from the session was played through the speaker, which reverberated in the empty room and was recorded back on the master mix, in the center track. When listening to the original three-track tapes, it is possible to drop out the left and right tracks during, say, a Coltrane solo, and hear a slight off-in-the-distance effect adding a subtle, resonant edge.

For the first session, instruments whose ranges would not collide were paired on the tracks: tenor saxophone and piano shared the left track, trumpet and bass the center, and alto saxophone and drums the right. As was customary with Miles's recordings from the late fifties, he was granted the "star" position of center track, almost always coupled with Chambers.

Because complete isolation between tracks was impossible, each instrument's sound—especially during solos—can be heard on all three tracks. As a result, the horns and piano are richly defined by three aural fields, adding a significant depth and completeness to their sound. During trumpet solos for example, one can make out Miles on the left and right tracks, as well as on the center with added echo. By fading out the center track on the master tapes, it is possible to discern the unique, acoustic dimension provided by 30th Street's vaulted interior.

FREDDIE FREELOADER
"Freddie Freeloader" is a 12-measure blues form given new personality by effective melodic and rhythmic personality. (From Bill Evans's liner notes to *Kind of Blue*.)

Ballplayers always stretch before a game. For jazz musicians, a straight-ahead blues has always been the exercise of choice to limber up both hands and ears. For this reason, and possibly to smooth over Wynton Kelly's ruffled feathers and minimize his waiting time, the first tune Davis called was a bouncy blues number, the only tune on which his newest sideman would play. Though recorded first, "Freeloader" would become the second track on *Kind of Blue*.

Of all the tracks that would endow the album with its bittersweet aspect, "Freddie Freeloader" was the least melancholy. At that point all the tunes were untitled; only at a later date would Davis be called on to name his new creations. As an adjunct to the job number, three consecutive "co" song numbers ("co" for Columbia) were assigned to the music of that session.

Townsend called for the session to begin, and identified the track. The mikes caught the musicians in mid-discussion about the song's structure:

IRVING TOWNSEND: The machine's on . . . here we go:
co 62290, no title, Take 1 . . .
UNIDENTIFIED MUSICIAN: . . . B flat on the end?
MILES DAVIS: Say Wynton, after Cannonball,
you play again and then we'll come in and end it.

Take 1 starts off at a jaunty pace, clearly a blues with its repeated four-bar opening. Unhappy with the tempo, Davis whistles after the eighth bar to cut off the take. Townsend immediately notices that Davis has shifted away from the microphone, and reminds the trumpeter that he is recording in a union facility.

MD: It was too fast.   IT: Miles, where you going to work now?   MD: Right here.
IT: OK, 'cause if you move back we don't get you. You were right where you played before . . .
MD: When I play I'm going to raise my horn a little bit.
Can I move this down a little bit? [moves microphone]
IT: It's against policy to move a microphone . . . [laughter]
Here we go. Ready? Number two . . .

Take 2 begins at a slightly slower pace. In the sixth bar Kelly hits a slight but noticeable clunker that might have been intended as a bluesy "grace" note. Though the take continues, by the turnaround at the end of the second twelve-bar cycle, Davis hits a flat note—a "clam" in jazz parlance—and the take is cut off.

Miles's impromptu approach in the studio was well known by 1959. "I've recorded with Miles and I know how he operates," stated J.J. Johnson, whose first session with Davis dated back to 1949. "Most of the time he goes into a studio and one take is it! . . . That's his philosophy on the recording bit." Miles's stop-and-start approach on the *Kind of Blue* sessions might seem to run counter to the album's, and his, first-take, only-take reputation. But as Evans later explained:

"Freddie" is how most musicians remember Fred Tolbert, the inspiration for the blues tune recorded at the first *Kind of Blue* session. Freddie was a colorful street character who worked as a bartender at a Philadelphia bar called the Nightlife and survived on handouts. It was a lifestyle he later freely acknowledged on his business card, which read simply "Freddie the Freeloader." Freddie befriended Miles during the heyday of the sextet, becoming a frequent hanger-on and errand-runner for the trumpeter. As Cobb remembers:

> *Freddie was from Philadelphia and he used to always imitate the way Miles talked. He worked at the bar near the Showboat, the place we used to work under the hotel. He used to give guys drinks, so everybody liked Freddie. He then decided to come to New York and hang out with Miles, so he'd be at all the gigs we played. If we were in New York he'd show up.*

"Freddie was kooky — harmless kooky," recalls Miles's ex-wife Frances Taylor. "He was always just kind of on the scene."

Herbie Hancock remembers Freddie from the early sixties.

> *I knew about Freddie [the] Freeloader first from the [Kind of Blue] song, and then when I was in New York. Freddie was very street smart, and Miles was always attracted to people who had brains and an interesting approach to life. All the musicians in New York knew him anyway, he was just another guy on the scene, you know.*

In 1979, a slightly inebriated Freddie offered New York radio station WKCR an alternative history of *Kind of Blue:*

> *One day I run into Cannonball, [when] Miles was working at the Showboat and his car had broken down so I took him down to the Ben Franklin Hotel on Ninth and Walnut — in Center City — to get the money to pay for his car, and Miles hired me. So Miles brought me to New York, in his little Mercedes Benz, and I stayed with him. . . . I was at the record date when they did "So What." I hummed "So What" out for him with Bill. That's when I hired Wynton and cut Bill loose. Wynton was more soulful. Yeah I'm a legend too. . . .*

In the interview, Tolbert mentioned Miles's frequent use of the dismissive expression that would become the title of *Kind of Blue*'s best-known track.

> *Miles is a beautiful person — if he loves you, he loves you. But you have to catch him when he's in love. Because if he's not in love he'll tell you "Get out of my face, I don't want to hear it." Then he'd also say . . . "Soooo what!"*

The first complete performance of each thing is what you're hearing. [*Kind of Blue*] is kind of remarkable from that standpoint, there are no complete outtakes. I think that is what accounts for some of the real freshness. First-take feelings, if they're anywhere near right, they're generally the best. If you don't take that one, generally, you take a dip emotionally and then it's really a professional, laborious process of bringing your self back up.

Miles's first-take philosophy was modified by a need to correctly lay down the opening head arrangement. When Herbie Hancock joined Miles in 1963 to record the album *Seven Steps to Heaven* at 30th Street, Miles used the same approach that Evans described for *Kind of Blue*. Hancock recalls: "Everything was a first take unless we screwed up the melody so what you hear on the record is the full first take. The five-and-a-half years I was with him that's the way Miles worked."

The tape starts up again, catching a brief run-through of the "Freddie Freeloader" theme by the horns and piano to tighten the theme's final phrase before the group proceeds without comment to Take 3. The horns play the head smoothly. Kelly hits his answer phrases and kicks into a slightly halting solo compared to his effort on the final take. Before the second chorus of Kelly's solo ends, Davis catches a mistake and whistles off the take.

"Hey, play that Irving . . ."

MD: Hey look Wynton, don't play
no chord going into the A flat . . .

Miles has been lauded for being an effective bandleader with a minimum of words. As Cannonball recalled in 1972, when he did speak, it was typically to react to something that seemed out of place. "He never told anyone what to play but would say 'Man, you don't need to do that.' Miles really told everybody what NOT to do. I heard him and dug it."

As the tape machine is turned on, a remnant of another take or rehearsal pops up for a moment. Then, preceded by a faint toe-tap counting off the tempo, the final (and first full) take of "Freddie Freeloader" is heard.

The tune shares an undeniable laid-back quality with the rest of the music on *Kind of Blue*. But if the remainder of the album was conceived around the subtle moodiness of Bill Evans's piano, "Freddie Freeloader" stands out as a showcase of Kelly's more upbeat, hands-on-the-tiller effect. As trombonist J.J. Johnson described the pianist, "he always projects a happy feeling, regardless of the tempo."

Kelly wraps up his solo neatly as Davis takes over with a three-note phrase echoing the piano's "answer riff" from the head of the tune. As Miles weaves his no-hurry-at-all solo around the blues changes, Kelly continues to lay in a soulful accompaniment, outlining the blues progression and giving the rhythm buoyancy. For Kelly, more often a sideman than a leader, "comping" was his first love. "In fact, at one time I didn't like to solo," he told *Down Beat*. "I'd just like to get a groove going and *never* solo." Miles recalled: "He could play behind a soloist like a motherfucker, man. Cannonball and Trane loved him and so did I." In fact, it is difficult to imagine the "Freddie Freeloader" theme without Kelly's loosely played blues notes wrapping themselves comp-like around the tail of each phrase. In this case, it is the filigree that makes the general design of the melody.

"I think Miles's blues solo on that track is one of my favorites," Evans stated years later. "There are a couple of places where just one note contains so much meaning that you can hardly believe it." Davis's improvisation, more bubbly than brooding as on the rest of the album, hits a startling moment two-thirds of the way through. He stops, and drops to a lower register in his horn, sounding like a reed instrument (one might think Coltrane was blowing for a second). Simultaneously, Kelly plays the same three-note riff that opens and closes Davis's solo.

Coltrane's solo kicks in with exclamation points. As precise a balance as Plaut may have achieved by arranging the band in the studio, he was unprepared for the startling power of Coltrane's tenor. "Fred absolutely had to turn down the knob there," commented Laico in listening to the master tape. Coltrane may well have crowded his microphone when his turn to solo arrived, but even at a distance he was known for being able to project strongly and possessing a powerful tone.

Kind of Blue finds Coltrane in transition. The prolixity of his previous recorded blues (such as "Sweet Sapphire Blues" on his Prestige album *Black Pearls* from the previous year) seems in check here. Miles recalled that in the last week of 1957, when Coltrane rejoined the band, the very first number they all performed together on stage had been a blues. On hearing Coltrane's tenor solo, Adderley "asked me what we were playing and I told him. . . . He says, 'Well, I ain't never heard no blues played like that!'"

In contrast, Coltrane's "Freddie Freeloader" solo shows a marked increase in attention to mood and the horizontal aspect of the music—melody and rhythm, rather than the harmonic gymnastics of the past. "I want to be more flexible where rhythm is concerned . . . most of my experimenting has been in the harmonic form. I put time and rhythms to one side, in the past," Coltrane admitted in an autobiographical sketch for *Down Beat* in 1960. The result on *Kind of Blue* is a more reflective tenor sound, wholly appropriate to the restrained blues of "Freeloader."

Cannonball follows Coltrane with a sax-to-sax handoff that reveals the degree to which Coltrane's more free-form style had affected him. "Trane had an extremely light, fluid sound and my alto sound has always been influenced by the tenor so it was sometimes difficult to tell when one instrument stopped and the other started," Cannonball recalled. (Conversely, it is no surprise that Coltrane himself had initially been an alto player.) "It sounded like a continual phrase."

The two saxophonists had perfected the trick over an abundance of gigs together by 1959. But not all jazz listeners were impressed by Coltrane's growing effect on Adderley. "Coltrane's playing has apparently influenced Adderley," complained a *Down Beat* reviewer of the sextet's Newport Jazz Festival performance the previous summer. "The latter's playing indicated less concern for melodic structure than he has illustrated in the past. . . ."

Another reason for their similarity may well have been their backgrounds: both saxmen began their careers steeped deeply in the blues. Coltrane toured with Texas alto saxophonist and blues singer Eddie "Cleanhead" Vinson's big band in 1948 and '49, while Adderley, commenting on the Fort Lauderdale group he co-led with his brother Nat, admitted: "We were strongly influenced by Louis Jordan, Eddie 'Cleanhead' Vinson, blues bands like that." Notably, his bebop-inspired runs on "Freeloader" resonate with a strong honky-tonk vibe.

As if to stress the blues connection, at the back end of his solo Cannonball slips in a quote from a popular 1957 R&B hit, Junior Parker's "Next Time You See Me," playing the melody to the line "and if it hurts you my darling, you'll only have yourself to blame." Adderley's penchant for quoting other songs and melodies was well-known. That the music of a Memphis (via Texas, since Parker recorded for Houston's Duke label) bluesman should be filtered into a cutting-edge jazz session in New York also speaks to the never-ending dialogue between jazz and blues (and the power of a good jukebox single).

A brief, under-recorded solo by Chambers showcasing the young bassist's agility and feel completes the cycle. With some excellent comping on piano, the band returns to the theme. Kelly fills in on top of the horn line and Cobb ends the tune with a *ra-ta-ta* punctuation on the cymbals.

IT: Want to hear it Miles?

As the tape stopped, a discussion obviously took place between Townsend and Davis, because the next voice is the producer's, announcing an "insert" take. Not fully satisfied with the out chorus, which they must have felt lacked the energy of the first completed take, the decision was made to record another take of the end of the tune, from the tail of the bass solo to the coda. Later, if it was deemed necessary, the producer could create a seamless edit by splicing the alternate ending onto the master tape.

Smooth splicing had become possible with the advent of magnetic recording tape at the end of World War II. But this was a mixed blessing to the purist ears of those like John Hammond. If it altered the sanctity of the improvised jazz moment, it was simply wrong. "It made it possible to make more dishonest records than there had ever been, through splicing." Mitch Miller, ever the studio craftsman, aired a more utilitarian view: "[Splicing] was just a tool to save a good performance. It wasn't the tool that became a crutch."

By 1959, tape splicing had long been common practice in the music industry, in jazz, and it certainly was on all of Miles's Columbia efforts to that point. On *Miles Ahead*, for instance, only one performance is a complete, undoctored take, according to jazz historian Phil Schaap. On Davis's more electronic albums of the sixties and seventies, editing and splicing would become an integral part of the overall production formula.

IT: This is Insert 1, Take 1   (sound of finger-snapping)

MUFFLED VOICE: . . . last four bars?

MD: No. Wait a minute . . . it's the last twelve bars.

Chambers plays the end of his bass solo again. The group follows with a relatively listless out chorus, finishing with a more abrupt ending than the smoother one of the first take.

MD: All right?   IT: Yeah.
        MD: Let's hear a little bit of it.   IT: Right.

Davis was less impressed by the insert than by the original full take, and the insert was never used.

SO WHAT

"So What" is a simple figure based on 16 measures of one scale, 8 of another and 8 more of the first, following a piano and bass introduction in free rhythmic style. (From Bill Evans's liner notes.)

IT: Here we go.
MD: Wait a minute.   IT: CO 62291, Take 1.
        MD: Wait one minute . . .   UNIDENTIFIED: One short minute . . .

"So What" is easily the best known and most covered tune on *Kind of Blue.* For many listeners, one has come to mean the other. When musicians and fans speak of the title track "Kind of Blue," invariably it is "So What" they are referring to.

The tune's perpetual popularity is explained at least partially by its memorable opening theme (following the dreamy prelude). It is simply the most identifiable and catchy melody off the album, a lyrical line as easy-going and natural and funky as a late-afternoon whistle heard from a passing stranger. "So What," though formally structured on a simple set of scales, displays a transparency of composition: it feels more natural and improvised than composed. That hovering tension between mood and mechanics furthers its lasting appeal.

Miles recalled drawing both melodic inspiration and feeling from two very specific sources, African folk and American gospel. The former came from a Guinean dance troupe his girlfriend Frances Taylor had introduced him to. "We went to this performance by the Ballet Africaine . . . Their rhythm! . . .They would do rhythms like 5/4 and 6/8 and 4/4, and the rhythm would be changing and popping." The troupe also featured a kalimba player using distinctive African scales in his playing. "When I first heard them play the finger piano that night and sing this song with the other guy dancing, man, that was some powerful stuff."

The church music came from an indelible memory of boyhood visits to his grandfather's farm.

> I added some other kind of sound I remembered from being back in Arkansas, when we were walking home from church and they were playing these bad gospels. That feeling is what I was trying to get close to . . . six years old, walking with my cousin along that dark Arkansas road.

Miles spiked his musical cocktail with a dose of modern classical music like Ravel and Rachmaninoff ("all that was up in there somewhere") but found that the final result did not exactly match his original vision.

> But you write something and then guys play off it and take it someplace else through their creativity and imagination, and you just miss where you thought you were going to go. . . . I missed getting the exact sound of the African finger piano up in that sound . . . but that's what I was trying to do on most of that album, particularly on "All Blues" and "So What."

The other distinguishing characteristic of the tune—which would be the first tune heard on the album—is its dreamy prelude, played rubato (i.e., out of tempo with the main body of the musical piece), atmospheric and charged with expectation. "On 'So What,' the introduction was written out single-line, and Paul and I played it and added a little harmony to it," Evans recalled. Who wrote that memorable prelude? It does not seem to have been Bill Evans, who, while adamant about his lost credit on "Blue in Green," never claimed authorship of any part of "So What," and whose words imply the music was given to him prewritten. All signs point to either Miles himself or Gil Evans. Gil was often found composing informally but intensely with Davis during this period, and it was Gil who would rearrange the prelude for a TV performance a month later and for the twenty-one-piece orchestra that performed "So What" at Miles's historic 1961 Carnegie Hall concert. The contention that the prelude was Gil's creation is furthered by his widow, Anita Evans, who recalls being told by her husband that he had written it. Cobb, when asked, puts it bluntly: "Man, it *sounds* like Gil's stuff."

With Bill Evans now at the piano and Kelly likely remaining to listen (many visiting musicians would sit in the studio during jazz recording sessions to witness and lend support), the tapes began rolling, catching Chambers bowing the "So What" theme. Instantly catchy, it's hummed by another musician in response as the sextet prepares to record what will be the leadoff track to the album.

IT: Number 2, Take 1.

Evans and Chambers work together, consolidating the vaporous bass-and-piano intro. Herbie Hancock described the rubato effect: "It sounded like Miles just gave [Chambers] an instruction to play this intro [prelude] out of tempo that's sort of floating." The lack of rhythmic resolution—not knowing where the downbeat will fall for the first half-minute of the tune—gives it an eerie, suspended feel.

With the miking of the bass noticeably improved from "Freddie Freeloader"—repositioning Chambers was probably all it took—the quiet prelude continues, though a musician's footsteps can now be heard in the studio.

IT: Start again please.

One can hear Evans and Chambers, lacking any specific instruction, "feeling" the music into place. The prelude still seems slightly out of sync, particularly at the point the piano and bass are to walk through a bluesy melodic line together. As the horns enter, playing the "So What" theme at a slightly slower tempo than the final, paper can be heard rustling. Townsend begins to complain of the background noise in the studio. Davis kids his producer, but for a reason. He says any sympathetic vibrations from the other instruments—in this case Cobb's snare drum, in which the snare has been rattling—should be considered part of the music.

IT: Hold it.   UNIDENTIFIED: Sorry . . .
        IT: Listen, we gotta watch it because if there's noise all the way through this . . . this is so quiet to begin with, that every click sound . . . MD: (unintelligible)
            IT: Watch the snare too—we're picking up some of the vibrations on it.
MD: Well that goes with it.
        IT: What?   MD: All that goes with it.
IT: All right (chuckles)—not all the other noises though . . . Take 2.

Two further attempts at Take 2 do not quite make it. The first ends as Evans's execution is noticeably sloppy; the second breaks off as Miles whistles and Adderley asks for further direction.

MD: Start again.   CA: When the horns . . .

The tape stops and restarts.

IT: Here we go Miles. Take 3. (Control room phone rings)

Two aborted tries at Take 3 follow, with an audible squeak on bass, and continuing background noise. Miles sounds slightly frustrated.

MD: Take it off. (unintelligible)

One more false start follows.

MD: Take it off.

The tape stops and restarts again, this time progressing sans interruption straight into the full and final take of "So What."

The timing of the prelude is tighter, yet still loose and dreamy. The final bass note played just before the theme resonates long and low with accentuated vibrato. Then Chambers takes a breath and plucks the familiar opening line.

"That's another thing," Hancock points out. "The melody is in the bass. How many people had done that before? There were some songs—'Two Bass Hit,' some Jimmy Blanton numbers [like "Jack the Bear" with Duke Ellington]. But there were very few things where the bass player plays the melody."

As innovative as the theme was, it was also quite traditional in its use of a call-and-response pattern common to countless blues and gospel numbers (evoking "Freddie Freeloader" to a degree). The theme gently passes through its AABA form, building gradually and logically, softly seducing the listener. Evans alone carries the two-note answer to Chambers' motif plucked in the first four bars, with Cobb lightly tapping the ride cymbal. Then piano and horns join together on the "Sooooo what" riff as the hi-hat begins to swing. By the third time, as the melody climbs a half-step, Miles, Coltrane, and Cannonball add a touch of insistence to their declaration. The intro backs down a half-step and the horns return to their original, subdued level.

If one moment encapsulates the restrained power of the entire album, the next may well be it. "When Miles comes in and starts his solo and Cobb hits that crash on the down beat," Hancock says, "you can't get any better than that." With dead-on timing, Cobb's one simple cymbal splash boosts the tune into top gear as Davis delivers one of his—and the idiom's—most unforgettable solos.

Like a whisper, Miles's playing insinuates with its distinct hushed, vocal quality. Languidly "spoken" in succinct, lyrical phrases, Miles's solo, over its almost two-minute duration, never strays far from the trumpet's middle register, notably in the same aural range as a human voice.

For George Russell the solo is the song. "It's one of the most beautiful solos ever. It *is* the melody." Russell was so convinced of this that in 1983 he arranged the solo as a chart for his twenty-one-piece Living Time Orchestra. "Why not have everybody join in regardless of their instruments and play this as a melody? Just let them all join in and be Miles." (At this writing, the Blue Note album on which the piece appears, *So What*, is out of print.)

Miles's "So What" solo is also a brilliant illustration of two other aspects of his trumpet sound. The first is his genius for simplicity. There is an almost exaggerated economy to his approach, juggling long tones and silence to achieve a disarmingly casual effect, and a palpable sense of drama.

Miles's other distinctive characteristic is a related tendency to push and play with the rhythm. His playing flits and delays, shifting on top and in between Cobb's propulsive cymbal work. His influence is clearly vocal. Davis's description of one of his favorite singers accurately reflects his own rhythmic approach: "[Billie Holiday] sings way behind the beat and then she brings it up—hitting right on the beat." He added: "Every once in a while you have to cut into the rhythm section on the beat and that keeps everybody together."

In contrast to Miles's back-of-the-beat feel, Coltrane's and Cannonball's solos on "So What" restlessly explore a new chord-free vista. Coltrane's solo works in fragments, urged on at one point by a shower of arpeggiated chords from Evans. Coltrane's concentration is audible: a pause occurs before the modal shift, then a new burst of energy as he launches into a new improvised line.

Cannonball takes a more fluid and melodic approach, injecting an exuberant rhythm in contrast to the subdued mood preceding him. His lyrical line is the least modal of the soloists', gliding through chromatic steps rather than the assigned steps of "So What"'s scalar form. But given the inherent freedom of a modal form, it's a creative license easily taken—and one that works. "The only ones who were really playing on the scales were Bill Evans, Miles, and Coltrane a little bit," commented Dick Katz, "but Cannonball was just playing Cannonball."

The sequence of solos, unvarying through most of the album, makes it easy to hear in Adderley's solo the references to what had come before; clearly the altoist was benefiting from hearing the approaches of his fellow horn players. As Adderley himself once said, "I listen to what Miles has done to a thing 'cause he always plays before I do, and after he has used something, I'll use the same technique—maybe not the same idea, but the same technique, and exploit it my way."

Evans seems to hold back a moment before entering his solo, as if checking to see if Cannonball is through, building lightly, then playing answering chords as the horns take over a support role, lightly punching in the "Soooo what" riff. He neatly announces the start of the solo with a calming, slightly syncopated note cluster, and delivers the goods.

Evans is typically understated on his debut outing on the album. His single note lines sound tentative at first. As the horn line continues to chug along, he allows the richness and nuances of a series of chords to ring, using the Steinway's "soft pedal" that allows a fine-tuned control at a quiet tempo—to add a warmth to his voicings. Only by the end of the solo does he unveil a strong, dramatic flair.

"I'm thinking of the end of Bill's solo on 'So What,'" Herbie Hancock says. "He plays these phrases, a second apart. He plays seconds." Playing two notes simultaneously—one only a second, or one major interval, above the first—startles with its dissonance. Evans plays several of these in sequence. "I had never heard anybody do that before. He's following the modal concept maybe more than anybody else. That just opened up a whole vista for me."

A short solo from Chambers leads into a restatement of the theme. As the horns exit, the rhythm section continues, Evans spurring on the close with slight emphasis, and the tune jaggedly ends. We haven't heard this ending; a gentle fadeout was used on the released album.

Immediately, the musicians fall out of performance mode, in high spirits after a masterful take. Cannonball breaks any somber spell the tune may have cast with his giddy humor and a Rodgers and Hart lyric, while "So What's" bass line is vocalized by another band member.

CA: (singing) With a sooong in my heart . . .
　　　UNIDENTIFIED: Dinga-dinga-dinga-doogong . . .

BLUE IN GREEN

"Blue in Green" is a 10-measure circular form following a 4-measure introduction, and played by soloists in various augmentation and diminution of time values. (From Bill Evans's liner notes.)

"Blue in Green" is the quiet miniature on an album of more extended meditations, five-and-a-half minutes of quiet, rippling solos over a ring of chords.

Its brief, ten-bar structure—breaking the standard thirty-two or twelve-bar mold for jazz composition—and steadily flowing tempo amplify its perpetual-cycle effect. "You can tell where it starts [but] you can't tell where it stops . . . I love that suspense. Not only does it sound good—it's unpredictable," Miles proudly stated.

Like the structured blues of "Freddie Freeloader," this tune breaks the absolute rules of modality. It follows a chordal pattern, but then structurally, it hardly offers anything else. "Blue in Green" is about placid mood and suspended feel, not apparent melody, and dovetails neatly into the overall feeling of the album.

> IT: Just you four guys on this, right Miles?
> MD: Five . . . No, why don't you play?

Barely audible is Davis's last-second invitation to Coltrane to play on a tune presumedly intended as a quartet piece. As the original album states, "Julian Adderly [sic] lays out on 'Blue in Green.'" For the sake of brevity and perhaps as a means of accenting the lugubrious, lower-register weight of the piece (his exuberant style might well have worked against its slow, somber feel), the decision was made to feature three soloists only: trumpet, piano, and tenor saxophone.

Also faintly perceptible in the background (though unintelligible) is Evans's voice, for the first time in the session taking charge and directing the layout of a piece.

> IT: CO 62292—Number 3, Take 1.

Evans, with Chambers's accompaniment, begins the piece's most recognizable element: the bright but bittersweet, four-measure introduction. The story of those introductory chords returns us to the question of the composition's creation.

Evans told writer Brian Hennessey of a visit he paid the trumpeter in late 1958. "One day at Miles's apartment, he wrote on some manuscript paper the symbols for G-minor and A-augmented. And he said, 'What would you do with that?' I didn't really know, but I went home and wrote 'Blue in Green.'"

Evans was not the first musician whom Miles challenged with written musical problems. Davis made it a habit, as David Amram tells it:

> I was at [Café] Bohemia with him late at night, and we walked around in Washington Square Park and he didn't say anything for like twenty minutes. Then he'd say, "Try this," and he had written some kind of scale, or five notes on a matchbook. "See what you can do with these."

The four-bar idea—an exercise in extended chordal suspension—that Evans developed from Miles's simple two-chord idea first came to light on December 30, 1958 when the pianist incorporated it into his loose, introductory sequence on a Chet Baker session. Compare the opening of the tune "Alone Together" off the album *Chet* with that of "Blue in Green": as Evans biographer Peter Pettinger points out, one will hear "exactly those chords."

Yet the introduction Evans carried into the *Kind of Blue* session changed and developed further with Miles's active involvement, captured as the tapes were rolling. Evans queries Davis on the length of the introduction, Miles decides to double its duration, and ultimately a co-composer credit seems due both musicians.

BE: We better do that again . . . do we start on the last four bars?
MD: Last four bars, but then you repeat it.   BE: Oh, do it twice.
MD: So it's eight.   BE: All right . . .
(Finger snap)   IT: Take 2.

Take 2 proceeds smoothly. The introduction finished, Miles's muted trumpet is heard as Cobb starts playing the brushes on his snare. Evans's minimal playing hands Chambers the key to the structure of "Blue in Green." More than on any other album track, the bassist holds the responsibility for outlining both its chordal and rhythmic structure. His unfamiliarity with the tune, however, proves problematic.

The take breaks down as musical signals apparently cross between Evans and Chambers, with the bassist hitting a wrong note. Miles requests that Cobb intensify the subtle effect of his playing.

(unintelligible studio chatter)
MD: Use both hands, Jimmy.   COBB: Huh?
MD: Just use both hands and play it the best way you can, you know. It'll be all right.
IT: OK, number 3.

Take 3 reaches Miles's solo again. As Cobb strikes two cymbal taps, Davis calls off the take. Again, Chambers fluffs a note and seems to be having trouble with the song form. Evans reconfirms the length of the introduction.

MD: Try it again Billy . . . one, two, three.   BE: Let's do that four?

The second try at Take 3 lasts roughly three minutes. The introduction leads to a gentler cymbal splash from Cobb and a crisp, muted solo from Miles. Evans takes over with a slightly halting passage, followed by Coltrane with a laid-back solo with slight vibrato. A rhythmic hiccup in his playing works slightly against the seamless, dreamy texture of the tune. Again Chambers hits a sour note and again the take is halted, though Miles is happy with the way the tune is working. Evans confirms that he and Chambers should follow the chord changes in unison.

MD: That's the idea.
BE: He [Paul] stays the same as me . . .

Take 4 runs to Miles's solo, but a crackling sound is heard that could have been a faulty microphone cord, or a loose connection within the mixing board. The take stops. Davis again plays at being contrary, teasing his control booth crew. As they start up again, Miles cedes the count-off to Evans.

IT: Sorry guys. It's our fault.
MD: No it isn't. I don't believe that. I don't believe that.
IT: It was a little static up here . . . go ahead.   BE: A one, a two . . .

Take 5 holds the charm, yielding the only complete version of "Blue in Green."

Evans's introduction is light and airy as originally conceived, creating a peaceful landscape for the group to enter into. The bass keeps a subtle beat while Cobb's two-handed brushwork on the snare drum offers tender reinforcement. Miles's muted solo arrives with an intensely languid, three-note phrase made even longer and more resonant by the natural echo of the studio (turn up the volume, and the vaulted ceiling is almost visible). Davis limits his vocabulary to long-held notes, dividing his phrasing into a series of whispered, two-part statements.

The unusual, palindromic order of solos on "Blue in Green" (trumpet-piano-tenor-piano-trumpet) further enhances the circular feel of the composition. In contrast to Davis's sparsity, Evans's "doubling up" (as musicians refer to tackling chord changes at twice the pace) creates a lighter feel with more movement. Even in a brief solo, he displays a daunting command of color and voicing in his chordal playing.

Coltrane finds a rhythmic middle ground between Davis and Evans, playing in a slow, deliberate tempo. His early love of Lester Young's light and airy feel is conjured to opportune effect in his brooding, fleeting statement. Evans, and then Davis reprise their initial approaches to the tune, Miles almost fading away at one point, then returning with a sequence of subdued flourishes. Evans restates the theme, building the intensity with one last escalation of note clusters, and permits the song to dissipate and fade over a prolonged, bowed note from Chambers.

"So What" and "Flamenco Sketches" may be lauded for their simplicity, but "Blue in Green"—in expression and construction—is the sole *Kind of Blue* composition bordering on absolute minimalism. Yet it possesses a totality other jazz players and listeners marvel at.

"If I was going to sit down and write a tune, it would have ten times more stuff going on than this," vibraphonist Gary Burton remarks, adding:

> Yet [Evans] made a memorable tune out of just practically nothing. I'm always impressed by someone who can write a very minimal piece that sticks in your mind and that's still interesting to play over and over again.

The song ends with a somewhat hushed statement of awe from the control room. Miles, still dissatisfied, rides Chambers for his handling of the ending.

IT: Beautiful.
            MD: Wake up, Paul . . .
UNIDENTIFIED: That's the idea . . .

IT: Beautiful. . . .

Second

Session

April 22, 1959, 2:30 pm

MILES HAD INTENDED to record more than just three tracks during the sextet's six hours in the studio on March 2—Evans has noted that he and Miles had worked on the structure of "Flamenco Sketches" that morning. But the group had used up their allotted time, so plans were made to reassemble in April to record the remainder of the album.

Fred Plaut and a studio assistant remained behind to prepare the studio for their late-night session with Lee Castle and the Jimmy Dorsey Orchestra. Bob Waller carefully collected from the tape machines the master reels containing the music that would yield the first half of *Kind of Blue*. He labeled the master and safety with the appropriate job number, then set the tapes aside to await transfer to "the Vault," as the staff called Columbia's tape storage facility uptown.

The engineers had no way of knowing it, but a motor problem on the master machine had caused the tape to be recorded slightly slower than fifteen ips. The resulting deviation was extremely subtle: the performances played back at a slightly sharper pitch. The mistake went undetected by Columbia's mastering staff, who used the master, not the unaffected safety, to generate the album. Over three decades and hundreds of thousands of pressings of the album, no musicians or music fans—and certainly not Miles nor his sidemen—ever reported hearing the higher pitch. Then, in 1992, the astute ears of engineer Mark Wilder caught the problem.

> The reissues had always been done with the "c" master reel, so I said, "Let's use the [safety] "D" reels since they've been played less." I always check the tapes against a copy of the album anyway, and the safety reels sounded different. I called in a trumpet player I knew to listen to Miles's solos and he confirmed what I heard—there was about a quarter tone difference.

All subsequent reissues of *Kind of Blue* have relied on the safety reels to correctly reproduce the album's first three tracks.

For the musicians it had been another day at the studio, one like many others. "We just really went in that day and did our thing," Evans told jazz writer Lee Jeske. And why would they have seen the first *Kind of Blue* session as a momentous occasion? Most of the group were thinking ahead to other recording projects over the next few weeks.

On March 10, Wynton Kelly, with Chambers and Cobb, completed a Riverside album, *Kelly Blue*. Two days later, Bill Evans joined fellow pianist Bob Brookmeyer on the double-keyboard concept *The Ivory Hunters* for United Artists. Coltrane, newly signed to Atlantic Records, entered the studio on April 1 with Chambers, pianist Cedar Walton, and drummer Lex Humphries. Cannonball, again with the Kelly/Chambers/Cobb rhythm

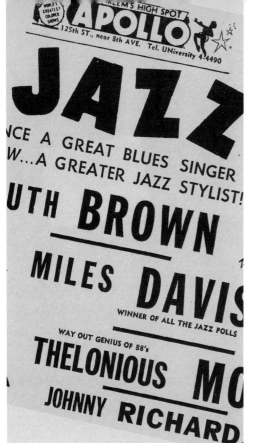

section, put down the tracks toward the Riverside album *Cannonball Takes Charge* on April 12.

Live performances kept the group close to home during that period as well. Miles's name appeared often on New York theater marquees and club ads. The sextet opened a week at the Apollo Theatre on March 13, sharing a mixed bill with Ruth Brown, Thelonious Monk, and the Johnny Richards Band. The gig was the reprise to a successful one-week engagement the preceding October that had also featured Sarah Vaughan. (At one of those late '58– early '59 Apollo shows, a young photographer named Jay Maisel snapped the intense mid-solo close-up of Miles that would become the cover to *Kind of Blue*.)

But in that six-week window between the two *Kind of Blue* sessions, something ultimately more consequential than a mere performance or magazine article would project Miles's name, face, and music coast-to-coast: Miles was taped for a national television broadcast in which he was the featured star.

The show was called "The Sound of Miles Davis." It was produced and directed by Robert Herridge, an intense, intelligent, cigarette-smoking Welshman who regularly invited CBS's late-night viewing audience to watch his in-depth, high-culture programming. With resourcefulness (and a sparse production style inspired by lean budgets), he had successfully adapted literature, drama, and musical performance to the small screen. Herridge's musical subjects had included the Philadelphia Orchestra, Ahmad Jamal, and an all-star group for his 1957 tour-de-force, "The Sound of Jazz." The program, a critical success that had drawn stacks of viewer response in the days before accurate TV ratings, had been produced with the input of noted jazz journalists Whitney Balliett and Nat Hentoff and featured once-in-a-lifetime performances and jams by Billie Holiday, Count Basie, Lester Young, Thelonious Monk, Ben Webster, Jimmy Rushing, and others.

Miles was Herridge's first choice for a follow-up to "The Sound of Jazz," but as Hentoff recalled, Davis had been burned by broadcast experiences before.

[He] had told me he would never do television again, saying, "They would fuck it up." But I talked him into meeting with Herridge, in whom Miles found somebody he could curse and respect.

With Hentoff credited as "musical advisor," America's premier modern jazz trumpeter became the subject of a half-hour TV program taped on April 2, 1959.

The taping of "The Sound of Miles Davis" took place in CBS-TV's Studio 61, a large room Herridge had intentionally left bare of any sets or other theatrical artifices. Jimmy Cobb recalled arriving at the studio:

> It was at Fifty-Sixth Street and Tenth Avenue. I walked in the door and it looked like a warehouse or something. The room stretched out and it actually had a terrible echo in it. I walked around it and there was a chalkboard with everybody's name up.

That small blackboard listing the band credits added to the low-tech feel of the show. Stage doors, electrical conduits, and hanging lights were visible behind the band as they played; musicians were free to stroll, chat, and smoke while others soloed, creating an informal mood not unlike that of a club. Miles had criticized a recent Jackie Gleason jazz gala as looking like "a Christmas tree on a plantation." The spare style of the Miles program forced the audience to focus on the music and the musicians. "Music we feel should be listened to and not talked about," Herridge stated curtly in his introduction, yielding the floor to Miles and his music.

Miles himself, dapper and cool in European casual wear, an ascot around his neck, never spoke on the show. The program was in two parts. In the second half, featuring Davis in an orchestral setting, a sweatered Gil Evans directed gems from *Miles Ahead*: "The Duke," "Blues for Pablo," and "New Rhumba." But the program's most compelling moment may well have been

OF MILES DAVIS

its opening sequence. The camera focuses on Miles playing a slow, haunting solo, then draws back to reveal Davis's working band: Cobb, Chambers, Kelly (taking his regular place at the piano) and Coltrane (Adderley was absent due to a migraine, despite his being credited at the end of the program). The camera pans over to Herridge announcing the show. Evans's orchestra in the background takes up Miles's melodic line, which becomes recognizable as the languid, atmospheric prelude to "So What." After a commercial break, the whole tune makes its broadcast debut, performed by the small group with the addition of three trombones.

This broadcast version is Miles's only recorded performance that comes so close to the original recording. The tempo was slightly more brisk—the tune had obviously evolved in just four weeks—but the mood was identifiably

the same. Even Miles's first solo (he takes a second swing through the tune, blowing in Cannonball's place) opts for phrasing similar to that of the recorded version, and settles in behind the beat much as it had a month previously.

Trombonist Frank Rehak, filling in for Cannonball, added weight to the opening theme, while he and two more trombonists extracted from the orchestra—Jimmy Cleveland and Bill Elton—helped propel the riffing behind Kelly's solo and the tune's out chorus. As would be expected, Kelly's playing is busier and funkier than Evans's on the recording, and Cobb was regrettably undermiked, but the performance remains a credit to the power and adaptability of Davis's composition.

Though it would not air until over a year later (when it would provide invaluable promotional support for *Kind of Blue* and the rest of Miles's catalog), "The Sound of Miles Davis" added several degrees to the steep angle of his career ascent. The eruptive success of *Miles Ahead* in 1957 had provided the first boost that propelled him from the narrow jazz world to a wider music audience. By 1959, the star-making machinery was firing on all cylinders. March alone had proved to be an especially hot month: *Porgy & Bess,* the long-awaited orchestral follow-up to *Miles Ahead,* was released on March 9, to instant acclaim and stellar sales. A full feature piece in *Esquire* (penned by Hentoff) was another feather in Miles's publicity cap.

By the time "The Sound of Miles Davis" aired, on July 21, 1960, 90 percent of American homes owned TV sets, quite a jump from 52 percent in 1956, the year Elvis Presley shook his way to stardom on *The Ed Sullivan Show.* By virtue of outreach alone, it was the most effective set Davis had played since his 1955 Newport appearance.

Television, unhampered by the stylistic segregation of record stores and radio stations, broke through established boundaries. Like Presley, the trumpeter was offered the rare opportunity to reach a huge portion of middle America that might never have thought to browse the jazz album section or tune in a late-night jazz radio show. Hentoff recalled Herridge's office being deluged with mail from viewers impressed by the show.

Critics hailed the program ("a model for future tele-productions in the jazz vein" wrote *Variety*) and Miles's performance ("the purest, finest jazz you ever heard," according to the Associated Press). Miles Davis the jazz phenomenon was becoming simply Miles the star.

SELECTION TITLE SPOT DATA	Take No.	F. S.	Master No.	OK	REMARKS
co 62293	1/2	1			TI NG prt FP
Sketches	1/2	8/9			
co 62294	5/6	8			
All Blues					

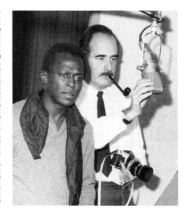

APRIL 22, 1959, 2:30 P.M.

Left: The *Kind of Blue* tape log, second session: note the "NG per FP" next to the first take of "Flamenco Sketches"

Right: Miles and Fred Plaut

Townsend scheduled the second session of Columbia project 43079 for the afternoon of April 22, a Wednesday, from 2:30 to 5:30. To maintain technical continuity, Columbia policy was that whenever possible the same staff would handle the various sessions of a given project. Accordingly, Fred Plaut and Bob Waller's initials appear on the various studio and tape logs for *Kind of Blue*'s second session, and the same handwriting shows up on the tape boxes. Laico mentions that in the fifties, 30th Street Studio engineers developed a logbook in which they kept track of different band setups, microphone placements and other pertinent information to aid their memory between sessions. (The register was lost when Columbia sold the studio in the early eighties.)

From close listening to the session tapes it appears Plaut followed the same audio setup as the first session. Seven microphones were again mixed down to three tracks, with one slight variation: alto and piano were now on the left, and tenor and drums on the right.

Again the musicians arrived separately and set up, and again the soloists converged to study the musical sketches that been prepared. The session was to be a brief one, with only two compositions being recorded. If the unused amount of tape at the end of the master reel for the second session is any indication, the group completed their recordings well before their cutoff time, and at least two hours before the next scheduled artist, Sylvia Sims, was due to begin a 7 to 10 P.M. session.

This time around, the proceedings would be well documented by Plaut's photography. Classical sessions were his usual oeuvre, but he was undoubtedly impressed enough to return to the project with camera in hand, and managed to get out from behind the mixing console to take about a dozen black-and-white shots. Columbia staff photographer Don Hunstein, not on specific orders but on general assignment, showed up as well and snapped three rolls during the session.

> It was understood that I should document the event: some long shots of the whole situation, the way the band was set up, then just walk around and if you see something shoot it. Individuals, two guys together, or in the case of that particular session, Miles leaning over the piano, then he sits down instead of Bill Evans, you know.

With Jimmy Cobb, Hunstein is one of the only two people living who experienced the second session of *Kind of Blue* inside the studio itself. When not clicking away ("Miles was indifferent for the most part, never bothered me"), Hunstein says he would "just hang around someplace or sit in the corner and listen . . . I'm grateful for that experience, God, nothing like that today." Along with the music, he found inspiration in the studio's well-lit if unadorned environment:

> There were no special effects, just ordinary ceiling lights—it was great for what I did because there was an overall lighting, nice and even. It was the plainest kind of situation.

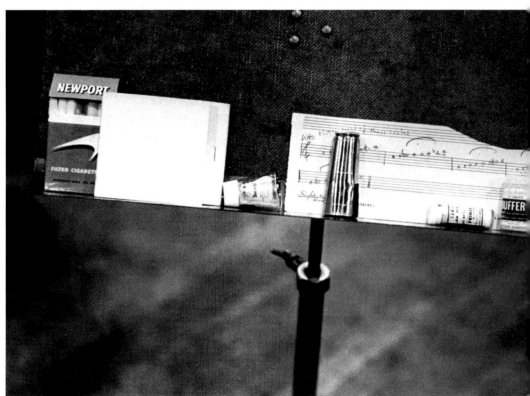

Hunstein's contact sheets capture much of the relaxed, unhurried air at 30th Street that afternoon: there are multiple exposures of Miles joking, smiling, walking around the studio, sitting at the piano, leaning over the keyboard, explaining a musical sketch. In fact, the entire band—by that point extremely familiar with the studio situation and each other—displays the same loose confidence. If a camera can be trusted to catch the essence of a moment, Miles and his sidemen were on common, comfortable ground that day.

Plaut's and Hunstein's lenses also captured the personalities of the band members. Adderley's open joviality is unmistakable as he enjoys a cup of coffee. Evans and Coltrane are their studied, introspective selves, their brows knit in concentration. Tall and looking very young, Chambers towers behind the rest, slightly aloof, eyes focused elsewhere. Cobb—off to the side at his baffled drumkit—somehow never made it into a frame.

Plaut captured one particularly telling image. In his close-up of Adderley's music stand, one can make out a page of sheet music, labeled "alto," that outlines a series of modes. It is the road map to the session's opening masterpiece, "Flamenco Sketches," and it is an extremely rare glimpse of the actual tabulature that helped define *Kind of Blue*.

FLAMENCO SKETCHES

"Flamenco Sketches" is a series of five scales, each to be played as long as the soloist wishes until he has completed the series. (From Bill Evans's liner notes.)

As Chet Baker's "Alone Together" did for "Blue in Green," a recording by Evans on another album in this period offered strong support for his author-ship of "Flamenco Sketches." The song's austere signature ostinato (an insistently repeated musical figure) bass pattern had been played by Evans on an album he recorded a few months earlier, in a song titled "Peace Piece." Originating as his take on Leonard Bernstein's "Some Other Time," a tune that was cut from the show *On The Town*, "Peace Piece" was recorded on December 15, 1958, and became one of the most celebrated tracks on Evans's second Riverside album, *Everybody Digs Bill Evans,* released in early 1959.

As Evans explained it, when he sat down to record a few solo pieces at the end of the *Everybody Digs* session, he began playing the introduction to

"Peace Piece," the inspiration for "Flamenco Sketches": The ostinato pattern as handwritten by Evans

"Some Other Time." But he never got past the two opening chords. "I started to play the introduction, and it started to get so much of its own feeling and identity that I just figured, well, I'll keep going."

According to the pianist, credit for "Sketches" should have been shared. Evans traced the birth of "Sketches" back to the morning of the *Kind of Blue*'s initial session, March 2:

> That morning before the [first session] date I went by [Miles's] apartment. He had liked the tune "Peace Piece" that I did, and he said he would like to do that. I thought that maybe, instead of doing one ostinato, we could move through two or three or four or five levels that would relate to one another and make a cycle, and he agreed and we worked at it at the piano until we arrived at the five levels we used. I wrote those levels out for the guys you know. That was all little sketches I made.

Whether composed alone or jointly, "Sketches" is *Kind of Blue*'s most purely modal composition. "Flamenco Sketches" is also the most prismatic tune on *Kind of Blue*, refracting a variety of influences (classical, impressionistic, exotic) into a haunting, pan-cultural theme covering a wide emotional range. As the outline on Cannonball's music stand shows, the modes used in "Sketches" ranged from the familiar and pleasant (Ionian) to the more tension-creating (Mixolydian) to the foreign (Phrygian). It was the last that lent "Sketches" its peculiar Iberian flavor during the solos. Townsend, lacking a name for the track after the session, wrote simply "Spanish" on his mastering notes to indicate the tune.

Spanish scales—or more correctly, Andalusian scales, which emanated originally from Morocco—were familiar to the general jazz community, as Amram relates.

> Dizzy was the one who spoke more than anybody about the concept of Pan-African music and how the music went from Africa all over the world. A part of that journey, of course, was when the Moors came to Spain and left some of those beautiful rhythms. The flamenco scale is actually the same as the *hijaz* [a Middle Eastern mode] and some of these sounds were part of the journey of African peoples around the world.

The tape for the fourth track starts rolling with a test tone to help with calibration of tape machines used for playback in the future. Townsend dubs the untitled track with a joking reference back to the recording of "So What" (when Davis had indicated any extraneous noise was intentional and should be left on the tape) and assigns the track its file number.

IT: OK Miles, "Surface Noise," CO 62293, Take 1.
UNIDENTIFIED: (laughter)

In a stunning example of impromptu mastery, the sextet turns in a complete, uninterrupted take on their first attempt of the day. This first take of "Flamenco Sketches" is now available as a bonus track on the CD reissue of the album—the final take was issued originally—and remains the sole complete alternate take from the *Kind of Blue* sessions.

Chambers's pedal point pattern (a repeated sequence of dominant notes) and Evans's opening chords neatly set a slow-walking, languid tempo, as Cobb's almost inaudible brushwork provides more ambient texture than rhythm. The tune opens with a two brief runs through the ostinato pattern, followed by Miles's muted trumpet, pensive and floating. Then we hear Coltrane, pensive and moody as he had been on "Blue in Green," and a carefully symmetric approach from Adderley.

As the soloists engage the tune's five-tier structure, the challenge seems to demand stealth and caution. "It was as though they were walking into this unknown territory and being very careful where they stepped," commented Herbie Hancock. "Nobody played too much—there was a minimalist approach to the material."

Chambers and Evans take on a modal traffic cop role, directing—sometimes just hinting at—the transitions from one scale to another. At times, particularly during Coltrane's solo, a gentle nudge from Evans is discernible; the pianist seems to request a modal change while the saxophonist stays with the scale.

The first take of "Sketches" also reveals a significant change from the first session. Perhaps through better microphone placement—but definitely through closer attention to the mixing—Plaut established a clearer, more defined bass sound. On both tracks recorded that second day, Chambers's bass sounds more rounded and present.

At the end of the take, the air of satisfaction is almost tangible. Miles requests a playback, and the tape stops recording.

> MD: Hey, play that Irving . . .
> IT: Nice Miles.

After hearing the first take, a decision is made to attempt another. The tape logs reveal that the judgment came from the engineering side: "TI—NG per FP" (i.e., "Take 1 is no good per Fred Plaut"). An arduous process begins in which the composition evolves over five more tries.

Recording continues, a short amount of studio chatter and bass riffing is heard, obviously to reset the level for the channel in which Chambers is recorded. Take 2 is announced. Miles calls Townsend's attention to an aspect of the studio's wooden details, and Adderley chimes in with an impromptu pun.

IT: Take 2.   MD: Wait a minute Irving . . . wait.

IT: OK.   MD: Hey when you raise up off the stool man . . . you get, oh yeah! (laughter) You know your floor squeaks,

you know. You know what I mean? Can you hear me?

IT: Yeah!   MD: Let's go!

CA: That's surf-ass noise you know . . . it's part of the tune, man . . .

UNIDENTIFIED: (laughter) Surf-ASS noise!

IT: Here we go—Take 2 . . .

Take 2 ends abruptly as Chambers, syncopating his line, hits a wrong note. He apologizes and explains why he lost his way.

MD: Start over again.

PC: I'm sorry.

IT: Ready?   MD: Yeah.

IT: 3 . . .   PC: I forgot—I thought I could close my eyes.

MD: Here you go Paul . . .

Take 3 starts off with Evans improvising more than ever on the simple introduction. Chambers begins embellishing his opening pattern, hitting and sometimes missing double-stops, and adding legato, letting the root note ring. Evans's chords become a little cleaner and assured, losing just a touch of the spontaneity of earlier takes. As Miles begins blowing, he hits a trumpet frack: a splitting of the tone usually caused by an unsteady lip. They stop playing.

MD: Can we start, uh, keep on, Irving?

IT: Let's do one more.   MD: OK . . . ready?

IT: Yep—Take 4.

The intricate and understated shift from one scale to the next during a solo is not as easy as it may look on paper. The first transition of Miles's solo is less than smooth, and the second simply falls apart as Chambers walks one way and Evans another. Miles cuts off Take 4 with a long trill.

Reissue producer Bob Belden has commented that since all the takes include a snippet of Miles's muted solos from the same opening scale, "Someone should splice together all of the [opening] C major sections from all of the takes of "Flamenco Sketches"; it would make a great melody."

MD: Let's try it again Irving.

IT: Ready . . . Take 5 Miles.

Chambers's double-stops sound less confident as the tune begins, the strings buzzing and his playing a little busier than before. At the first modal

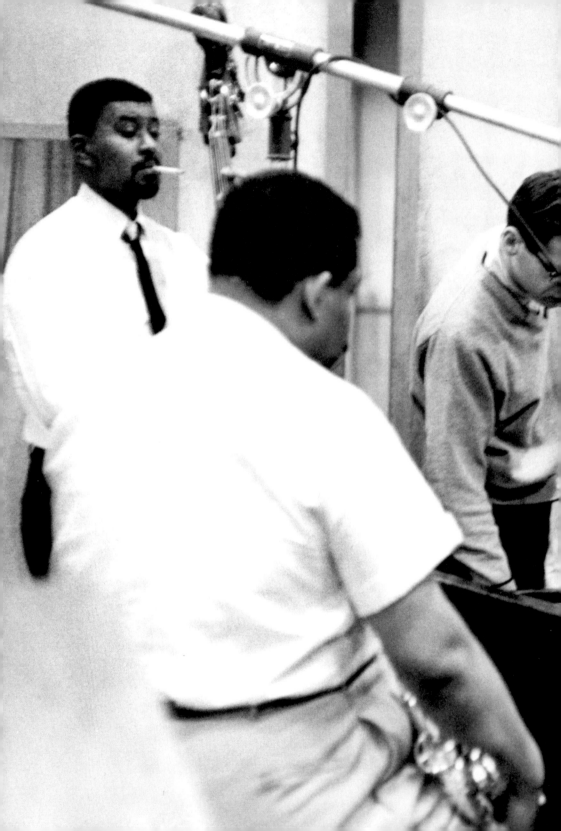

transition, the bassist again plays a gaffe. The take stops, and Miles offers a simple suggestion that solves the problem.

MD: (To Chambers) You're not watching Bill.

PC: I know. I'm sorry.   MD: Try it again Irving.

IT: Right, 6!

The band locks in together and Take 6 becomes the final, issued version of "Sketches," offering a satisfying mix of spontaneity and studied grace. Like the tune in general, Miles's solo is a blend of opposites. Exceedingly calm yet impassioned, halting while still melodic, he achieves dramatic effect at one point by leaning closer to the microphone and boosting his own volume.

Both saxophones follow suit, recording intimately close to their respective microphones, leaving little space for the ambience of the room to breathe in. Coltrane again takes his solo on an irregular path; at one point, expecting a transition, Evans steps out of the mode slightly and then returns, and all continues without fault.

If Miles's solo on "So What" is universally acknowledged as one of *Kind of Blue*'s improvisational high points, Coltrane's on "Sketches" must be celebrated for its emotional depth and subtlety. With hushed, tender nuance and a loose-knit approach prefiguring the spiritual intensity of his future recordings as a leader, he ranges from breezy and buoyant to somber, then bittersweet and melancholy, momentarily playing off the tune's plaintive Spanish sonority. It is impossible to be unaffected by his pristine passion.

Cannonball, true to his nature, arrives with a slight, exuberant push, doubling the scalar changes, stretching the structure of the tune, matching Coltrane's bluesy reach. Evans follows, inventing an extremely soft-and-slack lyrical line, much fainter than the first take, reaching a series of chordal splashes alternately bright, then brooding. Miles returns and—after his phrases become so hushed they threaten to disappear altogether—masterfully ends with a drawn-out note that suspends, rather than resolves, the tension of the entire performance.

A moment of calm follows. Knowing well that no further take is necessary, Miles, flush with satisfaction, gently ribs his producer. Townsend teases him in return, consoling Davis's feigned disappointment.

MD: That's terrible Irving . . .

IT: Don't worry about it.

"All Blues" is a 6/8 12-measure blues form that produces its mood through only a few modal changes, and Miles Davis's free melodic conception.
(From Bill Evans's liner notes.)

As the recording of the album began, so it ended: with a blues. However, the blues structure of "Freddie Freeloader" is more traditional than that of "All Blues." Tenor saxophonist Jimmy Heath, who would fill in for Coltrane for a brief month in 1960, learned that "All Blues" had a modal twist that preserved its link and feel to the album in general:

> When people play it other than in the Miles Davis band, a lot of people play it where they go from the G chord to C, a traditional blues. But when we played "All Blues," Miles would always say don't go to the IV chord on the second part of that. He wanted it to stay in a modal concept. So he'd go from G7 to a G minor sound, really playing that mode so that let his improvisation sound a little dissonant, and a little more sophisticated.

Compositionally, "All Blues" was all Miles, typically marrying different elements. The background riff of "All Blues," played insistently by Chambers throughout, is cited by Heath as "an old traditional blues lick on some different harmony." Speed it up with a slight Latin groove, and a Ray Charles sound emerges; throw it in 4/4 and one can almost hear "Do the Twist."

Evans remembered a point of instruction from Davis that created a transitional interlude acting as a sonic divider between solos. "On 'All Blues,' he said 'Play the chart, and then before each soloist, the [musical] figure will serve as a little vamp to enter the next soloist.'" In Miles's world, it is again the simple that proves the most effective: with one little directive, Davis departed slightly from established blues form, allowing each improvised section to begin anew, gathering its own energy and developing its own ideas, separate from what came before.

The other distinctive feature of "All Blues" is its waltz-like bounce, emphasized by a playful bass figure and a gospel-inspired inflection from Evans: an insistent, diatonic vamp jumping between the tonic and the V. Vamping—the repetition of a simple, usually two-chord pattern to hypnotic effect over which soloists improvise—is a feature that other, blues-based genres borrowed from jazz; countless R&B, funk, and dance recordings rely heavily on vamp sections.

Two noteworthy bandleaders, one funk-oriented and the other rock, have mentioned the influence of "All Blues" on their playing. Maurice White, drummer and founder of the soul group Earth, Wind and Fire, recalled:

I was fascinated with "All Blues" because being a drummer, having to master 3/4 time was something we wanted to do at an early age. But [Miles's] interpretation was not stiff, it was flowing like a river, effortlessly, the way the "one" [the downbeat] disappeared and it just flowed. There wasn't any stop and go.

Talking to Amiri Baraka, Miles recalled instructing Coltrane to inform Cannonball to disregard the "one"—the defining downbeat for funk and many other dance rhythms—when he joined the sextet:

This ain't no blues [presumably meaning R&B or other forms of popular blues]. Trane took Cannonball in the back and showed him what he was doin' . . . I told Trane to show him and stop him from accenting the first beat.

Donald Fagen, keyboardist and co-leader of Steely Dan, a rock band brimming with jazz influence, drew his own rhythmic inspiration from "All Blues":

It's essentially a blues vamp that goes on forever. If you go back to certain swing records, also on some rhythm and blues records at that time, you'll hear those kinds of vamps. You get this kind of rhythmic push that you only get when you only use a couple of chords.

Is it 6/8 or 3/4? It's not that easy to say, since the musician can enter into the time of the piece either way. One of Miles's last sidemen in 1991, trumpeter Wallace Roney, recalls Davis's comment regarding "All Blues": "It's just 'Milestones' in 3/4." Although Davis verbally invokes classic waltz time with a two-bar count-off in 3/4, 6/8 enables each player—particularly the soloists—to adhere to the traditional twelve-bar blues form (3/4 would create a twenty-four-bar melody), to count the six beat length of the vamp, and to feel through their solos accordingly. 6/8 is also a typical African rhythm (and incidentally is the foundation of most Afro-Cuban music).

The sound of Africa may have been heard by others too, or Miles may have referred to the tune as such. Either way, in the weeks after the session, Townsend, lacking a title, would write simply "African" for "All Blues" on his mastering notes.

IT: OK, CO 62294, Number 2, Take 1.
MD: One, two, three . . . one, two, three.

The take halts immediately as Chambers's entrance is uncoordinated and a little late. After the problems with "Sketches," the bassist seems particularly contrite. Miles again offers face- and time-saving advice.

PC: Let's start over again. I'm sorry, I'm sorry.

MD: Bill will start it off, you just come in.   IT: Ready?

MD: One, two, three . . . one, two, three . . .

Take 2 kicks off with Chambers locked in place, playing the consistent, jaunty eight-note part that stitches the entire tune together and defines its rhythm. As in "So What," Chambers and Evans join in setting an introductory mood, the pianist's a rolling piano figure marimba-like in its tremolo effect. Evans recalled it as a spontaneous addition: "On 'All Blues,' the little fluttering I play at the beginning is just something I threw in."

As the introduction continues, the horns appear with the long, languid-phrased riffs that define the "All Blues" theme. The horns play in harmony for one chorus; then Miles disengages to play a second melodic line that adds wings to the theme. Underneath, Cobb is on brushes, helping the tune shift through its blues changes slowly and subtly.

Cobb switches to drumsticks as Miles's solo begins. It is one of his most carefree improvisations on the album, rhythmically playful and dynamic. The set order of soloists changes slightly as Cannonball jumps in, exultant to be back in familiar blues territory, yet subdued a notch. Coltrane follows, handling the blues with a liberal sprinkling of his long-winded, sheets-of-sound imprint. Evans steps in lightly, staying with the tune's repetitive motif before building the energy while maintaining a rhythmic charge with his left hand.

For David Amram, Evans's solo generates a release that captures the magic of the entire album.

> What seems to go unnoticed with Bill Evans except by musicians is the way he plays those repeated figures perfectly on "All Blues," kind of like a master of simplicity. First you get hypnotized listening to him play that over and over and when he finally comes to playing his solo, it's one of those wonderful moments when you remember experiencing all those lost nights you'll never recover. It's there in the recording.

In the middle of his solo, Evans travels a modal path, playing in a "locked-hands" position, keeping his fingering the same as he moves both hands up and down the keyboard. "It's a brilliant moment where he plays fourths [striking notes three whole steps apart] like McCoy [Tyner] often did later with Coltrane," notes Bob Belden. "Evans stays close to just the white keys."

As Davis recalled in his autobiography, Evans's technique of avoiding the black keys was a simple and direct way of evoking the classical influences both were attracted to: "[Evans] used to bring me pieces by Ravel like *The*

Concerto for Left Hand and Orchestra. We were just leaning toward—like Ravel, playing a sound only with the white keys."

Following the piano solo, the band returns to the "All Blues" theme: Evans repeating the marimba-like tremolo, Chambers still on the same bass figure, and the two saxes in harmony on the pulsing out-theme. Miles plays the familiar melody over the saxophones, and then joins the theme. But Miles decides to delay the inevitable. After another vamp section on the last four bars—the turnaround of the blues form—he invokes a stuttering trumpet figure that echoes his solo. It is one last moment of invention, an impromptu send-off before the session ends.

As easy-rolling as it all sounds, the effort of playing the same musical phrase over and over—even for veteran musicians—is apparent as the tune ends. Perhaps most relieved is Chambers, who has played the "All Blues" defining ostinato pattern incessantly throughout the tune's 11:33 duration. Fingers and lips finally relax, and all breathe a sigh of relief.

> UNIDENTIFIED: Ssshhhhhoooooooo!
> (PROBABLY PC): (PANTING) Damn that's a hard mother!
> BE: Boy, if I didn't have coffee . . .   IT: What?

In one three-hour session, the two remaining tracks for *Kind of Blue* were completed, and the sextet packed up and went home. In later years, Evans recalled that "there was a good feeling on those dates. But I really had no idea—I don't think anybody did—that it would have the influence and duration it did." He added philosophically:

> Professionals have to go in at 10 o'clock on a Wednesday and make a record and hope to catch a really good day. The rest of it is being professional, reaching a high degree of performance in the area that you're trying to work.

It was the last time Miles Davis and Bill Evans would ever record together.

Selling *Blue*

FOR COLUMBIA RECORDS, *Kind of Blue* would be just one more golden egg in a nest full of pop, classical, soundtracks, and other profit-making jazz albums. Besides Davis, the label's other leading jazzmen were busy during the spring of 1959 as well. Duke Ellington had completed an album called *Jazz Party* with orchestral percussionists added to his regular band, and was gearing up to record the soundtrack to the new Otto Preminger film *Anatomy of a Murder*. On April 22, the same day Miles completed *Kind of Blue*, Dave Brubeck commenced recording a southern song cycle project in Hollywood entitled *Gone with the Wind*. Later that year he would record his career best-seller *Time Out*, with its smash single "Take Five." Columbia's newest signing, bassist/bandleader Charles Mingus, would enter 30th Street in May to record his label debut, the groundbreaking *Mingus Ah Um*.

Columbia was able to offer all its artists a full complement of support services. The company had become a powerhouse of mastering, packaging

and marketing since the early fifties. According to Stanley Tonkel, a tape editor during that period who would work on many Miles recordings in the sixties:

Miles and his sextet live at Birdland, 1959. Note Philly Joe Jones back on drums, temporarily substituting for Jimmy Cobb

Columbia was one of the few companies, outside of RCA, that was a complete recording company, not just a studio and an office. We did everything. We had a research and development office, we used to build our own [recording] equipment, we had a whole publicity staff, a photographic staff. We did all our own recording, all our own remixing, mastering and remastering. Everything was done in-house by Columbia staff.

At Columbia's main uptown offices at 799 Seventh Avenue, Irving Townsend, whose transfer to the West Coast was approaching rapidly, immediately began the process that would turn the unedited session tapes into a marketable product. He had accomplished such duties many times before, recently with Miles's *Porgy & Bess* tapes, which producer Cal Lampley had left with him after departing Columbia.

Townsend's task was made infinitely easier by the simple fact that—other than the first impromptu run through "Flamenco Sketches"—there were only single completed takes of each composition on the master tapes. His mastering instructions reveal that the three tracks from the first session were to constitute side A of the album, and the two from the later session side B. His simple plan seems to have been to open the album quietly and end the same way: "So What," with its wispy introduction, was chosen to kick off side A, while the gentle fade of "Flamenco Sketches" was placed at the close of side B.

As Cal Lampley had handed off *Porgy & Bess* to Townsend, so Townsend handed Teo Macero *Kind of Blue* sometime early that summer. This could well explain the miscommunication that resulted in the mislabeling of the tracks on side B: "All Blues" became "Flamenco Sketches." But the original error seems to have been Townsend's, as two separate notes reveal first the correct, then the incorrect order for the two tracks, identified by their co numbers, while the titles remain constant.

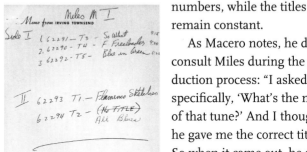

As Macero notes, he did consult Miles during the production process: "I asked him specifically, 'What's the name of that tune?' And I thought he gave me the correct title. So when it came out, he says, 'No that's not the way it goes.'" Though the roughly fifty thousand copies of the first pressing—an estimate culled from various Columbia alumni—were in error (and are now collector's items), a memo from Macero in October 1959 asked that the sequence be corrected. Nonetheless, confusion remains; to this day, many of the album's original fans still mention "All Blues" while meaning to describe "Flamenco Sketches" and vice-versa.

Townsend's notes reflect the fact that by early summer the album had a title, provided by Miles. Album names had not been much anticipated by Davis in the past. The titles of his first two Columbia albums had been chosen by George Avakian, and before that, the titles of most of Davis's LPs had reflected the concept behind the recording (*Miles Davis and the Modern Jazz Giants*, for example) or the standout track (*Milestones*). This time around Miles opted for a name that described more than just a song or the session.

The phrase "Kind of Blue" was typical of Davis. Other song or album titles of his had contained double-entendres—*Milestones, Miles Ahead*—and Davis obviously knew that *Kind of Blue* worked on at least two levels. The music—particularly "Freddie Freeloader" and "All Blues"—was structurally based on a "sort of" blues form, while the rest of the album insinuated an indistinct yet pervasive melancholy feeling that was indeed "kind of blue."

But beyond the punning, there was a socially conscious level to the name

Above left: Townsend's instructions on *Kind of Blue*'s sequencing. Note the confusion on the last two tracks

Above right: Townsend's mastering instructions for *Kind of Blue*

Bottom: A Columbia memo corrects the track listing gaffe on *Kind of Blue*'s first pressing

as well. "He wanted to connect with that old woman's voice [the gospel singer from Arkansas]," says Quincy Troupe, recalling how Davis repeatedly mentioned the sound of that faceless vocalist while working on his autobiography. As Troupe tells it, it was from that same childhood memory that Miles drew the inspiration for the album's title. "He told me that many times. He characterized her and the experience of most black people in this country as being a 'kind of blue' experience."

What of the names of the individual tunes? The naming of jazz instrumentals (as opposed to vocal songs, in which a title is usually suggested by the lyrics) has long been one fueled by extempore inspiration—a girlfriend's name, for instance (Miles's "Lazy Susan"), or even, as in "One O'Clock Jump," the time on the studio clock. To judge from their recollections, the musicians and producers involved in making *Kind of Blue* seem not to have focused much on the songs' titles. Avakian remarks that "Miles didn't care much about song titles at all." Cobb recalls that some of the names of the tunes on *Kind of Blue* were suggested by one of Miles's many girlfriends of the period, particularly "Freddie Freeloader": "She was going around saying she was the one who helped name that, and 'So What.' But the others—like 'Blue in Green' and 'Flamenco Sketches'—Bill [Evans] could have had something to do with that."

Two songs on *Kind of Blue* typify a penchant Miles was developing for naming compositions after friends and fellow musicians, and after slang, offhand expressions. "Freddie Freeloader" predates such titles as "Teo" (after Macero), "Mademoiselle Mabry" (after his wife Betty Mabry) and "Billy Preston." "So What"—a favorite off-putting expression of Davis's—calls to mind later titles like "Right Off" and "Call It Anythin'."

For the album cover, Townsend presented instructions to Columbia's art department noting the relative sizes of the textual information to be displayed. Miles's name was to be largest (100 percent) with the album title slightly smaller (80 percent), and for the first time on one of his Columbia albums, his sidemen were to be listed on the front cover as well (20 percent). As the back cover reveals, Townsend provided an odd mix of formal and informal names: Wynton became "Wyn" Kelly, Jimmy became "James" Cobb, and Cannonball was listed simply as "Julian Adderly." The misspelling of Adderley either was never caught by Columbia staff or was deemed too unimportant to warrant the expense of redoing the cover art; Cannonball's name was finally listed correctly on the 1997 CD reissue of *Kind of Blue*.

Townsend's instructions regarding the album cover were passed to the director of design and packaging for Columbia Records, S. Neil Fujita. Fujita had overseen the evolution of album covers from their very first incarnation in 1948, when they were called "tombstones" because they featured little artwork other than inscribed pillars that gave them a funereal look. By the late fifties, Columbia album covers reflected the art and styles of the time. The latest releases were wrapped in original, expressionist artwork (artist Ben Shahn created a few covers for Fujita), playful, colorful designs, and striking photography.

Fujita's normal strategy was to use an image-defining photograph for a Columbia artist's debut. "Earlier in [Miles's] career it had been photographs. Like Tony Bennett, also Johnny Mathis. It's best to show their face when they're new artists to the label. With Miles, I showed his face [on 'Round About Midnight] performing with a trumpet." Later, as an artist became established, Fujita chanced a more creative approach. The cover of *Porgy & Bess* displayed a couple side by side, cropped tightly so only their torsos were visible. Only the trumpet held between them connected the picture with Davis.

Fujita remembers that although his first instinct had been to employ an artist to fashion a new canvas for *Kind of Blue,* Davis insisted that he use a photograph instead. "Miles was very stubborn about his packages," he recalled. Previously, the trumpeter had caused Columbia to change the cover of *Miles Ahead* when it was reprinted, from a young swim-suited white woman on a sailboat to an energetic, mid-solo shot of the trumpeter. As Avakian recalled, Miles's objection when the album was released—"Why did you put that white bitch on there?"—had been more jibe than outraged challenge. But Davis saw the casual racism of Columbia's design policy. In his famous *Playboy* interview with Alex Haley in 1962, he spoke candidly about the problem and his own solution—putting his wife on the cover of 1961's *Someday My Prince Will Come,* rather than a white woman.

> I just got to thinking that as many records as Negroes buy, I hadn't ever seen a Negro girl on a major album cover unless she was the artist. There wasn't any harm meant—they just automatically thought about a white model and ordered one.

Fujita often used the photographs of Jay Maisel, whose black-and-white work appeared on album covers of such Columbia jazz greats as Duke Ellington and Louis Armstrong. From a series of color slides Maisel had taken of Miles performing at the Apollo, nattily attired in a sharp blue suit and diamond-patterned tie, Fujita chose a shot that captured an introspective, non-blowing moment—Miles's cheeks are relaxed—and that provided enough dark background for the cover text. Fujita notes that when thumbing through albums in a store rack, he had noticed that only the text on the upper edge of the cover was legible: "That's why I put the words up there, so they could read it even if it wasn't the first album on display."

Every Miles album Columbia had released bore an explanatory essay or at least words of praise from a noted critic or the album's producer (or, in the case of *Miles Ahead,* both). As Cal Lampley recalls, liner notes were also a way of circumventing a Columbia policy that applied to all production staff: "Nobody in those days got a production credit [on the album], but Avakian was smart because he always wrote the liner notes for his, so his name would be on them."

But the liner notes for *Kind of Blue* were by Bill Evans. With no critics present at the recording (as Hentoff would be on *Sketches of Spain*), nor a producer intimately familiar with Miles and his music (as Avakian had been on *Miles Ahead*), the task fell to the one person who both truly knew the music and could write well.

It is clear that Evans wrote the notes shortly after the recording sessions: the original handwritten manuscript bears no album or track titles. But with a sense of control and space not unlike that which he brought to his music, Evans neatly outlined his thoughts in blue ballpoint pen on three plain letter pages. From the fluidity of his handwriting the words seem to have been written quite spontaneously; Townsend edited them hardly at all. The only text not used on the album was Evans's final statement, an echo of a previous sentence: "Perhaps those that hear well will find something captured which escapes contemplation."

Evans did not offer biographies on the musicians, nor explanations of where the music fit into the jazz continuum. Instead, in an essay he called, simply, "Improvisation in Jazz," he compared the creation of the music through group improvisation to the creation of a Japanese painting. Like the music inside, his words have a directness that invites the uninitiated.

Evans's essay opens with a reference to a style of Japanese ink painting that Japanese art scholars identify as *suibokuga,* which first arrived in Japan from China with Zen Buddhist monks at the end of the fourteenth century. The choice of a Japanese art form as a point of comparison reflects the infatuation then current in New York artistic circles with Eastern art and mysticism. "It was very much in the air. Allen Watts's books [on Zen Buddhism]—we all read them," recalls Evans's friend and *Down Beat* editor Gene Lees. Evans's close familiarity with the subject enabled him, in a very brief space, to find a striking analogy with jazz:

> There is a Japanese visual art in which the artist is forced to be spontaneous. He must paint on a thin stretched parchment with a special brush and black water paint in such a way that an unnatural or interrupted stroke will destroy the line or break through the parchment. Erasures or changes are impossible. These artists must practice a particular discipline, that of allowing the idea to express itself in communi-

cation with their hands in such a direct way that deliberation cannot interfere.

The resulting pictures lack the complex composition and textures of ordinary painting, but it is said that those who see will find something captured that escapes explanation.

This conviction that direct deed is the most meaningful reflection, I believe, has prompted the evolution of the extremely severe and unique disciplines of the jazz or improvising musician.

Though Evans's imagery exaggerates slightly ("you'd have to punch through the paper with the wrong end of a brush to break through rice paper or parchment," one scholar said), he was spot-on in his use of metaphor. Sparseness, simplicity, and gentle texture are defining elements in both modal jazz and Japanese *suibokuga*.

Evans followed his metaphoric comments with a structural outline of each track offering a perspective normally shared only between musicians. His notes, studied by many budding musicians, were used like a trail of crumbs to follow the sextet's steps into modal jazz terrain. To this day Evans's liner notes are often quoted when the subject is improvisation or discipline in modern jazz, and they remain among the best-known words on any jazz album cover.

By the start of the summer, Macero, with Townsend still looking over his shoulder, had taken over the task of introducing *Kind of Blue* to the rest of Columbia. Following Columbia's established two-album-a-year strategy, the release of the album was scheduled for August 17, 1959, well over five months since the March 9 release of *Porgy & Bess*. (Another album from Miles in 1959, *Jazz Track*—comprised of the *Ascenseur* score and the four tracks recorded by Miles Davis sextet in 1958—was released only two months after *Kind of Blue*. When asked if this did not hamper Columbia's efforts to avoid competition between albums, one veteran explained that film soundtracks were considered in a different category, accounting for *Jazz Track*'s "off-cycle" release.)

Columbia had a long tradition of monthly meetings in which the Artist & Repertoire (A&R) department (basically, the label's in-house record producers) would convene with the heads of sales and marketing, and introduce the upcoming releases. The meetings were a sort of beauty pageant: music would be played, the covers would be displayed, and the various A&R men would each have a few minutes to win the hearts of Columbia's sales executives.

How an album ultimately fared in the field heavily depended on how it was prioritized by the New York office. At times—particularly when a jazz artist went up against a steady flow of pop stars—it was a tough sell. "You'd look at the expression on salesmen's faces and they'd be saying 'What the hell do we need all this for?'" remembers Lampley, who was present next to Avakian when Miles was first introduced to the Columbia sales heads in 1957. But Miles's reputation and a rave from a French writer deflected any opposition. "The French historian Andre Hodeir wrote a lovely article about [Davis] and George read it at the meeting and it made such a splash. One salesman named Stan Kavan I'll never forget because he took an interest in what George and myself had to offer," Lampley recalls.

Kavan, then a general merchandising manager on his way to a vice-presidency at Columbia, explains his enthusiasm: "Miles was really the first cool [jazz] artist we had on the label. We had a very good lineup of jazz people. But Miles brought us something we didn't have—the new, leading edge of jazz. It really was a breath of fresh air."

Mitch Miller leads the Columbia marketers in a Sales Convention singalong, 1959

By 1959, on the heels of Miles's incredible success with his first three albums, the Columbia sales force greeted the arrival of *Kind of Blue* with open arms. Kavan recalls:

> Miles was still early with us then, but was a stellar jazz seller . . . a jazz album that sold almost a hundred thousand copies in a year, that was extraordinary. Miles did that with *Porgy [& Bess]*. Any follow-up to a good album always gets attention, so we marketers were delighted to see a new Miles album. It had wings from the start.

After the monthly get-togethers with A&R, Kavan would hold a merchandising meeting to "develop the promotional plan for each album" in the two areas of his responsibility: retail and radio.

On the radio side, Kavan points out that *Miles Ahead* and *Porgy & Bess* had managed to break Miles out of the "just-jazz" radio format, though not as far as the playlists of pop stations on the more commercial AM band. "We had a very good list of jazz deejays but we realized after *Porgy* that there was a possibility of crossover into—I don't want to say "pop"—but "quasi-pop" feel, like FM stations. We serviced the popular FM stations when it became clear to us that Miles was beyond the hard-core jazz audience."

Del Costello, a Bay Area-based radio promotion veteran and jazz fanatic, was one of Kavan's soldiers-in-the-field when *Kind of Blue* was released. "I always had a head-start on everybody because Teo and I were great friends. Even before I heard the music [on *Kind of Blue*], he was saying that there was magic with the players. Even though the material was new they just hammered it—'A home run every time one of them soloed.'"

Costello recalls the success he encountered with *Kind of Blue*. "I took it over to Pat Henry, who ran the jazz station KJAZ and was known nationally, and we got on the air and started playing it and you could see the switchboard lights going, people wanting to know when it was available. He played the whole goddamn thing—in those days, that's not something they did." As Kavan predicted, Costello was able to get it played on a pop station as well.

A record store poster announcing the impending arrival of *Kind of Blue*

Jim Lang on KABC in San Francisco—he's now a game show host on TV—had a big audience after midnight. I remember specifically sitting in with him in the booth and convincing him to play "All Blues."

Phil Elwood, another Bay Area jazz deejay who received an advance copy of *Kind of Blue,* recalls:

Every Sunday I devoted the last half-hour to play what I considered the record of the week. *Kind of Blue* was the one I chose that week. I remember a call saying, "I just came in on that—who was that on piano? Who wrote that?" Afterwards, the whole two hours I was on every Sunday, somebody always phoned to make sure I would play it.

On August 17, 1959, the album's "street date," *Kind of Blue*—in its monaural (catalog number CL1355) and stereo (CS8163) versions—was shipped to an excited jazz community. Word had filtered through the grapevine about its impending release, and pianist Warren Bernhardt, then a student at the University of Chicago, was typical of those anxiously anticipating its arrival. "I remember standing at the record store, a little tiny place under the railroad tracks on the South Side, in the middle of the ghetto there. I was waiting with a bunch of other guys for the records to come in off the truck. We bought it the moment it was released."

As *Kind of Blue* hit the stores, Columbia publicist Deborah Ishlon succeeded in turning up the heat a final notch. She had already helped raise Miles's profile as high as that of any contemporary jazz artist by 1959. Some of the larger national publications had recently published feature pieces on Miles: *Time* and *The New York Times* the year before, and *Esquire* earlier that spring. Normally the others would have waited a year or two before refocusing on his career or recent albums. But a profile of the trumpeter appeared in the September issue of *Saturday Review,* including a few comments on *Kind of Blue:* "subdued stuff but nonetheless potent . . . it has a freshness, imagination and lack of strain rarely heard in studio work."

Ishlon also scored a number of favorable reviews for the album in daily newspapers and jazz and music trade publications. According to *Billboard, Kind of Blue* was a "Spotlight Winner" for the week of August 31, along with seventeen others, including the Count Basie LP (with Joe Williams) *Breakfast, Dance & Barbecue* and a jazz treatment of a well-known symphony, *Scheherajazz.* The trade magazine opined that Davis was "staying within the confines of what might be called the 'interior' style of cool jazz. . . ." *Metronome* caught up with the album in October and was ambivalent. The unsigned review praised its "fine ensemble playing" and "neat, simple charts," but mostly bemoaned the fact that "Miles seems to be limiting himself more and more all the time, that is playing within a smaller and smaller limit all the time, taking no chances at all."

Down Beat (also in October) was ecstatic. In an unsigned review, the journal proffered five (out of five) stars, stating:

> This is a remarkable album. Using very simple but effective devices, Miles has constructed an album of extreme beauty and sensitivity. This is not to say that this LP is a simple one—far from it. What is remarkable is that the men have done so much with the stark, skeletal material.

Perhaps the most emotive and prescient review came from *San Francisco Examiner* columnist C. H. Garrigues:

> This is one of Miles's great records . . . it is perhaps his greatest record since his days with Bird. . . . Buy it and play it, quietly, around about midnight . . . you will agree that this is jazz which, in all likelihood, will never be duplicated.

But Ishlon discovered that the more headlines and reviews she produced, the more interview-shy Miles became. The unfortunate downside of broader exposure and media attention was his increasing—and justified—distrust of most critics. Articles repeatedly took Miles to task for his onstage demeanor while misunderstanding his understated trumpet sound. Features appeared with titles like "The Enigma of Miles Davis" (in *Down Beat*), "Evil Genius of Jazz" (*Ebony*), or "Behind the cool indifference there seethes the man—Miles Davis a real toughie" (in the *Playboy* knock-off *Cavalier*). Miles

A rare promotional appearance by Miles. From left: Lieberson, Davis, Macero and Dave Brubeck at a Columbia jazz convention, 1963

would express his limited faith in jazz journalists to Haley in the *Playboy* interview: "I ain't going to name critics I don't like. But I will tell you some that I respect what they write — Nat Hentoff, Ralph Gleason and Leonard Feather . . . it ain't a long list."

Though a reluctant self-promoter, Miles was a realist. "He was one of the most intelligent people," remembers Lampley. "But I think he hated to show his intelligence." Outwardly, he seemed oblivious or disinterested. "The greatest thing I learned from Miles is not to pay attention to criticism," says trumpeter Hugh Masekela. But with a bottom-line pragmatism, he would read his notices and accept their value right or wrong: "He said that as long as they spelled his name right, he didn't give a shit."

Miles rarely participated in promotional or marketing appearances. Bruce Lundvall, now president of Blue Note Records, who began his career at Columbia as a marketing apprentice, remembers Miles as "never being involved with promotion of his product. He never did in-stores [free performances in retail record outlets]." Davis is markedly absent from count- less photographs of Columbia sales conventions during that era. Macero even recalls imitating Miles's voice on a tape to be played for sales represen- tatives at a Columbia Records convention.

None of which is to say that Miles was unaware of what was and was not being done to help sell his albums. At times, he could be extremely focused. While touring after the release of *Kind of Blue,* Davis discovered that juke- boxes in various nightclubs did not feature his music, but did offer selections by other jazz artists. A memo sent by Townsend to Kavan in April 1960 tells of "continuing requests from Miles Davis for representation in the EP [extended-play, 45 rpm single] market. He is primarily concerned with the amount of jazz now on jukeboxes in many areas of the country while he is not represented." The memo asked Kavan to "instruct our distributors to get them on jukeboxes and see what response we get. At the very least it will be good promotion."

Miles's urging resulted in a series of 45s created for coin operators only. Pianist Kenny Barron recalls: "You could hear those *Kind of Blue* things — especially "All Blues" — on the jukeboxes in clubs and restaurants and lunch- eonettes." Columbia files list the promotional singles as "It Ain't Necessarily So"/"All Blues," "There's A Boat Leavin' Soon"/"So What," and — one that Jimmy Cobb recalls — "I Loves You Porgy"/"Freddie Freeloader." "That was the one that I used to hear on the jukeboxes quite often. In fact, I remember going in a place where Freddie [Tolbert] was and he would be behind the bar working, and he'd be playing it all day because of his name, bragging, and he would be singing all the notes. He knew everybody's solo."

Despite Miles's ambivalence regarding conscious self-promotion, he was certainly comfortable pushing his music by continuing to do what he did best: performing live. As Townsend and Macero steered *Kind of Blue* through its release process at Columbia, Miles and the sextet dove into a busy touring itinerary assembled by Shaw Artists, playing to audiences in nightclubs and festivals. As a number of witnesses attest, it was an effective way of creating a buzz around his new album and around the new compositions from *Kind of Blue* that Miles adopted into his working repertoire—"So What" and "All Blues."

Shirley Horn was one fan of Miles who was impressed if slightly bewildered when first hearing the unfamiliar modal material performed live just after the *Kind of Blue* recording sessions.

> It affected everyone. Some people hated it, some loved it, some didn't understand it. I was totally confused at one point. I remember we were playing in New York at some hotel bar and I was on break and I went in to catch him and to say hello. There was a crowd, and I went up to Stan Getz who was there. We hugged and then we stood there and listened. I said "What do you think?" He said, "I don't know what to think. . . ." I said, "I don't either." It was beautiful but confusing.

The sextet was in the midst of a week of dates at Birdland at that point. As Cobb recalls, they were still performing the *Kind of Blue* material at a tempo similar to that on the record; "it was only much later that we started playing them faster."

Quincy Jones witnessed those dates at Birdland, and picked up on the languid pace of the new tunes in the band's repertoire.

> That is one of the striking characteristics of those *Kind of Blue* songs, you know—the tempos. [They] had almost a hypnotic trance to them. You know what it is? It's a junkie tempo. There's a very special mood that modal stuff creates, that reminds me of those nights at Birdland—all this brilliant music coming down on you.

Miles closed his Birdland engagement on April 29. A week later John Coltrane entered the studio to record the music for *Giant Steps.* Following so closely on the heels of the recording of *Kind of Blue,* the synchronicity seems almost scripted; very rarely do two flashes of connected brilliance occur in such short order (Atlantic would release *Steps* in 1960). Though divergent in musical style and execution—*Steps* was the result of much compositional trial and error and multiple takes—both albums resulted from a common intensity and drive to explore new musical territory.

Giant Steps stands as a personal leap forward for the tenor man, a declaration of musical independence foreshadowing his departure from Davis's group to form his own unit. In the album's liner notes, Coltrane revealed that his creative inspiration derived from a tireless spirit of self-education: "I sit there and run over chord progressions and sequences, and eventually, I usually get a song—or songs—out of each little musical problem." Like Evans and Davis, he was searching for a personal balance of the emotional and technical aspects of jazz: "I'm worried that sometimes what I'm doing sounds just like academic exercises, and I'm trying more and more to make it sound prettier."

The Miles Davis sextet returned to the road the day after Coltrane's second session, traveling to Chicago's Regal Theater (May 6–18); San Francisco's Black Hawk (May 29–June 11); Los Angeles' Jazz Seville (July 1–approximately July 15). But it was to be the swan song for the all-star lineup. Coltrane, offered a lucrative gig of his own back in New York, quit the band while in L.A. Though he would return intermittently for a few New York appearances, one European tour, and one more recording session, Coltrane stayed on only long enough for Jimmy Heath, his replacement and old friend from Philadelphia, to arrive.

The sextet had been running on borrowed time for a while. Since late 1958, Miles had made efforts to keep his all-star lineup intact—for example, by having his agent book Coltrane's first gigs as a leader—but the level of talent and the different stylistic directions in the band were simply too much to contain. Though Coltrane was the first to leave, Cannonball already had one foot out the door. Once the group finished their tour and returned to New York, Adderley would exit for good. The rhythm section of Kelly, Chambers, and Cobb had been moonlighting as a separate unit as well, recording on their own under Kelly's name, with Coltrane and alto saxophonist Art Pepper on separate albums in 1960 and with future Miles sideman saxophonist Hank Mobley in 1961.

It was to be expected. As Cobb commented:

> The *Kind of Blue* thing did separate into a variety of all-star groups because the band was an all-star kind of band in the first place, and most of it was different flavors. Bill [Evans] played a certain way, Cannonball had a thing he called funky, and Coltrane had his whole brand-new thing. [Kelly, Chambers, and I] had our little swing trio that everybody wanted to play with.

The surprise was that Davis was able to keep the band together as long as he did. As Macero commented nostalgically: "When you get a group like Miles had for a couple of months there, it was a miracle. Everything just sort of popped."

For the moment, though, Miles still had Cannonball. But Heath was

struggling to find his way into Davis's new modal-based material.

> I told Miles, because he could obviously tell, "Look man, I'm not having a problem with the tunes that have traditional cadences that end like 'Autumn Leaves' and 'On Green Dolphin Street.' This 'So What,' you know, I'm having a problem with that. Man, what do you play on that?" He said, "You play on the white keys on the outside, and all the black keys in the bridge." It's a wonderful analyzation. It's a simplification, but it's not.

The touring continued with Heath as a member of the sextet. Toronto was the next stop, for the Canadian Jazz Festival (July 22), where a young bassist from Detroit caught the performance. As Ron Carter remembers it, it turned his head around.

> I heard the band at the Toronto Jazz Festival. The Miles Davis songs at that time were "All of You," "'Round Midnight," "If I Were a Bell," and "Walkin'." Then he played this tune that had this different kind of order to it—the changes were not what we would call at the time normal changes. I couldn't figure out what was going on. I could *feel* the chords but I didn't know what they were doing. And the band was sounding comfortable. It took me a while to begin to understand that they weren't playing necessarily on changes as we knew them, but they were playing a form of scales. I thought I was pretty much behind the times so I said OK, I have to find out what this record is.

The Trio: Wynton Kelly, Paul Chambers and Jimmy Cobb in 1966

Miles and the group continued on to Chicago, then appeared at the French Lick Jazz Festival, another outdoor event produced by Newport Jazz impresario George Wein, on August 2. In the audience was the young vibraphonist Gary Burton, back home after his first year at the Berklee School of Music.

> I actually saw the *Kind of Blue* band play at a jazz festival near where I grew up in Indiana. It wasn't with Bill Evans, it was with Wynton Kelly. Of course I was listening to this and I didn't get it at all. I was seventeen years old and I'm thinking "Gee, you know, Miles is this famous guy, but his playing isn't nearly as impressive as other trumpet players I've heard who can play a lot faster." It wasn't until I got to hear the record that I began to understand and appreciate this whole new style and genre of jazz and improvising that had come along.

With a few days off, Heath returned home to Philadelphia, where, still dealing with the fallout from a drug bust, he found that his parole officer had decided to limit his travel to a fifty-mile radius from home. Miles was left with an empty tenor chair. He carried on without filling it through a festival date in Chicago sponsored by longtime jazz fan Hugh Hefner. Davis's *Playboy* Jazz Festival performance on August 7, 1959, was recorded and allows us to hear how far a tune like "So What" had progressed in the five months since the sextet recorded it in March. (Never officially released, the recording is a bootleg highly prized by Miles collectors.)

As the band launches into the familiar opening theme, it seems to burst with the energy of the classic Miles quintet. Cobb is nothing but explosive, propelling a jaunty rendition of a tune once tranquil and moody, summoning the same spirit—and dropping the same "bombs"—as Philly Joe Jones once had. Kelly's accompaniment is in the pocket, subtler than Garland would have been but as insistent. Miles machine guns his way into the tune, riding the front end of the rhythm, then drops back into his familiar, elongated phrasing. In no way pensive as he is on the studio recording, Davis takes chances; toward the end of his solo he reaches, Dizzy-like, for a high note and misses, blowing air. Cannonball then takes charge, pushing the energy to another, animated level, freewheeling through the tune's scalar shifts, paraphrasing a few of Davis's lines. Kelly's solo is furious: midway through, Davis and Adderley add a syncopated horn riff, then lay out as Kelly hits a series of Garland-like block chords and drops in a funky bass note motif. As the rhythm section closes the twelve-minute version with the theme, Miles harmonizes a lazy tone above the music.

The crowd's response—as it had been consistently on the tour—was nothing less than tumultuous. Whether or not all fans grasped the mini-malist structure of the new modal material, the sound and effect—sophisti-cated and smooth—piqued a hunger for Miles's impending album. The summer tour completed, Davis and his quintet returned to New York. Coltrane rejoined the group on August 13, the same week *Kind of Blue* was released, for a sold-out, two-week run at Birdland. The hometown audience proved just as enthusiastic as the rest of the country, and now comprised high society. Miles was, as he wrote, "feeling on top of the world. The new sextet with Wynton Kelly on piano opened at Birdland to packed crowds. People like Ava Gardner and Elizabeth Taylor were in the audience every night and coming back to the dressing room to say hello."

Toward the end of the engagement, on August 25, the triumphant mood was shattered. Between sets, Miles walked a white female acquaintance to a taxi in front of the club. As the cab departed, a beat cop told Davis to move on. The policeman and trumpeter exchanged confrontational words and looks; Miles assumed a boxer's defensive stance ("boxers had told me that if a guy's going to hit you . . . walk *toward* him so you can see what's happening") and the cop brought his billy club out and down on Davis's head. Miles was arrested and whisked away to jail. The next day front-page headlines told the story ("Probe into Birdland Beating Up") while dramatic photographs showed dark blood stains splattered on Davis's white jacket. Though Miles was exonerated two months later, he never forgot the humiliation and outrage he felt in that moment on the Broadway sidewalk. Decades later, he would title his last album for Columbia with the words he heard before being clubbed: "You're under arrest!"

Back at Birdland, Nat Adderley filled in for Miles, and Coltrane and Cannonball took charge of the sextet, finishing off an extra week at the club as Miles recuperated. Once Miles returned, Cannonball left Davis to join his brother. Though Coltrane remained for the time being, Davis was through with a sextet lineup. For the next eight years at least, Miles's working group would remain a quintet.

The end of 1959 saw Miles continuing to pack in the crowds and, supported by strong advertising placed by Columbia Records, *Kind of Blue* on its way to becoming a best-seller. In retrospect, the album, unique as it is, seems akin to a handful of enduring titles by veterans and youthful avant-gardists alike who, in tandem with Miles, were reaching back to jazz's birth-cry — the blues — while signaling the bends in the freeway ahead. A visit to the jazz racks that autumn revealed an array of new sounds, including Mingus's *Blues & Roots* and Ellington's blues-mood soundtrack to *Anatomy of a Murder*. Catching headlines and stimulating the most discussion, though, was the latest from a thin Texan with a plastic alto, Ornette Coleman's *The Shape of Jazz to Come*.

If there was one event that threatened to steal the spotlight from Miles's modal breakthrough that year, it was the arrival of Coleman in November at the Five Spot. Not since bebop had a single style or musician divided the critical and musical community as did the alto saxophonist with the pianoless quartet. The shock of this new, "free" approach to jazz was strong enough to propel it past the form's supporters (Martin Williams, John Lewis) and detractors (Leonard Feather, Louis Armstrong) to the attention of the mainstream press. *Newsweek* made it down to the East Village in 1960 to describe Coleman's "frazzled horn" and "snarling, snorting blats," and affirm, "Yes, modern jazz is controversial. But . . . jazz has never been more alive. And it still has something new to say."

By this time, Miles was a celebrity rather than a cause celebre: his name was not even mentioned in the article's wide overview. Whether this was a journalistic oversight or *Newsweek* actually felt his role in the "new jazz" was negligible, Davis's success by 1960 had certainly become singular and mainstream enough to place him in a category of his own.

As Martin Williams astutely pointed out:

> On the whole, Miles Davis was a lucky man, for apparently he can have it both ways: his records, like those of the Modern Jazz Quartet, seem to please people who want their music to be only a kind of fairly lively background sound issuing from their phonographs. But they also please those [who] expect the strongest kind of musical and aesthetic interest that the best jazzmen provide.

With no other project does this become more apparent than in the recordings Miles began in late November of that year. *Sketches of Spain* was his most outside-the-jazz-tradition album to date, transforming the exotic, modal promise of "Flamenco Sketches" into a full album based on flamenco-focused scales and sonorities. It was to be Davis's last great album project arranged by Gil Evans (1962's *Quiet Nights* never achieved the musical height or popularity of their other collaborations) and was the last of Miles's musical trifecta. "'*Porgy, Kind of Blue, Sketches*—that was a wonderful streak for us," Stanley Kavan comments, listing Miles's top-selling catalog titles through the sixties.

Whether the seed of *Sketches* was a track on *Kind of Blue* or, as Miles wrote, an album of Spanish guitar music played by "a friend of mine named Joe Montdragon, a studio bass player," or an old flamenco 78 called "La Niña de Los Peines" given to Gil Evans, as Avakian contends, it hit a common cultural nerve. As jazz fan and author Dan Wakefield remembers:

> Everyone I knew had bullfight posters on their walls . . . and went through a phase of heavy listening to flamenco music . . . to translate the essence of all that mythology—so central to our generation's imagination—into modern jazz, our time's music, was simply an act of instinctive genius.

The sessions turned into a Herculean, draining effort that critic Hentoff attended and chronicled for *Stereo Review*. Retakes followed takes which followed rehearsals; a tuba player kept delaying the recording by listening to a ballgame on his portable radio. The recording of *Sketches* was the extreme opposite of the spontaneous, one-take approach of *Kind of Blue*. The lightness of the former session, evident in Miles's studio chatter, disappeared under the perfectionism of the producer (Teo Macero, helming a Davis session for the first time) and the arranger. Bassist Bill Crow recalls the comment of a sideman who worked with Evans:

> I remember asking Joe Bennett, a trombone player, what a thrill it must have been to be on those dates and he said, "The only thing I can remember is the blood I was sweating trying to cut those parts."

When the last exhausting session of three ended the following March, Miles—who had not curtailed his touring, performing in and out of New York between the recording dates—commented, "After we finished working on *Sketches of Spain,* I didn't have nothing inside of me. I was drained of all emotion and didn't want to hear that music after I got through playing all that hard shit." Davis did not return to the recording studio until a year later, and would not tackle another collaboration with Gil Evans for another year after that.

Miles must have regarded his live engagements during the first part of 1960 as a relief from his ongoing studio activities. Still carrying Coltrane as part of his quintet, he played the Apollo in New York and the Regal in Chicago, finally settling into a two-week run at the Sutherland Hotel Lounge (in Chicago as well) in February. Warren Bernhardt was a budding pianist when he caught the quintet at the Sutherland:

> I got in and there was a circular bar with a real tall bandstand in the middle. I didn't know what Miles looked like, and this little guy in an Italian suit said, "What do you want?" I got a beer, sitting there at the bar, and all of the sudden he runs up the stairs and picks up the trumpet, and I realize, 'Holy shit, it was Miles.' He was tending bar while Coltrane was playing! Coltrane was playing forty-five-minute solos in those days. He would never take the horn out of his mouth. Then all through the breaks, there was a couch near the bar that went into the kitchen and Coltrane would lie down on the couch with his feet up, and practice real quietly, you know, it was just like this whisper. You go to the men's room, and walk by him [and hear] a lot of scales and stuff.

Already familiar with the music on *Kind of Blue,* Bernhardt was surprised to hear the difference on stage. But the effect lasted a lifetime; he had originally pursued a degree in science, but suffered a career shift after hearing Davis and the quintet that one night:

It was the magic of hearing "So What" live. It had already started to pick up speed, it was medium tempo by then, not breakneck yet. It must've been a tune that constantly went up in tempo, 'cause by the sixties it was [hums "So What" at fast tempo]. I was hoping Bill [Evans] was going to be with them, because by that time I had really fallen in love with his playing, and I wasn't that familiar with Wynton Kelly. Wynton made it different, a little more down home, less modal in approach and much more churchy. I fell in love with Wynton's playing that night, I still tell Jimmy Cobb about how it really changed my life that night—I decided to pursue music and not go into science.

By the spring of 1960, it was Europe's turn to hear the results of Miles's last effort with his sextet. In a series of well-coordinated album releases and a whirlwind three-week tour that, after much convincing, included a grumbling Coltrane, Miles's music swept through much of western Europe: France, Sweden, Norway, Denmark, West Germany, Italy, Austria, Switzerland, and Holland. The quintet's performance on March 22 in Stockholm's Konserthuset was recorded, documenting how far tunes like "So What" and "All Blues" had progressed in the full year since their recording. (The concert tapes have appeared in the States as import albums in a variety of formats over the years.) Brisk but still not yet overcharged—and with the freedom and space that one less saxophonist allowed—the tune unfolds from Cobb and Chambers's steady pulse. What had been a floating rhythm became a forceful beat set up by an insistent hi-hat and rim shots.

Cobb theorizes that the compositions had been kicked into high gear not only by familiarity but also because "Miles, playing them every night he probably didn't want to play them, figured he needed another challenge." Miles's solo in the Stockholm concert certainly holds up his image as a chance-taker. He maneuvers through a number of shifts in phrasing, playing in and behind the rhythm, as does Kelly in his superb variations on the song's theme.

But Coltrane is the standout improviser on this night, starting off slow and simple, building into an orgy of sixteenth-note runs and a fusillade of ideas. His solo foreshadows the musical intensity and spiritual heights he would reach on albums like *Live at the Village Vanguard* and *A Love Supreme*. Coltrane is nothing short of bristling; in an interview done that same evening, a local deejay queried him about his "angry sound." He answered matter-of-factly:

JAZZ NEWS

September 1960

Established 1956
VOLUME 4 No 31

Ninepence

IN
—
THIS
—
SSUE

...eek-end the Miles
Quintet arrives
British tour.

...ways this group
...e the most con-
...roup yet to tour

...m Colwell, who
...mpeter in Ger-
...s about Miles in
...article.

...our girl-about-
...ie Wilmer, cor-
Dill Jones on

...l and last part
Czechoslovakia'
Pages 6 and 7.

...also the regular
...ters pages plus
...rd reviews and
...ate news.

...pecial photo-
...zz group ap-
...back page.

...hotograph
of Miles

Opposite: European
magazine advertisements
for *Kind of Blue*

Left: Miles in Great Britain,
1960

The reason I play so many sounds—maybe it sounds angry—is because I'm trying
so many things at one time, you see. I haven't sorted them out . . . there are some
things that I know, some harmonic devices . . . that will take me out of the ordinary
path . . . but I haven't played them enough, and I'm not familiar with them enough
yet to take the one single line through them, so I play all of them. . . .

Up to the point of his departure from the quintet, Coltrane continued to take full advantage of the blank-canvas possibilities inherent in "So What" and "All Blues." When the tour ended, Coltrane departed the group for good. Davis had been considering a recommendation of Coltrane's named Wayne Shorter as a replacement, but Shorter was committed to a stint with Art Blakey's Jazz Messengers at that point. As Jimmy Heath was still limited by his parole board's decision on travel, Miles opted for saxophonist Sonny Stitt, who played both tenor and alto. A series of dates took the quintet through the summer, but Stitt proved less than satisfying to the trumpeter— particularly on the modal material.

Jimmy Heath remembers Miles's primary complaint: "He would say, 'You know, when Sonny Stitt was here, he was playing D minor 7 [instead of D minor] all the time on 'So What.'" Miles himself, in the midst of relating a run-in with Philadelphia traffic cops, recalled incidentally:

> So I picked up Jimmy and we were riding around talking about music and shit and I probably was complaining to him about Sonny Stitt playing the wrong kind of shit on "So What," because he would always fuck up on that tune and so I used to tell Jimmy this every time I'd see him.

Nonetheless, Stitt remained with the quintet through November, and another three-week tour of Europe, this one including a long-awaited visit to the United Kingdom. With much fanfare Miles played London on October 1. One perceptive critic at *Melody Maker*, Bob Dawbarn, noted his harsher, more experimental trumpet sound: "Miles surprised me by the violence of much of his playing and the angry swing he achieved."

In the audience—already a fan and familiar with Miles's older material— was trumpeter Hugh Masekela.

> It was the very first week that I came from South Africa. There was a great excite-ment, the thing about his mannerisms and other things. But I was already a big Miles nut. . . .

As Masekela recalls, the concert inspired him to pick up *Kind of Blue*:

> I bought it and it just blew me over. It was the simplest jazz — it had a lot of African overtones. Miles juxtaposed the modern, fantastically, against something very primitive on *Kind of Blue*. It had very deep Congolese overtones for me. Miles was already so far ahead, but I think that that was his, for me, his lasting and greatest revelation.

The year 1960 ended with Miles back in the U.S., Stitt replaced by tenor man Hank Mobley and plans afoot for the quintet to record two concerts during early 1961. The first location chosen was San Francisco's Blackhawk jazz club, an extremely popular venue Miles had grown to like. In late April, one weekend's performances yielded two energetic albums that reaffirmed Davis's ability to mix the right separate ingredients into the whole. Mobley's elastic tenor playing—smoother and less dark-toned than Coltrane's—changed the general complexion of the band. As British journalist Dawbarn had noted, Miles had already begun to reveal a more aggressive side to his playing with Stitt at his side. Now, partially in response to Mobley, Davis seemed to shift to an even higher gear, filling in the gaps that he had once left open, conjuring the intensity formerly provided by Coltrane and Adderley. "The presence of more conventional saxophonists like Stitt and Mobley, after five years when Coltrane carried the experimental weight in the band, may have pushed Davis himself into the role of the band's avant-gardist," wrote jazz critic Bob Blumenthal.

This new aspect of Miles's sound—which he would explore even further with his mid-sixties quintet—is in full evidence on his next recording. The Carnegie Hall concert of May 19, 1961, not only was his first public performance with an orchestra, but also symbolized the incredible ascent Davis had made in the four short years since his first studio efforts with Gil Evans. Though the evening featured performances with his quintet, it was—and still is—seen as a gala, "best of" event, celebrating his triumphs in an arranged setting.

Significantly, "So What" was chosen to open the program, just as it had on *Kind of Blue*. The twenty-one-piece orchestra performed the instantly recognizable rubato prelude, artfully rearranged by Gil so that the parts

Left: Symphonic "So What": Gil Evans's sketch for the renowned prelude

Right and opposite: The legendary May 19, 1961, performance at Carnegie Hall

originally played by piano and bass were tossed among the assembled instruments, but evoking Bill Evans's masterful performance in its understatement. Then, after a final, harmonized shriek from the orchestra, Miles and the quintet launched into the rest of the modal piece.

Miles had managed to ascend to a plane shared by very, very few. *Kind of Blue* was a top-selling jazz album, its sole competition at that point being Dave Brubeck's *Time Out* and Davis's other titles. Achieving star billing on the Carnegie stage symbolized an overdue public acknowledgment of his artistic merit, placing him in the pantheon of jazz masters and echoing the past breakthrough glory of Benny Goodman and Duke Ellington. Creating music he was proud of, that satisfied the hippest of the hip yet also appealed to both high- and middle-brow, Miles had made it on his own terms.

The Legacy of

Blue

Do you listen to records?
MILES: No, they're all in here [taps forehead] . . .
What do you see in the future?
MILES: Tomorrow.
— 1973

. . ."So What" or *Kind of Blue*—those things are there. They were done in that era, the right hour, the right day, and it happened. It's over, it's on the record. . . . I don't want you to like me because of *Kind of Blue*. Like me for what we're doing now, you know.
— Miles Davis, 1986

MILES HAD LITTLE use for jazz recordings, least of all his own. At home he might have a Rachmaninoff concerto on his stereo or a score of *Tosca* on his piano, as bandmates and intimates have reported. Davis's dismissive take on *Kind of Blue* allowed him to concentrate fully on the next gig, the next studio session, and the next career turn.

But like other works of art, *Kind of Blue* proved to have a destiny independent of its creator. In terms of its modal impact on the jazz world, of the popularity of its sound and compositions with other musicians, and of the apparently unstoppable trajectory of its success with music consumers, the album casts a long and wide shadow.

The ovation now so universally bestowed on *Kind of Blue* can give the impression that the album was the fuse to a stylistic tinderbox that exploded into the musical community, causing schisms of devotion and derision, creating diehard converts who carried the torch of modal expression bravely into the future. Yet the album arrived far more quietly than its reputation today would suggest—it worked its magic on the music through evolution, not revolution.

Apart from a few glowing reviews, the style and sound of *Kind of Blue* certainly did not generate much critical discussion immediately after its release. In the musical community, "as far as I'm concerned," states Orrin Keepnews, "there was no 'Road to Damascus' scene. . . . Nobody just woke up one day and said, 'Wow, Miles and Bill have just revolutionized the world.'" Dick Katz recalls: "I remember musicians were talking about 'they're just playing on two chords,' but it didn't come across as some kind of sea change—that change in improvisation seeped in gradually." An article on modal jazz in early 1960 in *Jazz Review* was one of the few that even tackled the subject, employing the term "tonal" to describe the new scalar focus in the jazz community: "Attention has settled around the tonal problem and those players who are working something out along this line (Coltrane, Bill

Evans, [Art] Farmer, Miles and Cannonball, to name a few) especially engage our interest at the moment."

Why this was so is easier to understand when one considers the album's historical context. The same year *Kind of Blue* was released, John Coltrane came into his own and, with one foot already out of Miles Davis's group, developed the charged, unbridled sound that would define the rest of his career. And Ornette Coleman arrived in New York. These three artists—Miles Davis, John Coltrane, and Ornette Coleman—are generally viewed as having been the instigators of a decade of turbulent change in jazz. As the fifties ended, they were the Mount Rushmore of jazz's new modern wave.

With music raw and stormy, Coltrane and Coleman drew—and still draw—most attention and credit for jolting the music forward. But Martin Williams, writing ten years after the dust of 1959 had settled, held that it was Miles who sounded the first bell before the impending gale.

> *Kind of Blue* was one of the most provocative events in jazz since the mid-forties. I have spoken of the surface simplicity of the jazz of the late fifties, of a cutting back, opening up and airing out of the density of modern jazz . . . when such retrenchments of style take place (an earlier example would be the Count Basie of the late thirties), major changes are probably at hand.

Quincy Jones speaks of how the Davis sextet was "pulling an incredible history with them." *Kind of Blue* can be heard as a recapitulation of almost every step of the jazz tradition that preceded it. (Though never one to review his own timeline, Davis was acutely aware of the common history behind him: "I don't like to hear someone put down Dixieland," he told *Down Beat* in 1950. "Those people who say there's no music but bop are just stupid.") The album subtly references elements of modal jazz (especially in "Flamenco Sketches"); Third Stream (in the impressionistic opening to "So What"); cool (in Miles's solos); bebop (particularly in Cannonball's solos); swing (in the unison horn lines and gentle rhythmic drive of "All Blues," a number that not surprisingly is often arranged for big bands); and the two springs at the fountainhead of jazz, blues ("Freddie Freeloader") and ballads ("Blue in Green").

It's the perfect jazz hub. If one simply follows the career paths of Miles's sidemen, as Ben Sidran suggests, an entire musical history opens.

> If you like *Kind of Blue*, turn it over, look who plays on it. If you particularly like the piano, go buy a Bill Evans record [or] buy a Wynton Kelly record. If you like the alto playing, buy a Cannonball Adderley record. That one record—it's not even six degrees of separation—is maybe two degrees of separation from every great jazz record.

Gary Burton notes the integrity of the music throughout.

> It wasn't just one tune that was a breakthrough, it was the whole record. When new
> jazz styles come along, the first few attempts to do it are usually kind of shaky. Early
> Charlie Parker records were like this. But with *Kind of Blue*, [the sextet] all sound like
> they're fully into it.

The speed with which cover versions of the material on *Kind of Blue* spread
attests to the album's immediate influence on the music (if not the critical)
scene. Within a year of its release, jazz bands began shuffling versions of
"So What" and "All Blues" into their songbooks. Younger players, especially,
began to favor the music, as Burton remembers:

> By the time I came to Berklee [School of Music in 1960] the students were already
> playing the tunes off the record. And for local jazz players . . . these modal tunes were
> the latest hip thing to add to your repertoire. The older players were not so comfort-
> able with them, because you didn't have a big progression of chord changes to hang
> on to, to guide your solo, and it was up to you to work with that scale.

Herbie Hancock echoes Burton's view, seeing *Kind of Blue*'s importance
to his generation as a portal from one era to another.

> It presented a doorway for the musicians of my generation, the first doorway that we
> were exposed to in our lifetimes. See, I was born in 1940, so I wasn't old enough to be
> around for the transition between swing and what we call the beginnings of modern
> jazz. Bebop was already on the scene by the time I ever paid any attention to it. When
> *Kind of Blue* came out, I had never even conceived . . . another approach to playing jazz.

The sound of *Kind of Blue* coming off jazz bandstands became common-
place soon after its release. "Once the record came out everybody wanted to
imitate ["So What"], you know. They wanted to play D minor, D minor, D
minor, then all of a sudden go up to E flat . . . I've been bugged by it since,"
laughs Teo Macero.

With club bands, jukeboxes, and FM radio disseminating *Kind of Blue*
from coast to coast, it wasn't long before the blues-based music broke out of
jazz circles and was picked up by R&B and even rock and roll groups. Keyboardist Donald Fagen recalls: "I had mentioned a Coltrane album to another
piano player at school, and he said, 'Heard it? That's the Bible, man.' That's
the way people also felt about *Kind of Blue*. It essentially became the Bible
about six months after it came out." Fagen adds:

> I was really an amateur player in high school [in 1963] and at the level I was starting
> at, I couldn't play the repertoire of standards, they were too hard to play or improvise
> at fast tempos. I could play "So What," though, and "All Blues." It was a great learning

thing for players that were not coming out of maybe from a formal point of view, from a formal background. If you met other musicians that's what they'd play to see how good you were, because everyone knew the tunes.

Beyond the ubiquitous covers of the album's tunes, *Kind of Blue*'s influence was heard more and more in the way the jazz community was performing, composing, and recording. "It had gotten to be where musicians would say, 'Hey, let's do one of those on this [recording] date—let's drop in some modal shit,'" recalls Keepnews from his vantage point as producer of many jazz albums. Adderley echoed: "Everybody started playing Lydian and Phrygian [scales] on compositions like that 'On the Trail' thing."

Part of the *Grand Canyon Suite*, which was written in the thirties by Ferde Grofe, an arranger with Paul Whiteman's orchestra, "On the Trail" was one tune that was well suited to scalar interpretation. Revived and arranged almost thirty years later by trumpeter Donald Byrd for a Blue Note record, it went unrecorded thanks to a disagreement between musician and label. But Jimmy Heath adopted Byrd's arrangement as the title track to a 1961 album.

Cannonball's *Know What I Mean?*

Jimmy Heath's *On the Trail*

He recalls that the track was typical of a number of "semi-modal" pieces that came forth in the early sixties, post-*Kind of Blue* period.

We wanted to experiment with modal pieces, not to the same degree as Miles, completely, like "So What." Not everyone else wanted to take those chances with some-

thing new. We weren't Miles Davis, so we said "OK, we'll do a little of that." A lot of the modal pieces we wrote were modal for a while and then they ended on a sequence of chords to get back to a certain point to be more communicative to an audience.

Keepnews, Adderley's producer during the early sixties, remembers the altoist consciously choosing to conjure the scalar freedom and delayed tempo of *Kind of Blue* on the title track to his 1961 album with Bill Evans, *Know What I Mean?* "What I do recall on that particular tune, which has no musical relationship with anything else on the album, was that musicians thought of it not so much as modal with a capital M, but as a more customary use: being another tool, another thing in the bag of tricks."

That same year, Joe Zawinul—who had already been composing with a minimal number of chords—joined Adderley's rhythm section, bringing a modal sensibility that would dovetail with Cannonball's later, mid-sixties soul jazz sound.

I wrote many modal pieces for Cannonball, usually the up-tempo tunes, like the song called "Scotch and Water" that was based on two chords. And some other tunes that were totally built on modal structure, like "Doctor Honoris Causa" [and] "74 Miles Away." [The latter] was a very natural groove based just on one chord. The whole tune is in A flat minor, it never changes.

"74 Miles Away" explored a funky, extended 7/4 vamp (hence the title). As Zawinul remembers, the tune had an impact on Miles.

We were in Detroit at the Cobo Hall in 1967 and it was Cannonball's band and the Miles Davis quintet [on the same bill]. Miles always liked to open the show. We knew how tough they were to follow and they played their asses off, people were screaming. Cannonball had the habit, when it was a really big event, to let me call the set. So I said, "Let's open with '74 Miles.'" So when we started playing people in Detroit were going off! They were already so high from Miles's stuff. Miles, I remember he was leaning on the bandstand, man, right behind the piano. And I turned because I wanted to see his reaction, and he said, "*Motherfucker.*" (laughs)

Already aware of Zawinul's talent on piano—Miles had considered him to replace Bill Evans before settling on Wynton Kelly—Davis began employing his compositional abilities in 1968, leading to Davis's groundbreaking album *In a Silent Way*. Zawinul relates that their collaborations were a natural—if unconscious—outgrowth of earlier modal forms.

When I composed, I never thought of scales. I just use what I feel. All the music was improvised first, and then written down. In those days I wrote very fast, just like "In a Silent Way," in about two minutes. That's a modal tune, you know. There were a couple of chords in my version, and then Miles didn't want any chords at all.

As bebop's harmonic breakthroughs informed both the cool jazz and hardbop that came after it, so various aspects of modal jazz were worked into soul jazz recordings and Miles's proto-fusion experiments of the late sixties.

Zawinul, who founded Weather Report, perhaps the leading light in the parade of fusion bands descending directly from Miles's tutelage, was one of many who carried a modal approach well into the seventies. He recalls a lesson he imparted to Weather Report's (then) new bassist.

Let me tell you something man—when Jaco [Pastorius] first came into the band, after about a week or so, he said, "You know, Joe, this one chord stuff is great, I love it, but I run out of licks." I told him, "Jaco, all you have to do is NOT play licks then you cannot run out of them." He became very good at playing on one chord, an excellent player on this kind of modal thing. It started opening things in his head and he had much more room to go.

For all the modally influenced music that Davis, Cannonball, Heath, Zawinul and others would ultimately produce, no musician was more transformed by the modal experience of *Kind of Blue*, and none would prove more influential with what he did with that experience, than John Coltrane. As biographer Lewis Porter noted:

> [Coltrane's] "So What" solo indicates the direction that Coltrane's music was to take during the 1960s, more so than "Giant Steps." He became more and more concerned with structural aspects of improvisation; as he did so, he concentrated more exclusively on modal backgrounds, which gave him the time he needed to develop his ideas at length.

By 1961, by reducing chord changes to a minimum on such recordings as "My Favorite Things," the tenor man applied the idea of scalar improvisation to trance-like, hit-making effect. In 1962, Coltrane explained to the French magazine *Jazz Hot* how he adapted the waltz-like song from *The Sound of Music* to a more modal form: "This piece is built, during several measures, on two chords, but we have prolonged the two chords for the whole piece." ("Only he could do that and make it work," commented Miles in 1988, referring to the tune's modal section.) By simplifying the chord pattern of songs into a set of modes, Coltrane was refashioning chordal songs for his own modal purposes.

The modal model of improvisation provided the launch pad for Coltrane's ever-more experimental forays over the next few years. As Cannonball explained it, his former bandmate was now following a guideline of his own. "What John began to do really escaped from the modal thing. He got into other types of exploration, free sounds [that] were perfectly disciplined associations for him." One open-ended structure led to another. With modality as his foundation, Coltrane pushed the boundaries of group jazz with increasingly experimental albums that flowed into the new musical area then known as "free": *Impressions* (particularly on the modal title track), *A Love Supreme* (employing a scale of Coltrane's own design), and *Ascension* (on which Coltrane directed a large ensemble through a four-scale form).

Looking back in 1972, Cannonball praised Coltrane's late-career explorations, emphasizing that his leading role in the free jazz movement derived directly from his past modal and bebop-based experience.

> [Free players] are playing what they believe in and what they hear, what they feel. But you can't put them all in the same bag because they're coming from various directions. Like Marion Brown is a college graduate, majored in music, he used to play like Charlie Parker and now he plays free. But I don't think anybody was as basically trained as Coltrane. [A free player would have] had to be his contemporary to have his

kind of discipline and training because that kind of stuff is not available to young musicians.

Other than Coltrane's singular pursuits, did the modal inform approach free jazz as a whole? To Jimmy Heath, modal territory became a greenhouse for a variety of free players, though—as Adderley had mentioned—it exposed a certain lack of experience and training.

> A lot of free players relished in modal playing, because they couldn't connect the changes like their predecessors, you know. You can get right in the groove, because you're not thinking about, "Well, this is F minor 7, this goes here, the B minor there." People who could play tonally and inside the changes were able to play in the modal style more convincingly to me than the free guys. I can't speak generally, because *some* of them could play very good in the free style. Ornette [Coleman] could play anything and it was swinging. But I'm speaking of some of the followers.

Coltrane might have been a guiding light to many free jazz players, but he was not the first pioneer in that new stylistic territory. Back in 1959, free jazz had already rocked the jazz scene, catching everyone unaware— Coltrane and Miles included. In marked contrast to *Kind of Blue*'s slow and subtle sonorities, the sound of Ornette Coleman was the sound of revolution.

When Coleman, a Texas-born alto saxophonist, blew in to New York from Los Angeles with his quartet—cornetist Don Cherry, bassist Charlie Haden, and drummer Billy Higgins—he turned on an entire generation of impro-visers. Most timelines now trace the breakthrough of free jazz to that moment. Coleman and his quartet had in a sense been on the same quest as Miles: seeking freedom from chord changes and other structural devices that defined jazz up to that point. But their raw sound and dalliances with atonality and countermelodies were more jarring than any modal endeavor. Ornette, like Miles, maintained focus on melody, but unlike Miles he did not rely on scales as the underpinning of his music. His group still followed chorus-based structures; on recorded tunes like "Lonely Woman" and "Congeniality" (both off his 1959 album *The Shape of Jazz to Come*) one can hear the song itself cycling through the performance. Rather, Coleman's revolution was founded on individual and collective initiative; if the soloist felt like continuing an improvised line, or taking some other liberty with the song's form, the ensemble was trusted to intuit and follow that course.

Ground zero was the Five Spot in New York City's East Village, where Coleman's debut occurred only a few weeks after the release of *Kind of Blue*. For those priming for the cutting edge, it was the former that signaled the breakthrough to a new modernity in jazz. Zawinul witnessed the arrival of both.

Kind of Blue was a nice, mellow album, but I don't really remember it really turning my head around. Then when Ornette came on, he really sounded like he was from another age, from another planet. The new thing was here, man.

Miles was among a jazz fellowship that was somewhat miffed and very mystified at first. Orrin Keepnews recollects that "Cannonball, and most of the guys on the scene, were very scornful when Ornette first appeared. It had to do not only with the way he was playing but the way he had become the darling of the critics in about five minutes." To Miles, it must have seemed Ornette Coleman, live in 1966 eerily familiar. Just as his modal debut was released, another pianoless jazz group arrived from the West Coast (shades of '52: Mulligan, Baker, and the coming of cool) to snatch the attention of the press and public. Pianist Paul Bley, who had gigged with Coleman in Los Angeles prior to his New York debut, was present at the Five Spot for Coleman's historic opening. He told writer Francis Davis: "Everybody was there, including Miles Davis, who stood talking to the bartender with his back to the stage, as though he was thirsty and just happened to stop in for a drink."

However Miles felt about what he heard over his shoulder, he was not ready to toss out the rule book and embrace atonality or structural freedom as enthusiastically as Coleman did in '59 or Coltrane would later. Davis never turned his back completely on melody and rhythm. As Zawinul points out, despite his many stylistic twists and turns, he retained a basic musical troika that was his lifelong signature: "Miles always played differently but, of course, you could always recognize his tone, his incredible phrasing, and his rhythm. Those were his three keys." Coleman stressed an opposing ideal that reads as a direct repudiation of Miles's: "My phrasing is spontaneous, not a style. A style happens when your phrasing hardens."

As late as 1969, when the message of free had long been accepted and absorbed, Miles would still tout a need for a musical outline and foundation.

> You have some kind of form. You have to start *somewhere* . . . you have walls and stuff, but you still come in a room and act kinda free. There's a framework, but it's just—we don't want to overdo it, you know. It's hard to balance.

So many years later, the question of distance between Davis and Coleman (and—by later experimentation—Coltrane), of who provided the more revolutionary musical statement at the time, of modal versus free, seems to dissipate into a simple comment on stylistic differences. Ultimately, Coleman and Davis seem more philosophically akin than musically opposed. Both dedicated their careers to rewriting the rules of jazz—one more completely than the other—and their own words, though spoken separately, complement each other in an implied dialogue.

> DAVIS: Maybe a guy wants to play out of key for about four or five bars . . .
> "Why should I be afraid to play that?"
> COLEMAN: You can play sharp in tune and you can play flat in tune.
> DAVIS: [I'd] rather hear a guy miss a couple of notes than hear
> the same old cliches all the time . . . even if it's skillfully done.
> COLEMAN: From realizing I can make mistakes,
> I have come to realize there is an order to what I do.

There's a theory that all great stories follow one of two plots: A hero takes a trip or a stranger comes to town. In the context of late fifties jazz and our three modernist heroes, it seems that both plotlines converged. Coltrane departed for a late-career musical journey whose discoveries still resonate over three decades after his death. Coleman appeared with little warning and fractured a community slightly splintered to begin with, helping to launch an avant-garde still battling for respect, like a distant cousin in the extended jazz family.

At first, Miles's post–*Kind of Blue* narrative seems to parallel Coltrane's. With a new quintet featuring Herbie Hancock, saxophonist Wayne Shorter, bassist Ron Carter and drummer Tony Williams (a group that is now as legendary as his quintet of the mid-fifties), Davis sought ever more freedom from structure.

But Miles, like Coleman, eventually began reworking not just the structure but the sound of jazz itself. By 1968 and '69, Columbia Records memoranda reveal him requesting electric instruments for his group; within a few months, he successfully shotgunned the marriage of jazz with funk and rock rhythms and sparked a fire called fusion that would sweep jazz into the seventies, and remains as factious and divisive as free jazz.

No, *Kind of Blue* did not spark any musical revolutions. It did not lead, define, or come from the avant-garde. It did not launch an entire school of jazz style, as did *The Birth of the Cool*, *Walkin'*, or *Bitches Brew*. But as Bill Evans would tell *Down Beat* editor Len Lyons in the seventies, the emphasis on such criteria could obscure what was really of value in new jazz sounds.

> It's this preoccupation with "who's the most modern" instead of "who's making the most beautiful, human music." [The most beautiful] may very well be the most modern thing as well, but to make just avant-garde the criteria has gotten to be almost a sickness, especially in jazz.

In 1959, in *Kind of Blue*, Miles was a crystallizer rather than an originator like Coleman. Evans drew a precise parallel in the classical world:

Most iconoclasts are contributors to progress, but usually it's the person who organizes those things—an eclectic who comes along and organizes the work of a few iconoclasts. It really has happened a lot in music. One example would be Debussy and Ravel, who crystallized and brought to real refinement the raw conception that Satie had.

After the wild ride Bird and Diz had taken jazz on in the mid-forties, pushing the envelope of harmonic and rhythmic invention as far as it would go at that point, Miles and other cohorts had pulled jazz back to a cooler, blues-spirited extreme. That pendulum swing, from the apogee of bebop to the high-water mark of modal jazz, constitutes a period of unparalleled creativity in jazz. From that perspective, many see *Kind of Blue* as more of a goodbye to an age that had passed than a vision of the future.

"That album was really the end of the bebop era, you know?" remarks Quincy Jones. "*Kind of Blue* was the voice of that era—from '48 to '59—it was the highest culmination of the standards of the time." Amram adds: "I've always felt that *Kind of Blue* was Miles's valentine to Charlie Parker . . . a farewell, a moving on from that whole experience."

In 1986 Miles delivered what was more of a eulogy than a love letter to modal jazz, telling *Musician* magazine:

> What I used to play with . . . Cannonball, Bill Evans, all those different modes, and substitute chords, we had the energy then and we liked it. But I have no feel for it anymore. Other people still do it, but it doesn't have the same spark. It's more like warmed-over turkey.

Four decades on, the sound of *Kind of Blue* is woven so tightly into our musical tapestry that it is difficult to distinguish its traces. Herbie Hancock sighs, "Name me some music where you don't hear echoes of it. I hear it everywhere—some of the modality in rock could be directly from *Kind of Blue*." Critic Robert Palmer, who wrote the liner notes to the 1997 CD of *Kind of Blue*, discovered that very link backstage at the Fillmore East in 1969.

> Duane Allman [was] the only "rock" guitarist I had heard up to that point who could solo on a one-chord vamp for as long as half an hour or more, and not only avoid boring you but keep you absolutely *riveted*. . . . "You know," he told me . . . "that kind of playing comes from Miles and Coltrane, and particularly *Kind of Blue*. I've listened to that album so many times that for the past couple of years I haven't hardly listened to anything *else*."

Allman was only one of a number of sixties rockers under the spell of *Kind of Blue*. Ray Manzarek, keyboardist of the Doors, comments:

"[Drummer] John [Densmore] and I were big Coltrane and Davis fans, and we tried to bring a lot of their modal influence to rock." Successive generations admit the inspiration as well; Police guitarist Andy Sommers states, "['So What'] was very influential in my trying to take in the idea of modal jazz rather than the usual harmonic changes." Blues Traveler frontman John Popper notes that "Miles's *Kind of Blue* is a great example of [Coltrane and Davis] at the height of their playing."

To Donald Fagen, whenever a cool, loping, Mancini-like theme plays in a movie theater or on TV, *Kind of Blue* is implied.

> In the early sixties, there was a certain kind of music you'd hear on television and in films, where guys would just play over the same chord for a long time, creating atmosphere. After *Kind of Blue* came out, I think that sort of legitimized that kind of writing even further so that you have to this day a lot of extremely static film music: repeated ostinatos and the spooky-sounding, "Pink Panther" kind of stuff that evolved from the same group of arrangers and players who came up with that cool, modal sound.

For some, like Ben Sidran, certain contemporary groove-and-texture music conjures the album.

> One of the things that's been so prevalent the last ten or fifteen years, is trance, the concept of trance, and this hypnotic thing. If you look at this movement in Britain, the drum-and-bass stuff, or the trance music [coming] out of Europe. I think that it's not a stretch to say that a lot of that goes back to what *Kind of Blue* did: the enforced elan, hovering, staying on the vamp.

"So What" was the very specific inspiration for the anthem of yet another musical style: funk. The tale began in 1959 in Rochester, New York. A high school tenor saxophonist named Alfred Ellis "was hanging out with the local musicians and I heard that album [*Kind of Blue*] at a friend's house—it made an impression on me . . . very moving, kind of haunting almost. Miles was so melodic. And his use of space—it had a gentle drive."

Eight years to the month after the release of *Kind of Blue*, Pee Wee (as he was then called) Ellis hooked up with the godfather of soul, James Brown, becoming his primary musical collaborator. Their first studio effort together yielded "Cold Sweat," one of the seminal—and not coincidentally, minimal—themes of funk. As Ellis tells it, the subconscious inspiration for the song's signature horn riff came from what he heard in '59.

> The night before this one session, James calls me into his dressing room after the show and hummed me this bass line. So overnight, [driving] down to Cincinnati, we put together this horn line on the bus . . . it was a one-chord thing and [that two-note riff] fit perfectly with the melody of "So What." In the back of my mind it made sense

to fit it there . . . Dee-Dum . . . Dee-Dum. Later it occurred to me that's what it was . . . "So What," just kind of inverted.

In 1989, speaking at the Studio Museum of Harlem, Miles himself publicly acknowledged the connection and—characteristically—either innocently or intentionally confused who influenced whom. "I love James Brown —you know that number I wrote called "So What"? I think I got it from him or he got it from me: DAH-Dunh-ti-ti-ti-ti-ti-ti-ti-DAH-Dunh." In any case, given Davis's use of Brown's distinctive funk rhythms in the late sixties and seventies, it's clear that the inspiration flowed both ways. As trumpeter Wallace Roney recalls from a conversation with Davis in the year he passed away, there was one more chapter to the tale. Miles recycled a James Brown rhythmic figure that his drummer inverted:

> [Miles] re-borrowed that "So What" thing. He told me that on [his 1968 album] *Filles De Kilimanjaro*, he wanted [drummer] Tony [Williams] to play a "Cold Sweat" beat on "Frelon Brun." Miles said (imitates Miles's whisper): "That motherfucker, he played 'Cold Sweat' upside down!" Man, he was so proud. He thought that was the hippest thing in the world. I mean 1991, and he was still floored by that.

If the sound of *Kind of Blue* is woven inextricably into the musical fabric of our culture, its influence is even more unmistakable within the common thread of jazz. To jazz-attuned ears, echoes of Miles's album can be heard whenever, say, a muted trumpet solo is heard over an atmospheric background, or when a pianist plays classically inspired voicings on a slow-moving blues. "I hear it in a whole generation of young piano players," says Bill Crow. Jason Moran, a young pianist currently recording for Blue Note Records, is typical of his current crop of improvisers channeling the strains of *Kind of Blue*. "Most of the songs from that record I learned as a beginner. . . . Some of the upper register stuff that I do is done intentionally with Bill Evans and what he was playing on 'Flamenco Sketches' in mind."

Moran points to "Root Progression," the last song on his record *Soundtrack to Human Motion* (1999), as having "the same type of mood that 'Flamenco Sketches' has." Brad Mehldau, another newcomer whose piano style reflects an intense understanding of both pre- and post-modal jazz traditions, and the ability to bounce between the two, admits:

> Some of the approaches that have developed in my trio over the past few years have their predecessor in *Kind of Blue* in an indirect but important way . . . we often abstract the harmony—that hyper-chordal movement—in a variety of ways, enjoying the simplicity of the 32-bar AABA form. This kind of thing is happening on a live record of ours, *Art of the Trio, Vol. 4*, on the rhythm changes in a tune of mine called "Nice Pass".

Some jazz educators point out a downside to the album's influence. The argument holds that the simplicity of *Kind of Blue*—and of modal jazz in general—lets young musicians bypass such components of jazz training as understanding of chordal structures and harmonic relationships. "*Kind of Blue* is where younger players start listening," complains Crow. "They don't go back before." Cannonball felt the style did not provide enough challenge for younger musicians.

> All you had to do [to play modal material] was just be able to play your instrument well enough to make [the improvisations] more complex from a technical point of view. But there was nothing to do but play those [scales in] different ways. So it gave vent to a lot of people who didn't have anything to say in terms of thought.

Dick Katz agrees: "A big hunk of jazz education right now is based on that [modal] concept, to teach kids to improvise even if they have only mastered their instrument halfway well. To me, it's a little like doing it by the numbers." In 1988, Miles himself warned against playing modal jazz exclusively: "I don't like guys who make a livin' playin' in the mode . . . We just did it because it's one style . . . [modal jazz] would get monotonous if you'd sit there a long time."

But modal compositions—not requiring fluency in complicated harmonic theory—do allow students to jump in earlier and start soloing, giving them an early chance to garner valuable practice on improvisational elements like phrasing and tone. Most important, as the scalar-based form relies on immediate and convincing invention of a lyrical line, younger musicians are challenged to assert and expose their creative selves, generating compelling melodies on the spot. As such, Gary Burton, now head of Berklee School of Music, sees a need for a balance of all approaches in a jazz curriculum, including the modal approach of *Kind of Blue*. "We need both simple tunes and complex tunes for playing experience, and for learning."

As Burton acknowledges, knowing the material from *Kind of Blue* is now a must for any self-respecting, working jazz musician. Fake books, which guide countless musicians through countless gigs at clubs, dances, and events like weddings, are sure to include sheet music for at least "So What" and "All Blues." Burton recalls, "I saw those tunes from *Kind of Blue* start showing up in *The Real Book*, one of the well known fake books, around 1970 or so."

Taking stock of the recorded interpretations of "So What" and the rest of *Kind of Blue* is a rough science at best. The fact that the publishing rights to the music on *Kind of Blue* have been sold repeatedly from one corporate entertainment giant to another does not facilitate the task. As of this writing,

Sony-ATV, a music publishing division of Sony Music based in Nashville, has held partial rights to all five tracks—and countless other Miles Davis originals—for barely three years.

Of the original sextet, only Bill Evans and Miles ever continued performing or rerecorded any of the songs on *Kind of Blue*. Conceivably as a means of reinforcing his claim on the tune, Evans recorded a version of "Blue in Green"—slightly more strident than the original—with bassist Scott LaFaro and drummer Paul Motian in December of 1959 for his album *Portrait in Jazz*. Orrin Keepnews, the session producer, recalls:

> When Bill recorded it himself subsequent to the release of *Kind of Blue*, it was his absolute and quite uncharacteristic insistence [that] I list him as co-composer on his initial recording of it. Bill said Miles took sole credit for the song: "Miles put it in his publishing company and there's nothing I can do about that." Bill felt the only recourse he had was to insist, and Bill seldom insisted I do anything, but he said I had to list him [as composer].

To this day, "Blue in Green" is credited intermittently to "Davis-Evans" on various albums by the pianist. The composition became part of Evans's repertoire for the rest of his career. In 1974, he recorded it again along with "So What" (with an impressionistic prelude different from the original recording) live at an outdoor concert in Canada for the album that bears its name: *Blue in Green*.

Davis, for his part, revisited "So What" and "All Blues" on multiple live albums for Columbia as his sound and style evolved through the sixties. But once he entered his fusion period, he never again recorded the *Kind of Blue* material, and only rarely performed it live. While Miles was contributing his trumpet playing to a Shirley Horn album in 1990, she asked him, "Why don't you come on back and play some of that old stuff?" Horn still remembers the excuse Davis offered: "Nah, it hurts my lip."

Recordings of the tunes from *Kind of Blue* by other musicians have become a thriving cottage industry. According to Ron Carter, "Each song on that record has more covers than most pop tunes. Everybody records 'So What,' 'Blue in Green,' and 'All Blues,' and you hear an occasional version of 'Freddie Freeloader.'" The list of musicians and groups who have recorded one of those tunes is numbing in number and variety. Take "All Blues." It has been recorded by jazz legends like Milt Jackson, Chet Baker and George Benson; contemporary avant-gardists like the World Saxophone Quartet and Steve Turre; and a variety of trumpeters from Freddie Hubbard and Chet Baker to Doc Severinsen and Mark Isham. The tune's inherent funk possibilities have been explored by fusion and soul-jazz survivors like

Stanley Clarke, Jimmy McGriff, and Les McCann; Latin musicians like Tito Puente and Bobby Enriquez; and even New Orleans' Rebirth Brass Band. Few of the reworkings were to Miles's liking, especially if the version denied the tune's simplified, modal intent. A funky and hard-driving version by Les McCann and the Jazz Crusaders led Davis to comment to Leonard Feather in 1964:

> What's that supposed to be? . . . They don't know what to do with it—you either play it bluesy or you play on the scale. You don't just play flat notes. I didn't write it to play flat notes on—you know, like minor thirds. Either you play a whole chord against or else . . . but don't try and play it like you'd play, ah, "Walkin' the Dog." You know what I mean?

Saxophonists young and old seem drawn to "So What," no doubt because of Coltrane and Adderley's mastery. Dexter Gordon, Frank Morgan, Benny Golson, John Stubblefield, and Donald Harrison have all revived it. Meanwhile, trumpeters (Art Farmer, Mark Ledford, Wallace Roney), pianists (Fred Hersch, John Hicks), bassists (Charlie Haden, George Mraz), and various other instrumentalists (violinist Jean-Luc Ponty, vibist Gary Burton, and harmonicist Toots Thielemans) have put their stamps on "Blue in Green."

The ease with which *Kind of Blue*'s blues-structured tracks translate to stringed instruments has led a wealth of guitarists to reinterpret the material. Grant Green's 1961 and George Benson's 1971 treatments of "So What," and Wes Montgomery's 1963 take on "Freddie Freeloader," are all considered minor classics. Ronny Jordan, fresh out of London's acid jazz scene, logged a UK hit with a funk-fueled version of "So What" in 1991, while classic rockers like Robby Krieger (of the Doors), Jerry Garcia (of the Grateful Dead, in the company of mandolinist David Grisman), and Derek Trucks (of the Allman Brothers) have all recorded it as well. The list of stringmasters

Bill Evans's *Blue in Green*; Oscar Brown Jr.'s *Tells It Like It Is!*

recording "Freddie Freeloader" (Philip Catherine, Stanley Jordan), "All Blues" (Kenny Burrell, Jim Hall), or "Blue in Green" (John McLaughlin, Kevin Eubanks) continues to grow.

Kind of Blue has also been recorded in a host of vocal covers with inspired lyrics. Perhaps the most amusing is Eddie Jefferson's dig at the critical obsession with Miles's onstage behavior ("Miles has left the stage—SO WHAT!"). Two different poetic approaches to "Blue in Green" have appeared on two different Miles tributes: Cassandra Wilson's *Traveling Miles* and Shirley Horn's *I Remember Miles*. Oscar Brown, Jr.'s popular, impressionistic take on "All Blues" from 1963 has been redone by an array of jazz-oriented singers, from the cabaret/ nightclub stylists (Joe Williams, Morgana King), to the more R&B-tinged (Ernestine Anderson, Kevin Mahogany), and the smoother, pop-inflected (Dee Dee Bridgewater, New York Voices).

Brown recalls the inspiration that brought forth the song: "I was in a United Airlines plane, leaving Los Angeles, and the sky was clear and blue, the ocean was blue, and the plane had a blue décor and that's how that lyric ['The sea, the sky and you and I/we're all blue . . .'] started." Brown, who was also a Columbia Records artist, explains that he auditioned the words for Miles while they were on the same bill a few months later:

> I had a conversation with Miles between breaks at Cecilia's Lounge, a restaurant that was directly across from the stage door of the Howard Theater in Washington, D.C. I sang it to him and he was cool, otherwise I wouldn't have done it.

Arguably the most outstanding vocal treatment of *Kind of Blue* material yet recorded is Jon Hendricks's vocalese summit on "Freddie Freeloader." In 1989, he and Bobby McFerrin, Al Jarreau, and George Benson vocalized the original solos of Coltrane, Kelly, Miles, and Adderley, respectively. The singers are uncannily accurate in their renderings of those timeless improvisations, and the entertaining lyric evokes bar talk and street hustle: "Freddie, Freddie/Free booze, free blues, free dues."

To put a number to the phenomenon—insofar as data from music and publishing databases can be trusted for accuracy—there have been close to one hundred fifty covers recorded of "All Blues" and "So What," almost one hundred of "Blue in Green," and (surprisingly) only fifteen or so of "Freddie Freeloader." The most challenging and most purely modal track, "Flamenco Sketches," has been covered only five times. Tenor man Joe Henderson is one of the few artists who took that challenge, featuring his rendition on *So Near, So Far (Musings for Miles)* in 1992.

In return for the initial production costs of a few thousand dollars in 1959 (contractual advance to Miles, union scale payment to six sidemen, nine hours studio time, four reels of tape, one piano tuner), Columbia Records certainly struck a gold mine of profit with *Kind of Blue*. The album's self-perpetuating popularity causes record executives and retailers to grow giddy. An album with staying power is said to have legs; *Kind of Blue* has been running a forty-year marathon with no signs of fatigue. Despite little promotional effort, and no consistent marketing strategy over the album's forty years, sales figures, particularly those of in the latter nineties, are steadily ascending. "It averages five to seven thousand [copies sold] every week, like clockwork," marvels one record label head. "During the Christmas season last year [1998] I remember *Kind of Blue* was hitting as much as 25 thousand in a week."

Although much of the information on the album's past retail performance is buried or has been lost, enough exists to reveal a most impressive picture of *Kind of Blue*, the product. In the U.S., the music of *Kind of Blue* has been issued over nine times in almost every format of sound recording popular since 1959: LP, 45 rpm single, reel-to-reel tape, cassette tape, CD, and most recently SACD (Super Audio CD); current discussions are considering DVD audio. (Sony Music can find no record of it ever being issued as an 8-track.) From the moment of its release until it was overtaken in 1969 by the phenomenal success of *Bitches Brew*, *Kind of Blue* was Miles's most popular album. A comparative sales study from Columbia's files reveals that of all Davis's LPs to January 1962, *Kind of Blue* was his leading seller by far, with over 87,000 copies sold. *Porgy & Bess* was the only album that came close.

Since 1959, the album's sales trajectory in the U.S. shows an incredible exponential growth: approximately 87,000 copies sold by 1962; 420,000 by 1984, when CDs were introduced; and 445,000 by the end of 1986. *Kind of Blue* took over thirty years to reach gold album certification—500,000 copies sold—in August of 1993, and then it doubled those numbers in less than four years, becoming platinum (1 million copies sold) in February of 1997. In that same year, Sony Legacy—the arm of Sony Music established in 1990 to reissue music from the company's extensive back catalog—brought forth *Kind of Blue*, catalog number CK64935. At this writing, this latest incarnation is well on its way to triple platinum status in the U.S.

Credit for this recent explosion of sales is attributable to at least a few business and cultural factors: increased musical knowledge and appreciation through an expanded and stratified media (e.g., more cable stations, more specialty magazines, more rock stars touting their favorite jazz albums); larger music stores with well-stocked selections; and a more complete computerized tracking of retail sales. As well, the advent of compact discs in 1984 taught all labels the value of catalog exploitation; reissues of almost all archival music revitalized an industry that was still hurting from the post-disco collapse of the late seventies. Reissue programs are taken very seriously today and have become part of the financial backbone to the music business; currently, there is no major label that does not boast a well-coordinated program for repackaging and re-promoting the treasures from its vaults.

It's a formidable forty-year sales history. But in a way *Kind of Blue*'s success has happened despite Columbia Records. Before the eighties, there had been little attempt to re-promote what was slowly becoming, on its own, Miles's most popular album (other than his million-seller *Bitches Brew* in 1969). In fact, Columbia did little other than keep the record on the market, sometimes with cursory attention to the album's repackaging.

Here's an example. Columbia debuted *Kind of Blue* in compact disc format for the first time in 1984. Two years later, the label unveiled its "Columbia Jazz Masterpieces" series, offering thirty-two classic album titles from the vaults in new covers with a distinctive purple border, in both LP and CD formats. *Kind of Blue* was chosen to join various Louis Armstrong, Benny Goodman, and Billie Holiday titles in the first wave, but was ignominiously repackaged: unable to locate the original artwork from '59, the company decided to use an extremely out-of-focus, live photograph of Miles from the late sixties. Not only was it an anachronistic gaffe—fashion-conscious as Davis was, he was not sporting loose, wild patterned white shirts in 1959—but worse, the photograph was printed in reverse. So many jazz fans remain convinced that a left-handed Miles Davis graces the original cover of *Kind of Blue*.

(One other point regarding that edition: the back cover credits Teo Macero as "Producer." As confusing as that may be, the listing is actually half correct—Macero was indeed producer of that reissue. However, the most recent CD edition of *Kind of Blue* is the first to accurately note: "Original Recording Produced by Irving Townsend.")

Tracking the sales history of *Kind of Blue* outside the U.S. is an even more difficult task. The album has been licensed, as a whole and piecemeal, to almost every territory in the world since 1960, when it was released throughout western Europe on the Fontana label, a subsidiary of Philips Phonographic Industries, a Dutch company then operating with a two-way licensing agreement with Columbia Records. (It was from Philips—later part of Polygram and now part of the

#1 from the outset: a 1962 Columbia sales study shows *Kind of Blue* as Miles's best-seller

Bottom: The unfortunate left-handed Miles cover

MILES DAVIS SALES STUDY 1961

		TOTAL 1961	GRAND TOTAL
		7,259	61,825
	Round About Midnight	6,916	45,285
..9	Miles Ahead	6,720	51,829
..041	Milestones	9,165	42,981
..193	Jazz Track (Frantic)	10,489	83,579
..268	Porgy and Bess	22,269	87,932
1274/CS 8065			
1355/CS 8163	Kind of Blue	22,632	61,302
1480/CS 8271	Sketches of Spain	31,979	31,979
1669/CS 8469	In Person - Friday Night	31,316	31,316
1670/CS 8470	In Person - Saturday Night	7,289	7,289
20/CS 820	In Person - Friday & Saturday Night	(January 1, 1962)	
1656/CS 8456	Someday My Prince Will Come		
	TOTAL	156,034	505,311

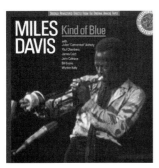

MILES DAVIS Kind of Blue
with
Julian "Cannonball" Adderley
Paul Chambers
James Cobb
John Coltrane
Bill Evans
Wynton Kelly

multinational Universal Music—that Columbia licensed Miles's soundtrack to *Ascenseur Pour L'Échafaud*.) Many music companies have folded or been bought and absorbed into larger firms; initially, record keeping on a consistent, universal scale simply did not happen.

But if current sales are any indication, it is safe to assume that as in the U.S., *Kind of Blue* proved a popular international seller through the sixties. By the 1970s, it was possible, through a global arrangement of licensing and sublicensing deals, to purchase at least the music from *Kind of Blue*, if not the entire album, in almost any corner on the planet. A survey of various album covers from around the world shows how little certain territories had to work with; in the old Soviet Union they would have been happy to have had any photograph at all to print on the cover.

Kind of Blue goes worldwide. From left: USSR, UK and French editions of the album

At the dawn of the digital age in the early eighties an unfortunate thing occurred: a glut of repackaged back-catalog titles in the new compact disc format swept through the world, each promising higher-quality digital audio than the next. This would not seem to be a bad situation at first glance. But then Columbia executives in New York began noticing that their foreign licensees were actually issuing inferior product and exporting it into the U.S. Steve Berkowitz, vice president of A&R at Sony Legacy, describes the situation:

> In the late fifties and sixties, Columbia was a domestic record company and there really wasn't such a thing as an international music business yet. So when Japan or France wanted to put out a record, Columbia would just take it as gravy. The idea of copying and sending a tape abroad to a licensee was, "Hey, by the way, make a copy of that *Kind of Blue* record, we gotta ship it out to Japan tomorrow." So an engineer would take a copy of *Kind of Blue*, maybe the master, maybe a copy, maybe it was Dolby-ed, maybe it was equalized specifically for LP, maybe it wasn't, and it would be sent abroad. Japan or France would get it, and it's forever their original master. It was at best a second or third generation copy of what maybe was the original.

The end result?

So it's 1992 and you walk into Tower Records in downtown New York, and there's seven different versions of *Kind of Blue*. For $7.95 there's a bootleg, for $10.98 you've got the one from Columbia that's got the purple border around it and he's a left-handed trumpet player, and how many 'E's are there in "Adderley"? And for $40 the Japanese half-speed original 24 bit-direct stream. And you get that CD, and though it's a perfect mastering of their tape, their tape is from the sixties that's a third-generation copy to begin with.

Berkowitz explains that blame can be partially laid on the shifting responsibilities in a growing company, and on bottom-line motivations: "Sony is a corporation, not a library or a museum. There was an ebb and flow of different departments handling reissues like these." Today, with the advent of multinational corporations like Sony Music, the creation of Legacy to oversee a global, consistent reissue strategy is an overdue but welcome development.

The latest version of *Kind of Blue* is a good example of Legacy's more

focused and conscientious efforts. CK64935 is a worthy salute to the album, featuring the original music with the speed problem corrected and the first take of "Flamenco Sketches" added. In a rare example combining old musical information with new media technology, this reissue connects to a website dedicated to *Kind of Blue*, at www.sonymusic.com/thelab/ConnecteD/Miles Davis, featuring session photographs and an interactive analysis of Miles's "So What" solo. (Unfortunately, the site remains slow and difficult to access, and may or may not be compatible with various operating systems.)

Recent research has shown that since 1997, over one million copies of *Kind of Blue* have been purchased outside the U.S. Not surprisingly, the album is most popular in countries where jazz has long been held close to the hearts of music fans: England, France, Germany, Japan and Greece. Assuming the same three-to-one ratio of albums sold domestically compared to the rest of the world, it is a safe bet that *Kind of Blue* will reach a world-wide total of over five million copies sold before its forty-first birthday on August 17, 2000.

The week of August 7, 1999, *Billboard* ran a front-page feature titled "Miles Davis's True 'Blue,'" to mark *Kind of Blue*'s fortieth anniversary. In it, an employee at Tower Records' downtown Manhattan flagship store related that it was their "best-selling catalog album, period. More people buy that than any record by the Beatles, Frank Sinatra, anybody." The article went on to describe the centrally located aisle-end display—the premier location in retail real estate—"regularly devoted to nothing but *Kind of Blue*."

I've seen that display: CDs by Coltrane, Adderley, Evans and any number of major and minor jazz legends lie a few yards away in any direction. Its placement seemed almost too symbolic, the album as a serene blue beacon radiating its invitation to new listeners, an aural stepping-stone for many into the world of jazz.

Not long ago, as I stood in that music superstore, I watched as a young woman—no older than twenty-five, as I recall—walked briskly past me, honed in on the *Kind of Blue* rack, and picked up a copy. Long after she disappeared toward the cashier, I began to wonder how she had come to make her selection that day. Did she already know the album? How had she first come to hear about it? Was the purchase for herself or someone else?

But I was not interested in conducting a marketing survey—all that leads to a different kind of research and study. I prefer just to imagine that copy of *Kind of Blue* finding its way into the hands of some first-time listener, working its magic.

EVERY AGE ADOPTS its own cultural touchstones, and very few are passed on. But since 1959, no other jazz album—and there have been many outstanding candidates—has succeeded in removing *Kind of Blue* from its premier position. Future music lovers might nominate a different album as their masterpiece of choice—Coltrane's *A Love Supreme,* perhaps, or a ground-breaking effort by some musician yet to gain notice. One can't help but wonder if somewhere, another *Kind of Blue* is being recorded that will resonate into the next century.

Epilogue

Almost all the elements that made *Kind of Blue* possible—the musicians, producer, record company and even the studio—have passed on or been transformed. Of Miles Davis's fabled sextet-plus-one, Jimmy Cobb dolefully said, "I'm the only one left out of the session so they talk to me about it." John Coltrane was the first member of the *Blue* brotherhood to pass away, succumbing to liver cancer in 1967. Tuberculosis took Paul Chambers two years later, when he was only 34, and Wynton Kelly followed in 1971 at forty. Cannonball Adderley, a lifelong diabetic with an attendant weight problem, was suddenly felled by a stroke in 1975. Bill Evans passed away in 1980 from an ulcer and pneumonia, his demise hastened by decades of drug abuse.

Producer Irving Townsend, retired from Columbia and living in Santa Ynez, California, died in 1981, the same year that 30th Street Studio, home to so many timeless recordings, was sold off by CBS Records following the financial downturn of the record business in the late seventies. 30th Street's Steinway pianos, vintage microphones, and other equipment were auctioned, as was the building, for a song. The once-busy studio, under-used in its latter years as the label began to purchase or lease master recordings from artists rather than subsidize the creation of its own music, was razed less than a year later. A condominium building now stands at 207 East 30th Street. Columbia Records is part of an international empire driven by pop and rap multi-platinum success albums. Its jazz department is relatively small and conservative when compared with the roster of the fifties; it is comprised primarily of trumpeter Wynton Marsalis and tenor saxophonist Branford Marsalis, trumpeter Terence Blanchard, pianist Marcus Roberts, and a few lesser-known artists (such as bassist Kyle Eastwood and keyboardist Frank McComb).

Miles Davis—the tireless explorer—was beset with a multitude of ailments in the seventies and eighties. He died in 1991 of a massive stroke.

When I listen to *Kind of Blue,* it always brings to mind a magazine photograph I clipped years ago. Still tacked to my bulletin board, the picture of maple leaves poking through a weathered bamboo fence is captioned:

"When beauty reaches great subtlety . . . the Japanese call the effect *shibui* . . . restrained elegance." The term *shibui* has no simple equivalent in English, but a little research reveals that it means more than mere subtlety or elegance. It is—as the caption reads—an effect rather than an attribute, referring not to a canvas, or to a piece of music, but to the act of appreciation itself.

When artistic talent of the highest order creates a work that achieves a timeless balance of opposites, perfectly merging the yin of the emotional and the yang of the analytical, it evokes *shibui*, recognizable by the strong emotional response it draws forth. There is melancholy in its suggestion of impermanence, serenity in its deep reserve and simplicity.

Eastern examples of such masterworks lean to the natural, the uncluttered, and the implied. A single flower in an old, tarnished vase. A faint, mountainous vista caught in a misty morning as defined by a few brief brushstrokes on a rice paper scroll. A lonely, evocative motif played on an unaccompanied bamboo flute. Western culture might offer a vintage claret that, once tasted, can be neither forgotten nor precisely recalled. A morose, blue-hued painting of a guitarist from a style and period that a master painter would never repeat. A recording of Ravel's *Concerto for Left Hand and Orchestra* by Arturo Benedetti Michelangeli (which Miles appraised: "When he plays, he plays like he's never going to play that again").

And I would add *Kind of Blue*.

Bibliography

For the sake of convenience, books, articles and other written sources have been arranged by subject category.

Jazz in the fifties

Amram, David. Vibrations: *The Adventures and Musical Times of David Amram*. New York: The MacMillan Company, 1968.

Balliett, Whitney. *The Sound of Surprise*. New York: E. P. Dutton & Co., 1959.

Cerulli, Dom and Burt Korall, Mort L. Nasatir, eds. *The Jazz Word*. New York: Da Capo Press, 1960. Many of these essays are by jazz musicians themselves, such as Gunther Schuller's "Is Jazz Coming of Age?" and George Russell's "Where Do We Go From Here?"

Dawson, Fielding: *Krazy Kat & 76 More: Collected Stories, 1950–1976*, Black Sparrow Press, Santa Barbara, 1982. In the short story "Pirate One," Fielding provides a vivid walk-through of various New York jazz clubs and Greenwich Village bars of the fifties.

Gleason, Ralph J. *Celebrating the Duke: And Louis, Bessie, Billie, Bird, Carmen, Miles, Dizzy and Other Heroes*. New York: Da Capo Press, 1995.

Goldberg, Joe. *Jazz Masters of the 50s*. New York: The MacMillan Company, 1965.

Halberstam, David. *The Fifties*. New York: Villard Books, 1993.

Hentoff, Nat. *The Jazz Life*. New York: Da Capo Press, 1961. An eyes-open look at the economic realities and career expectations of a jazz musician's life fill the chapter "The Changes."

———. *Speaking Freely*. New York: Alfred A. Knopf, 1997. Includes a rare and informative chapter on Robert Herridge and his pioneering role in the fledgling television scene of the late fifties.

———, and Albert J. McCarthy, eds. *Jazz*. New York: Da Capo Press, 1959. Concludes with Hentoff's excellent "Whose Art Form? Jazz at Mid-Century."

Hodeir, Andre. "Perspective of Modern Jazz: Popularity of Recognition?" *Down Beat* (August 20, 1959): 40–42.

Keepnews, Orrin. *The View From Within: Jazz Writings, 1948–1987*. Oxford University Press, New York, 1988.

Lhamon, W. T. Jr. *Deliberate Speed: The Origins of a Cultural Style in the American 1950s*. Washington D.C.: Smithsonian Institution Press, 1990.

Maguire, Roberta S., ed. *Conversations with Albert Murray*. Jackson: University Press of Mississippi, 1997.

Rosenthal, David. *Hard Bop: Jazz and Black Music, 1955–1965*. New York: Oxford University Press, 1992.

Smith, Charles Edward. "A Summing Up: 25 Years of Jazz." *Down Beat* (August 20, 1959): 37–39.

Sukenick, Ronald. *Down and In: Life in the Underground*. New York: Beech Tree Books, 1987.

Wakefield, Dan. *New York in the 50s*. New York: St. Martin's Press, 1992. Devotes an entire chapter, "Graduating to the Five Spot," to the levels of hipness through which a jazz devotee could advance.

Williams, Martin. *Jazz Masters in Transition, 1957–1969*. New York: Da Capo Press, 1970.

———. *The Jazz Tradition*. New York: Oxford University Press, 1970. Offers a particularly insightful chapter on Miles.

Wilson, John. Jazz: *The Transition Years, 1940–1960*. New York: Appleton-Century-Crofts, 1966.

Miles

As the research into Miles's history is an ongoing process, inaccurate information does crop up in these books, and others listed below. Nonetheless there is enough historical accuracy to be, as the adage goes, "close enough for jazz."

Carner, Gary, ed. *The Miles Davis Companion: Four Decades of Commentary*. New York: Omnibus Press, 1996. Of particular interest are Ben Sidran's "Talking Jazz," Amiri Baraka's "Homage to Miles Davis" and Pearl Cleage's "Mad at Miles."

Carr, Ian. *Miles Davis: The Definitive Biography*. New York: Thunder's Mouth Press, 1998.

Chambers, Jack. *Milestones: The Music and Times of Miles Davis*. New York: Da Capo Press, 1998.

Davis, Miles with Quincy Troupe. *Miles: The Autobiography*. New York: Simon and Schuster, 1989.

Ephland, John, "Miles to Go: Miles Davis," *Down Beat* (October, 1988): 16–54.

Fisher, Larry. Miles Davis and David Liebman: *Jazz Connections*. Lewiston, NY: The Edwin Mellen Press, 1996.

Gleason, Ralph J. "Composed for 6 Months, Then Made Tune a Waltz," *San Francisco Chronicle* (June 20, 1959).

Green, Stanley, ed. *Kings of Jazz*. New York: A. S. Barnes & Co., 1978.

Haley, Alex. "Playboy Interview: Miles Davis." *Playboy* (September 1962): 57–66.

Harris, Pat. "Nothing But Bop? 'Stupid,' Says Miles," *Down Beat* (January 27, 1950): 18–19.

Hentoff, Nat. "An Afternoon with Miles Davis." *Jazz Review* (December, 1958): 9–12. Miles's most revealing commentary on his modal path of the late fifties.

———. "Miles." *Down Beat* (November 2, 1955): 13–14.

———. "Miles Davis: Last Trump." *Esquire* (March, 1959): 88–90.

Kirchner, Bill, ed. *A Miles Davis Reader.* Washington, D.C.: Smithsonian Institution Press, 1997.

Lohmann, Jan. *The Sound of Miles Davis: The Discography.* A listing of Records and Tapes—1945–1991. Copenhagen: JazzMedia Aps, 1992.

Losin, Peter. *Miles Ahead 2.0* (website). www.wam.umd.edu/~losinp/music/miles_ahead.html.

Morgenstern, Dan. Liner notes to *Miles Davis Chronicle, The Complete Prestige Recordings.* PCD–012–2, 1987.

Taylor, Arthur. *Notes and Tones: Musician-to-Musician Interviews.* New York: Da Capo Press, 1993.

Tomkins, Les. "Miles Davis Talking." *Crescendo* (December 1969): 20–22.

Vail, Ken. *Miles' Diary: The Life of Miles Davis 1947–1961.* London: Sanctuary Publishing Limited, 1996.

Williams, Richard. *The Man in the Green Shirt: Miles Davis.* New York: Henry Holt & Company, 1993.

KIND OF BLUE bandmembers

If only there were studies on all the band members as thorough and informed as Pettinger's (on Evans) and Porter's (on Coltrane) are. Many of the albums listed in the discography—particularly the box sets—include well-researched and annotated liner notes with information not found elsewhere.

JOHN COLTRANE

Coltrane, John. "Coltrane on Coltrane." *Down Beat* (September 29, 1960): 26–27.

Fujioka, Yasuhiro, Lewis Porter, and Yoh-Icho Hamada. *John Coltrane: A Discography and Musical Biography* (Studies in Jazz; No. 20.) Scarecrow Press, 1993.

Gleason, Ralph J. "Coltrane's Sax Blows Instant Art." *San Francisco Chronicle* (November 24, 1963): 30.

"John Coltrane Talks to Jazz News." *Jazz News* (December 27, 1961): 13.

Porter, Lewis. *John Coltrane: His Life and Music.* Ann Arbor: The University of Michigan Press, 1998.

Woideck, Carl, ed. *The John Coltrane Companion: Five Decades of Commentary.* New York: Simon & Schuster, 1998.

CANNONBALL ADDERLEY

Gitler, Ira. *Jazz Quarterly.* (Summer, 1959): 197–211.

Adderley, Cannonball. "Paying Dues." *Jazz Review* (May, 1960): 12–15.

DeMichael, Don. "The Responsibilities of Success." *Down Beat* (June 21, 1962): 13–15.

BILL EVANS

Aikin, Jim. "Bill Evans." *Contemporary Keyboard* (June, 1980): 44–55.

Gottlieb, Robert, ed. *Reading Jazz: A Gathering of Autobiography, Reportage and Criticism from 1919 to Now.* New York: Pantheon Books, 1996. Excerpts Gene Lee's exemplary overview of Evans's life and career, "Meet Me at Jim and Andy's."

Hennessey, Brian. "A Person I Knew." *Jazz Journal International* (March, 1985): 8–11.

Jeske, Lee. "Bill Evans, Trio Master." *Down Beat* (October, 1979): 18–21.

Lyons, Len. *The Great Jazz Pianists.* New York: Da Capo Press, 1983.

Pettinger, Peter. *Bill Evans: How My Heart Sings.* New Haven: Yale University Press, 1998.

Wilner, Paul. "Jazz Pianist: Life on the Upbeat." *New York Times* (September 25, 1977).

WYNTON KELLY

Lees, Gene. "Focus on Wynton Kelly." *Down Beat* (January 3, 1962): 16.

Columbia Records

Dannen, Fredric. *Hit Men.* New York: Vintage Books, 1991.

Fox, Ted. *In The Groove, The People Behind The Music.* New York: St. Martin's Press, 1986.

Gillett, Charlie. *The Sound of the City: The Rise of Rock and Roll.* New York: Pantheon Books, 1983.

Hammond, John. *John Hammond On Record: An Autobiography.* New York: Penguin Books, 1977.

Kohler, Eric. *In The Groove: Vintage Record Graphics, 1940–1960.* San Francisco: Chronicle Books, 1999.

Soundtrack for a Century (companion book to CD Box set), Sony Music, New York, 1999.

Modal jazz

Kernfeld, Barry Dean. *Adderley, Coltrane and Davis at the Twilight of Bebop: The Search for Melodic Coherence.* Ph.D. thesis, Cornell University, 1981.

Porter, Lewis: *John Coltrane: His Life and Music.*
The subject of modal jazz is found in the chapter

"Giant Steps and Kind of Blue."
Sadie, Stanley, ed. New Grove Dictionary of Music
and Musicians. Washington D.C.: MacMillan
Publishers, 1980.

Other topics

KIND OF BLUE

Bambarger, Bradley. "Miles Davis's True 'Blue.'"
Billboard (August 7, 1999): 1.
Dollar, Steve. "Re-Release of Davis' Kind of Blue
Well Worth the Wait." Atlanta Journal-Constitution
(April 13, 1997).
Garrigues, C. H. "Recapturing the Magic of Miles."
San Francisco Examiner, October 11, 1959.
Heckman, Don. "Kind of New." Los Angeles Times
(March 30, 1997).
Kahn, Ashley. "At 40, Still a Vital Portal to Jazz."
The New York Times (August 15, 1999, Section 2):
27–33. A personal testimonial, on the fortieth
anniversary of its release, to the dog-eared vinyl
album I have kept since high school days.
Kahn, Ashley. "Cast a Giant Shadow." Mojo
(September, 1999): 52–57. Includes three errors
herein corrected: Macero was not the original
session producer, 30th Street was not formerly a
Russian Orthodox church, but Greek, and there
was one alternate take.
Kolodin, Irving. "Miles Ahead or Miles' Head?"
Saturday Review (September 12, 1959): 61.
"Miles Davis." Metronome (October, 1959): 29.
"Miles Davis." Down Beat (October 1, 1959): 28.
Mirapaul, Matthew. "Living Liner Notes for Classic
Miles Davis." The New York Times (July 16, 1998).
"Spotlight Winners of the Week." Billboard (August
31, 1959): 28.
Straub, Bill. "Miles Davis' Kind of Blue Turns 40."
Scripps Howard News Service (April 25, 1999).

SUIBOKUGA AND JAPANESE ART

Mason, Penelope. History of Japanese Art. New York:
Harry N. Abrams, Inc., 1993.
Shimizu, Yoshiaki and Carolyn Wheelwright, eds.
Japanese Ink Paintings. Princeton, NJ: Princeton
University Press, 1976.

GENERAL JAZZ REFERENCE

Bley, Paul with David Lee. Stopping Time: Paul Bley
and the Transformation of Jazz. Canada: Vehicule
Press, 1999.
Cook, Richard and Brian Morton. The Penguin Guide
to Jazz on CD. New York: Penguin Putnam, Inc.,
1998.

Crow, Bill. Jazz Anecdotes. New York: Oxford
University Press, 1990.
Erlewine, Michael, et. al., eds. All Music Guide to
Jazz. San Francisco: Miller Freeman Book, 1998.
Jones, LeRoi. Blues People. New York: Morrow Quill
Paperbacks, 1963.
Jost, Ekkehard. Free Jazz: The Roots of Jazz. New
York: DaCapo Press, 1994.
Meltzer, David, ed. Reading Jazz. San Francisco:
Mercury House, 1993.
Sidran, Ben. Black Talk. New York: Da Capo Press,
1971.

Discography

The following is a subjective survey of albums that define a roadmap outward from the "musical hub" that is *Kind of Blue*. Dates denote the latest reissue of each album.

Miles Davis

EARLY YEARS (1946–1950)

First Miles. Denon/Savoy SV–0159, 1992. Features his first session as a leader in 1947.

Yardbird Suite: The Ultimate Collection. Rhino 72260, 1997. Features "Donna Lee" and "Now's the Time."

The Complete Birth of the Cool. Capitol Jazz CDP 7243–4–94550–2–3, 1998.

PRESTIGE/BLUE NOTE YEARS (1951–1956)

Miles Davis: Volume One and Volume Two. Blue Note CD 781501–2 and CD 781502–2, 1990.

Walkin'. Prestige OJCCD–213–2, 1999.

Miles and the Modern Jazz Giants. Prestige OJCCD–347–2, 1991.

Miles (The New Miles Davis Quintet). Prestige OJC–006–2, 1992.

Cookin'. Prestige OJC–128–2, 1990.

COLUMBIA YEARS (1957–1962)

with Quintet/Sextet:

'Round About Midnight. Columbia, 65359, 1997.

Milestones. Sony, 65340, 1997.

Kind of Blue. Columbia/Legacy, CK64935, 1997.

In Person, Friday Night (and Saturday Night) at the Blackhawk. Columbia CK 44257 (and CK44425), 1990.

with Gil Evans:

Miles Ahead. Columbia/Legacy, CK65121, 1997.

Porgy & Bess. Sony 65338, 1997.

Sketches of Spain. Columbia/Legacy, CK65121, 1997.

Miles Davis at Carnegie Hall—The Complete Concert. Columbia/Legacy, CK65027, 1998.

in France:

Ascenseur Pour L'Échafaud. Phonogram 8225662, 1987.

BOX SETS

Miles Davis Chronicle: The Complete Prestige Recordings. PCD–012–2, 1987.

Miles Davis & Gil Evans: The Complete Columbia Studio Recordings. Columbia/Legacy, 2 67397, 1996.

Miles Davis with John Coltrane: The Complete Columbia Recordings. Columbia/Legacy C6K 6583, 2000. Includes all of *Kind of Blue* (including the alternate take of "Flamenco Sketches"), the complete 1958 "Fran-Dance" session (with the sextet featuring Bill Evans) and all live recordings of the same sextet from that year (Newport Festival and "Jazz at the Plaza").

John Coltrane

Blue Train. Blue Note CDP 7460952, 1996.

Black Pearls. Prestige OJCCD–352–2, 1992.

Giant Steps. Rhino 75203, 1998.

My Favorite Things. Rhino 75204, 1998.

Impressions. Impulse! 314–543–416–2, 2000.

A Love Supreme. Impulse!/GRD 155, 1995.

Ascension. Impulse! 314–543–413–2, 2000.

The Heavyweight Champion: The Complete Atlantic Recordings (box set). Rhino R2–7 1984, 1995.

The Classic Quartet: Complete Impulse! Studio Recordings (box set). IMPD 8–280, 1998.

Cannonball Adderley

The Summer of '55. Atlantic/Savoy Jazz 92860–2, 1999.

Sophisticated Swing: The EmArcy Small Group Sessions. Verve, 314–528–408–2, 1995.

Somethin' Else. Blue Note, 7243–4–95329–2–2, 1999. Miles's title track contribution features the same subtle, call-and-response take on the blues as is prevalent on *Kind of Blue*.

Cannonball Adderley Quintet in Chicago. Verve, 314–559–770–2, 1999.

Know What I Mean? (with Bill Evans). Riverside OJCCD–105–2, 1987.

The Best of Cannonball Adderley: The Capitol Years (with Bill Evans). Capitol Jazz, CDP 7–95482–2, 1991.

Bill Evans

Everybody Digs Bill Evans. OJCCD–068–2, 1987.

On Green Dolphin Street. Milestone, MCD–9235–2, 1995.

Portrait in Jazz. Riverside, OJCCD–088–2, 1987.

Blue in Green. Milestone, MCD–9185–2, 1991. (A live set from 1974.)

The Complete Riverside Recordings (box set). Riverside 018, 1991.

Wynton Kelly, Paul Chambers and Jimmy Cobb

Chambers, Paul. *Bass on Top*. Blue Note B2–46533.
Kelly, Wynton. *Kelly Blue*. OJCCD–033–2, 1991.
Kelly, Wynton. *Someday My Prince Will Come*. Vee Jay 902.
Wynton Kelly Trio–Wes Montgomery. *Smokin' at the Half Note*. Verve 829–578–2.

Covers

The albums listed feature many of the interpretations of *Kind of Blue* material mentioned in the book.

Benson, George. *Beyond the Blue Horizon*, Sony 40810, 1990.
Brown, Jr., Oscar. *Tells It Like It Is*, Columbia CL 2025, 1963.
Green, Grant. *Sunday Mornin'*, Blue Note, CDP–7243–8–52434–2–4, 1996.
Henderson, Joe. *So Near, So Far (Musings for Miles)*, Verve 517 674, 1993.
Hendricks, Jon. *Freddie Freeloader*, Denon, CY–76302, 1990.
Horn, Shirley. *I Remember Miles*, Polygram, 557199, 1998.
Jefferson, Eddie. *Heart and Soul*, Prestige OJCCD–396–2, 1989.
Jordan, Ronny. *The Antidote*. Fourth & Broadway/ Island 162–444047–2, 1992.
Montgomery, Wes. *Portrait of Wes*, Riverside OJCCD–144–2, 1990.
Williams, Joe. *Joe Williams Live*, Fantasy OJCCD–438–2, 1990.
Wilson, Cassandra. *Traveling Miles*, Blue Note, 7243–8–54123–2–5, 1999.

Jazz in the fifties

To give a sense of the width and breadth of the jazz scene in the fifties—including the sounds that directly informed the making of *Kind of Blue*—I offer the Ellington, Mingus and Coleman titles (in addition to Coltrane's *Giant Steps* above) as a sampling of the progressive jazz being made concurrent with the recording of *Kind of Blue* in 1959. I also submit four albums that constitute a strong hard bop starter's set (beyond the Davis titles mentioned above.) In respect of home entertainment budgets that may be over-burdened by these recommendations, I have purposefully avoided box sets.

Ammons, Gene. *The Gene Ammons Story: The 78 Era*, Prestige, PCD–24058–2, 1992. Includes "Walkin'."
Bernstein, Leonard. *What is Jazz*, Sony Classical SMK 60566.
Blakey, Art. *The Jazz Messengers*, Columbia/Legacy, CK–65265, 1997. Hard Bop Classic #1, produced by George Avakian.
Brown, Clifford and Max Roach. *Study in Brown*. EmArcy, 814–646–2. Hard Bop Classic #2.
Coleman, Ornette. *The Shape of Jazz to Come*, Atlantic 1317–2, 1959.
Ellington, Duke. *Anatomy of a Murder*, Sony 65569, 1999.
Farmer, Art and Benny Golson. *Meet the Jazztet*. Hard Bop Classic #3: Features the minor hit (and cousin to "Freddie Freeloader") "Killer Joe."
Gillespie, Dizzy. *The Complete RCA Victor Recordings*, Bluebird 07863–66528–2, 1995.
Holiday, Billie. *Lady in Satin*. Sony/Legacy 65144, 1997.
Kenton, Stan. *The Best of Stan Kenton*. Capitol Jazz CDP 7243–8–31504–2–7, 1995.
Mingus, Charles. *Mingus Ah Um*, Columbia/Legacy CK 65512, 1998.
Modern Jazz Quartet. *Fontessa*, Atlantic Jazz 1231–2, 1989.
Monk, Thelonious. *Genius of Modern Music*, Volumes 1 and 2. Blue Note CDP–7–81510–2 and CDP–7–81511–2, 1989.
Mulligan, Gerry and Chet Baker. *The Best of the Gerry Mulligan Quartet with Chet Baker*, Pacific Jazz CDP 7–95481–2, 1991.
Rollins, Sonny. *Sonny Rollins Plus Four*. OJCCD 243–2, 1987. Hard Bop Classic #4.
Russell, George. *The Jazz Workshop*, Koch Jazz, KOC-CD–7850, 1998.
———. *New York, NY*, Impulse! IMPD–278, 1998.
Sinatra, Frank. *In the Wee Small Hours*, Capitol, C2–968626, 1991.
Thornhill, Claude and his Orchestra. *The 1948 Transcription Performances*. HEP CD 17, 1994.
Tristano, Lennie. *Intuition*. Capitol Jazz, CDP–7243–8–52771–2–2, 1996. Features "Intuition" and "Digression," arguably the first recorded instances of "free" jazz.
Various. *The Birth of the Third Stream*, Columbia/ Legacy, CK 64929, 1996. Includes Miles soloist spot on John Lewis's "Three Little Feelings" and J.J. Johnson's "Poem for Brass."

Source notes

All interviews were conducted by the author unless otherwise noted. When possible, all liner notes are referenced by catalog numbers of the most recent edition of the album.

INTRODUCTION

17 "Miles Davis is my definition of cool": Bob Dylan, interview by Scott Cohen, "Not Like a *Rolling Stone* Interview," *Spin* (December 1985).

17 "I remember at Berklee School [of Music in Boston]": John Scofield, interview, tape recording, 6 December 1999.

17 "In some of the movements of Beethoven's *Ninth Symphony*": Elvin Jones, interview, tape recording, 29 November 1999.

17 "It's like listening to *Tosca*": Shirley Horn, interview, tape recording, 28 November 1999.

17 "In the fin-de-siecle frenzy": In the months before December 31, 1999, *The Los Angeles Times*, *Vibe*, *Entertainment Weekly*, and Amazon.com were among the countless publications and websites that featured *Kind of Blue* on their lists counting down the Top 10, Top 100 or "Greatest Albums of All Time."

19 "That will always be my music, man": Quincy Jones, interview, tape recording, 21 June 1999.

19 "It's one thing to just play a tune": Chick Corea interview, tape recording, Sony Music *Kind of Blue* website, 1998.

20 "*Kind of Blue* is just one of those amazing albums": George Russell, interview, tape recording, 10 November 1999.

20 "Clearly it was just a great seduction record": Ben Sidran, interview, tape recording, 31 October 1999.

20 "For slow action, I put on *Kind of Blue*": Anthony Kiedis quoted in "What's Your Favorite Make Out Music?" *Jane* (September, 1998).

20 "The trance-like atmosphere": Donald Fagen, interview, tape recording, 5 November 1999.

20 "I will confess that I spent many memorable evenings": Pearl Cleage, "Mad at Miles," *Miles Davis Companion* (London: Schirmer Books, 1996), 214.

THE BIRTH OF THE TONE: MILES 1949–1955

25 "I prefer a round sound": Davis interview by Quincy Troupe, tape recording, Studio Museum in Harlem, New York City, 6 May 1989.

25 "Now's the Time": All recordings mentioned prior to the early fifties were originally single 78 rpm releases and are listed in text simply by song title; recordings after 1951 note album as well.

"Now's the Time" was first issued as a 78 on the Savoy label and is now available on *The Immortal Charlie Parker*, as listed in the discography. Tip of the fedora to Seth Rothstein for reminding me of this particular Miles solo.

25 "Almost like an invitation": Miles Davis with Quincy Troupe, *Miles: The Autobiography* (New York: Simon & Schuster, 1989), 11.

25 "Miles is . . . more or less a late arriver": Bill Evans, interview by Bill Goldberg and Eddie Karp, tape recording, Fort Lee, NJ, WKCR-FM, 1979.

26 "I was in the sixth grade": Miles Davis, interview, "Miles Ahead," *Great Masterpieces*, Public Broadcasting System, 1986.

26 "St. Louis then was like a conservatory": Ibid.

26 "I spent my first week in New York": Davis, Miles, 52.

26 "Miles talks rough": Dizzy Gillespie quoted by Dan Morgenstern, liner notes to *Miles Davis Chronicle*, The Complete Prestige Recordings, PCD-012-2, 1987.

26 "He had that little cold exterior": Quincy Jones, interview.

27 "The shit they was talking about was too white for me": Davis, Miles, 52. Miles might have had other reasons to discontinue his studies, as a source close to Davis who prefers anonymity writes:

> "Miles was badly out of place at Juilliard. I've seen his 1944–1945 transcript, and he failed piano, theory, dictation, orchestra and chorus, although he started with an A in dictation and orchestra. His trumpet teacher William Vacchiano—first chair with the New York Philharmonic—gave him a B in his spring exam, after B-minuses earlier. In the 1945 summer session, Miles got a D in Elementary Sight-singing and a B in Elementary Dictation." (Letter to author.)

27 "I couldn't believe that": Davis, Miles, 61. Note must be made that many of these world-class jazz legends were in fact very attuned to classical music and stylistic elements, while Davis may simply have not been aware of their enthusiasm or interest.

27 "His taste was just world-class, innate": Quincy Jones, interview.

27 "The way he carried himself": McCoy Tyner, interview, tape recording, 10 November 1999.

27 "Composers Alban Berg, Bela Bartok": George Russell quoted by Burt Korall in original liner notes to *New York, N.Y.*, Impulse!, IMPD-278, 1998.

27 "modal jazz": Russell's composed introduction to Gillespie's 1947 recording "Cubana Be" is often hailed as one of the first conscious attempts at playing jazz based on modes, rather than chord changes. "The whole opening movement was in an auxiliary diminished

chord mode," recalled Russell. Russell, interview.

27 "We were very close friends": John Lewis, interview, tape recording, 19 November 1999.

28 "It was so bad I thought I'll go study dentistry": Miles Davis, interview by Steve Rowland, *Miles Davis Radio Project*, part 2 of 7, American Public Radio, 1990.

28 "I wanted to quit": Davis, interview, Studio Museum of Harlem.

28 "He said, "Bird told me": David Amram, interview, tape recording, 14 January 2000.

28 "Miles was quoted": Ibid.

29 "Now on that break that Bird made": Roy Porter, interview, *Miles Davis Radio Project*.

29 "I love Dizzy, but": Davis, Miles, 163.

29 "Davis's outlook": A majority of music historians hail the fifties as the most gilded era of small group jazz, and the backdrop to the birth of *Kind of Blue*. See Bibliography for a list of valuable sources describing the state of jazz during that creatively fertile decade.

29 "For the younger musicians": John Lewis quoted in Nat Hentoff, *The Jazz Life* (New York: Da Capo Press, 1961), 13.

29 "There was something about the times": Quincy Jones, interview.

30 "I first met Gil": Marc Crawford, "Portrait of a Friendship," *Down Beat* (February 16, 1961): 18. In his interest to provide an accurate transcription of "Donna Lee" for Thornhill's band (itself highly unusual as the bebop tune was not yet an accepted part of the jazz repertoire of the time), Evans needed not only Davis's permission to record the number, but his confirmation that the written arrangement was correct. Davis—already a fan of the Thornhill band—must have been pleasantly surprised and impressed by Evans's interest and attention to detail.

30 "The sound hung like a cloud": Gil Evans quoted in Mike Zwerin, "Birthday of the Cool," *Forbes* (November 15, 1999): 322.

30 "We wanted that sound but": Davis, Miles, 118.

31 "When I noticed Miles Davis": Mike Zwerin, liner notes to Miles Davis, *The Complete Birth of the Cool*, Capitol CDP 7243-4-94550-23, 1998.

31 "Unsure of how to be boss": Mike Zwerin, "A Most Curious Friendship," *Down Beat* (March 10, 1966): 18.

31 "Cracked the whip": Gerry Mulligan, original liner notes to Miles Davis, *The Complete Birth of the Cool*, Capitol CDP 7243-4-94550-23, 1998.

32 "Left to our own devices": Gerry Mulligan interview by Charles Fox, BBC 3, quoted by Ian Carr, *Miles Davis: The Definitive Biography* (New York: Thunder's Mouth Press, 1998), 50.

32 "[Duke] tells me I'm in his plans for the fall": Davis, Miles, 121.

33 "It was the same old story": Davis, Miles, 141. Years later, Gerry Mulligan validated Davis's take on the cool/hard-bop schism, recalling:

> I always felt that to a certain extent it was kind of a journalistic pigeon-holing that made this kind of polarization. I suppose it was later on that I realized that there was some reaction among the musicians themselves, some of whom resented the success of cool jazz in California, and that broke down into the white guys against the hard-blowing black guys in New York.
> —Gerry Mulligan quoted in Kenny Mathieson, "Cool Ruler," *The Wire* (November 1991): 28.

33 "I was never into": Ibid.,130.

33 "that was the beginning": Ibid., 132.

33 "I couldn't wait to tell Bird": Frank Morgan in *People* (1987), quoted by Joel Lewis, "Junk Bonds," *The Wire* (October 1991): 24–26.

34 "couldn't buy a job anywhere": Davis, Miles, 163.

34 "Some thought he was playing saxophone on the level of Bird": Ibid., 134.

35 "Miles was knocked out by Coltrane's playing": Joe Theimer, letter, 1946, quoted in Lewis Porter, *John Coltrane: His Life and Music* (Ann Arbor: The University of Michigan Press, 1998), 50.

35 "I wanted to use two tenors": Davis, Miles, 155. According to Lewis Porter's Coltrane chronology, the date of this unusual two-tenor engagement is thought to be March 11, 1951 (not 1952 as *Miles: The Autobiography* alleges.) See Porter, 348.

35 "He's a trickster": Jimmy Cobb, interview by Mark Masterson and author, videocassette, TV documentary-in-progress, 13 November 1999.

35 "He played nice ballads": Jimmy Cobb, interview, tape recording, May 1999.

35 "Miles and I had been barnstorming": Philly Joe Jones, quoted in Ken Vail, *Miles' Diary: The Life of Miles Davis 1947–1961* (London: Sanctuary Publishing Limited, 1996), 53.

36 "He knocked me out": Davis, Miles, 178.

36 "Everybody bought his records": Bill Crow, interview, tape recording, 10 November 1999.

36 "When he did 'When Lights Are Low'": Ibid.

36 "Nodding out": Davis, Miles, 164.

37 "People started looking": Ibid., 163.

37 "I came back to New York in February 1954": Ibid., 174–5.

37 "The metallic Harmon mute": Ian Carr, *Miles Davis: The Definitive Biography* (New York: Thunder's Mouth Press, 1998), 81.

37 " 'Walkin'' is credited": The question of authorship of "Walkin'," whether written by Ammons,

Davis or Carpenter (who at one point also managed Ammons) is one obscured in the wash of time, and seems to be one that will remain unanswered.

38 "Beginning now, one passionate note": Martin Williams, *The Jazz Tradition* (New York: Oxford University Press, 1970), 190.

38 "I got J.J. Johnson and Lucky Thompson". Davis, *Miles*, 177.

Though Miles wrote that he chose Clarke over Blakey for the former's brushwork, no brushes are heard on either "Walkin'" or "Blue n'Boogie". Davis likely was thinking of a session three weeks earlier when Clarke used brushes on "Solar", "You Don't Know What Love Is" and "Love Me or Leave Me"."

38 "That record was a motherfucker man": Ibid.

40 "I asked Dizzy 'Why can't I play like you?'": Davis, interview, Studio Museum of Harlem.

40 "When you're not technically a virtuoso": Art Farmer quoted in Hentoff, *The Jazz Life*, 208.

40 "Listening to Miles": Cannonball Adderley, quoted in Ira Gitler, *Jazz Quarterly* (Summer, 1959): 203.

40 "Monk: When am I supposed to come in?": *Miles Davis Radio Project*. This dialogue has been included on various reissues of the material from this momentous 1954 Prestige Records session, most often under the title *Miles Davis and the Modern Jazz Giants*.

41 "He was an aggressive, innovative player": Davis, *Miles*, 134.

41 "Philly Joe was the fire": Ibid., 199.

42 "A very drunk Charlie Parker" – Session producer Ira Gitler maintains that though Parker drank heavily before the session, the saxophonist performed with full command when the tape rolled; the music confirms Gitler's contention.

42 "Red knew I liked Ahmad Jamal": Ibid., 190.

42 "Round Midnight": The proper title for the Monk classic-does it start with an apostrophe? does it include "about"?-has long been a mystery, and the loose, varied manner in which it has been used in song, album and book titles has only added to the confusion. Avakian explains the title of Miles's first album for Columbia:

> The word "about" does not appear in the lyric which Bernie Hanighen set to Thelonious Monk's melody. He wrote the words after the song had already been copyrighted as "Round About Midnight" (including the apostrophe), and the publisher insisted that I print the album title to conform with the copyright. Many musicians and fans still think it's an error or an affectation.
> —George Avakian, liner notes to *Miles Davis with John Coltrane: The Complete Columbia Recordings*. Columbia/Legacy C6K 6583, 2000.

That said, this book employs *'Round About Midnight* for the Miles album, "'Round Midnight" for the song, and an apostrophe in both.

42 "Miles played thrillingly": Jack Tracy, "Newport!" *Down Beat* (August 25, 1955): 24.

43 "The next time I saw him": Jack Tracy, interview, tape recording, 3 December 1999.

43 "Miles got a crazy idea": George Avakian interview by Mark Masterson and author, videocassette, TV documentary-in-progress, 13 November 1999.

43 "I said, 'If you can get a group together'": Ibid.

44 "Jack had more faith in Miles": Ibid.

49 "Miles called to say": Ibid.

49 "I could almost hear him playing": Davis, *Miles*, 193.

49 "I don't think we would've had Coltrane's": Bill Evans, interview.

50 "I wasn't excited": Davis, *Miles*, 195.

50 "I think the reason we didn't get along at first": Ibid.

50 "He is . . . able to really control": Dave Liebman quoted in Larry Fisher, *Miles Davis and David Liebman: Jazz Connections* (New York: The Edwin Mellen Press, Lewiston, 1996), 127.

50 "I recognized it in": Miles Davis, quoted in Ben Sidran, "Talking Jazz," in Carner, Gary, ed., *The Miles Davis Companion: Four Decades of Commentary* (New York: Omnibus Press, 1996), 188.

50 "On September 27": Most Davis and Coltrane biographies agree that Coltrane's official debut as a member of the Miles Davis quintet was in Baltimore in late September (the 27 or 28). Porter points out that as Davis had toured through Philadelphia earlier that summer and appeared with a local pick-up band (July 18–24), he may well have auditioned Coltrane at that time. See Porter, 352.

50 "Miles himself had not played": Nat Hentoff, "Jeri Southern, Miles Davis, Terry Gibbs; Birdland, NYC," *Down Beat* (November 30, 1955): 6.

50 "Faster than I could have imagined": Davis, *Miles*, 196.

50 "[Miles] said "come on down"": Avakian, interview by Masterson and author.

53 "In 1955, Columbia represented": Davis, *Miles*, 206.

INTERLUDE: COLUMBIA RECORDS

45 "I have this poster": Dave Brubeck, interview, tape recording, 29 February 2000.

45 "The long-playing record": "Lieberson Cities Col. Disk Sale Leadership," *Billboard* (December 23, 1957): 15.

45 "My Fair Lady": Much of this information was culled from Fredric Dannen, *Hit Men* (New York: Vintage Books, 1991), 60–61.

46 "With its development": "Lieberson Cities Col. Disk Sale Leadership," *Billboard* (December 23, 1957): 15.

46 "When you have the president of a company": Brubeck, interview.

46 "Before 1950 when I came on board": Mitch Miller, interview, tape recording, 7 December 1999.

46 "It was the first time a musician": Ibid.

46 "We're not going to second guess you": Mitch Miller quoted in Ted Fox, *In The Groove, The People Behind The Music* (New York: St. Martin's Press, 1986), 52.

47 "Columbia had originally hired Avakian": Avakian adds:

My hiring in 1940 was to produce the first-ever reissues, both in albums [78 rpm multi-disc collections] and singles–Hot Jazz Classics: The Original Recordings that Made Jazz History. *And when I returned from the Pacific [Theatre in World War II], I was hired as an all-around pop producer but the following year was put in charge of both Pop Albums (a new department, anticipating LP) and International: two jobs nobody was interested in at the time, but which became the company's biggest money-producers a few years after the LP. (Avakian, letter to author.)*

47 "The catalog was doing incredibly well": George Avakian, liner notes to *The Birth of the Third Stream*, Columbia/Legacy 64929, 1996. Avakian describes a general creative license wherein all profit-making departments enjoyed the same degree of freedom: "The money was rolling in and neither Mitch nor I had any problem about how each of us spent our separate budget dollars." (Avakian, letter to author)

47 "A widening public for jazz may result": Robert A. Perlongo, "Jazz in 1959", *Metronome* (February, 1959): 16.

47 "These styles weren't vying": Barry Ulanov, interview, tape recording, 22 November 1999.

48 "You have to imagine the setting": Quincy Jones, interview.

48 "He said 'I thought you were in charge of jazz'": Avakian, interview by Masterson and author.

48 "Jazz was never thought about": Ibid.

THE QUINTET, THE SEXTET, AND THE RISE OF MODAL JAZZ

57 "When I first joined Miles in 1955": Coltrane quoted in *Jazz News* (December 27, 1961): 13.

57 "I was playing my horn": Davis, Miles, 198.

57 "Nobody knew what to expect": Sy Johnson quoted in Porter, 99.

57 "The intricacy of the linkage": Ralph J. Gleason, *Celebrating the Duke: And Louis, Bessie, Billie, Bird, Carmen, Miles, Dizzy and Other Heroes* (New York: Da Capo Press, 1995), 137.

58 "The Louis Armstrong Hot Five": Bob Weinstock quoted in Joe Goldberg, *Jazz Masters of the 50s* (New York: The MacMillan Company, 1965), 76.

58 "All the tremendous cohesion": Ralph Gleason, *Down Beat* (September 19, 1957): 25.

59 "Davis got into a yelling match": Davis, Miles, 202.

59 "his hoarse rasp": Avakian adds: "Miles used to emphasize the rasp for effect, especially in his later years. A couple of times when he did it in front of somebody, he'd turn to me and wink." (Letter to author.)

60 "Miles was an icon": McCoy Tyner, interview.

60 "Kind of guru for a lot of people": Herbie Hancock, interview, tape recording, 23 November 1999.

60 "In the fifties": Bill Cosby interview, "Miles Ahead," *Great Masterpieces*, 1986.

60 "Not only in music": Hugh Masekela, interview, tape recording, 27 November 1999.

60 "There were guys walking around": Cobb, interview by Masterson and author.

60 "I had to play a solo": Quincy Jones, interview.

61 "'With the Italian suits'": George Avakian, liner notes to *Miles Davis with John Coltrane: The Complete Columbia Recordings*, Columbia/Legacy C6K-65833, 2000.

61 "When 'Round About Midnight came out": Ibid.

61 "I was very fond of the Miles Davis nonet recordings": Avakian, interview by Masterson and author.

62 "Miles came and listened": George Avakian, liner notes to *The Birth of the Third Stream*, Columbia/Legacy 64929, 1996.

62 "I don't keep any of my records": Miles Davis, "Self Portrait," *Down Beat* (March 6, 1958): 47. Though Miles would alter his opinions of what his favorite recordings were over the years, most scholars believe he was referring to his first date as a leader (on which Parker played tenor saxophone). The date was August 14, 1947, the record label Savoy and the group a quintet—including John Lewis (piano), Nelson Boyd (bass), and Max Roach (drums)—that recorded "Milestones" (a Lewis original), "Little Willie Leaps," "Half Nelson" and "Sippin' at Bells."

62 "I had told [Miles and Gil]": Avakian, interview by Masterson and author.

62 "*Miles Ahead* had the right level of sophistication": Avakian adds:

Miles unexpectedly chose to play fluegelhorn on Miles Ahead, *the only album he ever played it on and a decision I never asked him about. [Miles credits Clark Terry for first introducing him to the instrument while still in St. Louis, in* Auto-biography, *44.] Sometimes he seemed to be not at home with it, like on "Springsville" and "I Don't Wanna Be Kissed (By Anyone But You)," but I decided not to suggest that it might be easier if he played some passages on trumpet. Even before*

Miles Ahead, *I have always felt that the solo part written by John Lewis for fluegelhorn that Miles played on "Three Little Feelings" (from* The Birth of the Third Stream*] may have encouraged Miles to still greater refinement in his trumpet playing. He had a more delicate sound on [fluegelhorn,] even uptempo.* (Avakian, letter to author.)

63 "Limp whimpering and fumbling uncertainty": John S. Wilson, "Promising Jazz Talents Fulfilled," *New York Times* (January 12, 1958).

63 "You have to keep in mind": Orrin Keepnews, interview, tape recording, December 1999.

63 "They were running up tabs at the bar": Davis, Miles, 212.

63 "On April 28": Vail, 97.

63 "As much as I loved Sonny": Ibid., 216.

64 "I had two things in mind": Adderley, quoted in Gitler, *Jazz Quarterly*, 201.

64 "Miles hired me essentially": Cannonball Adderley, interview by Jack Winter, tape recording, KCFR-FM, Denver, 1972. Reel-to-reel copies of Winter's interviews with a variety of jazz artists—most from the early seventies—are now housed at the Institute of Jazz Studies, Rutgers University, Newark, New Jersey.

64 "I had this idea in my head": Davis, Miles, 217.

64 "*Ascenseur*": Malle's first feature was released in the U.S. under the title *Frantic*, and in England as *Lift to the Gallows*.

65 "He said, 'Wait a minute'": Kenny Clarke, quoted in Vail, 108.

65 "By the time he came back": Adderley, interview.

66 "I felt I learned from him in every way": John Coltrane, "Coltrane on Coltrane," *Down Beat* (September 29, 1960): 27.

66 "Sheets of sound": Ira Gitler in liner notes to John Coltrane, *Soultrane*, Prestige 7142.

66 "On returning . . . I found Miles": Ibid.

66 "Coltrane's words": Much of the information that follows regarding modal jazz was culled from a variety of written sources (see Bibliography), as well as conversations with Bob Belden, jazz bandleader and reissue specialist, and Suzanne Eggleston, Public Services Librarian, Yale University Library, New Haven, Connecticut.

67 "Bebop's discipline means": Adderley, interview.

67 "When Gil wrote the arrangement": Miles Davis quoted in Nat Hentoff, "An Afternoon with Miles Davis," *The Jazz Review* (December 1958): 11–12.

68 "It's like a structured cadenza": Dick Katz, interview, tape recording, 17 November 1999.

68 "Leonard Bernstein wanted me to give him": Avakian, interview by Masterson and author.

68 "Playing changes was the sign of elegance": Ben Sidran, interview, tape recording, 31 October 1999.

69 "When I asked him in the forties": Russell, interview.

69 "I felt that Miles was saying": Ibid.

69 "In most jazz pieces": Porter, 160.

69 "I think that was a happy development": Ulanov, interview.

70 "One day when Miles came back": Gil Evans, interview by Bill Goldberg and Ed Karp, tape recording, WKCR-FM, New York City, 1979.

70 "Coltrane said the reason": Jimmy Heath, interview, tape recording, 8 February 2000.

70 "A detail of a photograph" (caption): Identification of these scales was made with the assistance of Bob Belden and Lewis Porter, and by consulting an in-depth analysis of "Flamenco Sketches" in Barry Dean Kernfeld, *Adderley, Coltrane and Davis at the Twilight of Bebop: The Search for Melodic Coherence*, Ph.D. thesis, Cornell University (1981): 137–144. It should be noted that Evans's tabulature does not necessarily reflect the order of scales as performed by the soloists on *Kind of Blue*.

71 "A lot of the scalar material": Joe Zawinul, interview, tape recording, 26 January 2000.

71 "I knew about some of those primary modes": David Amram, interview.

71 "Egyptian minor scales": Davis, Miles, 64.

71 "I want [my solos] to cover as many forms of music": "Coltrane on Coltrane," 27.

71 "In the early fifties": Joe Zawinul, interview.

72 "We were just leaning toward": Davis quoted by Ben Sidran, *Miles Davis Companion*, 190.

72 "We were trying to incorporate": McCoy Tyner, interview.

72 "At that time, Bill sounded": Bill Crow, interview.

74 "The music we heard at home was Khatchaturian": Frances Taylor Davis, interview, tape recording, 9 November 2000.

74 "He would usually play classical music": Peri Cousins quoted in Peter Pettinger, *Bill Evans: How My Heart Sings* (New Haven: Yale University Press, 1998), 24.

74 "Coltrane and I call it the 'implied reference'": Adderley, quoted in Gitler, *Jazz Quarterly*, 203.

76 "This was the first record": Davis, Miles, 225.

77 "We used to go to Philadelphia": Adderley, interview.

78 "When he had to fill a spot in the band": Cobb, interview.

78 "One night I looked up": Bill Evans, interviewed by Brian Hennessey, "Along Came Bill," BBC Radio, 1990, quoted in Pettinger, 25.

78 "We got in my Volkswagen": George Russell, interview by Bill Goldberg and Eddie Karp, tape recording, WKCR-FM, New York City, 1979.

78 "Bill had this quiet fire": Davis, Miles, 226.

78 "I played with [Miles] once": Elvin Jones, interview.

78 "Philly Joe had drawn up": Adderley, interview.

79 "When I first got the call from Miles": Cobb, interview.

82 "Little Foot Right Out": Avakian adds: *"Fran-Dance' is not really an original; Miles lifted it from "Put Your Little Foot,'" which comes from a lyric somebody put to an old central European waltz tune which I have always known as "The Varsoviana," which suggests Poland as its country of origin. Lehman Engel used a recording of "Varsouviana" (it can be spelled many ways and often is) extensively in the original stage production of* A Streetcar Named Desire, *for which I was in charge of the jazz background.* (Avakian, letter to author.)

82 "Miles occasionally might say": Bill Evans, interview.

83 "Paul Chambers and Jimmy Cobb": Bill Evans, interviewed by Sy Johnson, quoted in Pettinger, 57.

83 "Especially when he started": Cannonball Adderley, "Paying Dues," *Jazz Review* (May 1960): 15.

83 "I like the piano player to stroll": Adderley, quoted in Gitler, *Jazz Quarterly*, 204.

85 "His status as a racial minority": Pettinger, 62.

85 "Miles made him uncomfortable": Adderley, interview.

85 "You got to make it with everybody": Davis, Miles, 226.

85 "I'd like to please everyone": Ibid.

85 "It was more of an issue with the fans": Paul Wilner, "Jazz Pianist: Life on the Upbeat," *New York Times* (September 25, 1977).

85 "Bill put in his notice": Adderley, interview.

85 "Miles hired Red back": Ibid.

85 "Bill is a fine pianist": Adderley, *Jazz Review*, 15.

86 "He said Bill was really the guy": David Liebman quoted in Larry Fisher, 137.

INTERLUDE: 30TH STREET STUDIO

75 "Acoustically one of the finest recording spaces": John Hammond, *John Hammond On Record: An Autobiography* (New York: Penguin Books, 1977), 217.

75 "30th Street Studio was a hundred feet": Frank Laico, interview, tape recording, 12 November 1999.

75 "30th Street was in operation": Miller, interview.

76 "It had something you don't find": Mike Berniker, interview, tape recording, 10 November 1999.

77 "I used to record down": Quincy Jones, interview.

77 "There wasn't any metal in there": Berniker, interview.

77 "Teo Macero, who was first hired": George Avakian says, "I hired Macero, but not for A&R. I brought him in to replace Cal Lampley [in 1957], who I wanted to switch from the engineering department's [crew of] score-reading classical tape editors. Teo then replaced Cal a second time, coming into the A&R department when I brought Cal to Warner [Brothers Records]." (Letter to author.)

77 "All the engineers were top notch": Interview with Teo Macero, May, 1999. Avakian adds: Fred Plaut and Harold "Chappie" Chapman should be credited as the engineers who established the 30th Street sound." (Letter to author.)

77 "All of us [engineers]": Frank Laico, interview.

FIRST SESSION

91 "successive departures of George Avakian . . . and Cal Lampley": Avakian explains further: *After I left [Columbia Records] there was no longer a Pop Album department. The album and single departments joined and Mitch Miller became the titular head of all Pop A&R. I went to Warner Brothers [Records] to become the company's first A&R director . . . Lampley left [Columbia] to join me at Warners; I later took him with me to RCA.* (Avakian, letter to author.)

91 "Townsend . . . joined Columbia as an advertising copywriter": George Avakian, interview, tape recording, 7 March 2000.

92 "What stands out": Brubeck, interview.

92 "Brubeck beat the shit": Bob Waller, interview, tape recording, 18 November 1999.

93 " . . . and the *Kind of Blue* session was no exception": Avakian notes that the same creative license that brought forth *Miles Ahead* was still enjoyed by Townsend and Davis in 1959. "Townsend was free to let Miles do anything he wanted, and it was Miles who called the *Kind of Blue* shot all the way. Obviously, it did not originate with anyone else." (Letter to author.)

93 "He said, "Cal, I'm sitting": Cal Lampley, interview, tape recording, 5 November 1999.

93 "Frances [Taylor] was dancing": Davis, Miles, 229.

94 "You know, I was playing after Philly Joe": Cobb, interview by Masterson and author.

95 "The call I got from Miles for that record": Ibid.

95 "Had already planned that album": Davis, Miles, 233.

95 "Wynton used to come": Cobb, interview by

Masterson and author.

96 "I remember Miles": Cobb, interview.

96 "Miles conceived these settings": Bill Evans, original liner notes to *Kind of Blue*, Columbia/Legacy, CK 64935.

96 "We had played ['So What']": Jimmy Cobb, liner notes to *Miles Davis with John Coltrane: The Complete Columbia Recordings*, Columbia Legacy, C6K 65833.

96 "I wrote it in 4/4": Miles Davis quoted by Ralph Gleason, "Composed for 6 Months, Then Made Tune a Waltz," *San Francisco Chronicle* (June 20, 1959).

98 "It was the first time Miles recorded": Bill Evans, interview.

98 "Some people went around saying": Davis, Miles, 234.

98 "'Blue in Green'": Miles Davis, interviewed by Quincy Troupe, tape recording, 12 December 1986. This tape and other original recordings made by Troupe that resulted in the writing of *Miles: The Autobiography* now reside in the permanent sound recording division of the Schomburg Center for Research in Black Culture, The New York Public Library, 515 Malcolm X Boulevard, New York, NY, 10037.

98 "One colleague recalled being told by Evans": Herb Wong, quoted in Pettinger, 83.

98 "Evans's approach to the piano": Miles Davis quoted by Ben Sidran, *Miles Davis Companion*, 190.

98 "You play 'Confirmation'": Adderley, interview.

98 "I think, on the part": Dick Katz, interview.

98 "Wanted the music this new group": Davis, Miles, 220.

99 "He was prolific": Teo Macero, interview, tape recording, May 1999.

99 "Oh fuck you": Ibid.

99 "A composer-musician-performer": Teo Macero, quoted in Gregg Hall, "Teo . . . the Man Behind the Scene," *Down Beat* (July 18, 1974): 13.

99 "It could have been done on a napkin": Bob Belden, conversation with author, 2 December 1999.

99 "Like 'Freddie Freeloader'": Bill Evans, interview.

99 "I didn't write out the music": Davis, Miles, 234.

99 "Mostly he would just say": Cobb, interview.

99 "Miles ran over the charts": Bill Evans, interview.

100 "Normally you get a cartload of tapes": Mark Wilder, interview, tape recording, 31 January 2000.

101 "Our control room at that point": Laico, interview.

101 "To see each other": Cobb, interview.

101 "We would insist on a test": Laico, interview.

102 "Ever since about 1948": John Hammond quoted in "Talk of the Town," *The New Yorker* (July 17, 1954): 17.

102 "Just a bit of sweetening": Laico, interview.

103 "I've recorded with Miles": J.J. Johnson quoted in Goldberg, *Jazz Masters of the 50s*, 76.

105 "The first complete performance": Bill Evans interview.

105 "Everything was a first take": Hancock, interview.

106 "He never told anyone what to play": Adderley, interview.

106 "He always projects a happy feeling": J. J. Johnson quoted in Gene Lees, "Focus on Wynton Kelly," *Down Beat* (January 3, 1962): 16.

106 "In fact, at one time": Wynton Kelly, quoted in Ibid.

106 "He could play behind a soloist": Davis, Miles, 233.

106 "I think Miles's blues solo": Bill Evans, interview.

106 "Fred absolutely had to turn": Laico, interview.

107 "Asked me what we were playing": Adderley quoted in Davis, Miles, 221.

107 "I want to be more flexible": "Coltrane on Coltrane," 27.

107 "Trane had an extremely light": Adderley, interview.

107 "Coltrane's playing has apparently": Don Gold, "Newport Jazz 1958," *Down Beat* (August 7, 1958): 16.

107 "We were strongly influenced": Adderley, interview.

110 "It made it possible": John Hammond, quoted in Fox, 24.

110 "[Splicing] was just a tool": Mitch Miller, quoted in Ibid., 41.

110 "On *Miles Ahead*": liner notes to Miles Davis and Gil Evans.

111 "We went to this performance": Davis, Miles, 225–6.

112 "I added some other kind of sound": Ibid., 234.

112 "But you write something": Ibid., 235.

112 "On 'So What'": Bill Evans, interview.

112 "Man, it sounds": Cobb, interview.

113 "It sounded like Miles": Hancock, interview.

115 "That's another thing": Ibid.

115 "When Miles comes in": Ibid.

116 "It's one of the most beautiful": Russell, interview.

116 "[Billie Holiday] sings way behind": Davis quoted in Hentoff, "An Afternoon with Miles Davis," *The Jazz Review*, 10.

116 "The only ones who were": Katz, interview.

117 "I listen to what Miles": Adderley quoted in *Jazz Quarterly*, 202.

117 "I'm thinking of the end": Hancock, interview.

118 "You can tell where it starts": Miles Davis, interview by Quincy Troupe, tape recording, 12

December 1986.

118 "One day at Miles's apartment": Bill Evans quoted in Conrad Silvert, liner notes to Bill Evans, *Spring Leaves*, Milestone M-47034, 1976.

118 "I was at [Café] Bohemia": Amram, interview.

119 "Exactly those chords": Pettinger, 82.

121 "If I was going to sit down": Gary Burton, interview, tape recording, 30 November 1999.

INTERLUDE: FREDDIE FREELOADER

104 "Freddie was from Philadelphia": Cobb, interview with Masterson and author.

104 "Freddie was kooky": Frances Taylor Davis, interview.

104 "I knew about Freddie": Hancock, interview.

106 "One day I run into Cannonball": Fred Tolbert, interview by Bill Goldberg and Ed Karp, tape recording, WKCR-FM, New York City, early summer 1979.

SECOND SESSION

125 "The reissues had always been done": Wilder, interview.

125 "We just really went in that day": Bill Evans, quoted in Lee Jeske, "Bill Evans, Trio Master," *Down Beat* (October, 1979): 19.

126 "At one of those late '58/early '59 Apollo shows": In the search for appropriate photographs for this book, I found two live shots of Miles with the same unique background: a distinctive, hand-drawn, palm-leaf pattern. One was taken by Chuck Stewart and one by Jay Maisel (the latter was part of the same series of color slides from which the *Kind of Blue* cover photo was taken). As Stewart knew his photo was taken at the Apollo Theater in late '58 or early '59, and as Maisel was not aware of the venue but recalled shooting Miles on more than one occasion at the Harlem venue, logic dictated that the cover of *Kind of Blue* depicted Miles in performance at the Apollo.

127 "[He] had told me": Nat Hentoff, interview, tape recording, 1 November 1999.

127 "It was at 56th Street": Cobb, interview.

127 "A Christmas tree on a plantation": Davis, quoted in Nat Hentoff, "A Letter to Timex—and others," *Metronome* (March, 1959): 43.

130 "A model for future tele-productions": Howard H. Prouty, ed., *Variety Television Reviews, 1923–1988* (New York: Garland Publishing Inc., 1988), 211.

130 "The purest, finest jazz": Charles Mercer, Associated Press, quoted in "Review and Preview," *Daily Variety* (July 22, 1960).

131 "April 22, 1959, 2:30 PM": The second session has been mistakenly reported as taking place on April 6, due perhaps to the fact that Columbia's stu-dio reservation log reports a Miles Davis session that day. After much research, I have concluded that entry was in fact a cancelled studio reservation; to date, no Miles Davis recordings from April 6, 1959, have been found. However, that studio log—plus all tape logs, mastering instructions and even the tape box containing the master reel of "Flamenco Sketches" and "All Blues"—reference April 22 as the accurate date of the second session.

131 "Laico mentions": Laico, interview.

132 "It was understood": this quote and all following credited to Don Hunstein, from Don Hunstein, interview, tape recording, 3 November 1999.

133 "He began playing the introduction": Pettinger, 68.

134 "I started to play": Bill Evans quoted in Jim Aikin, "Peace Piece," *Contemporary Keyboard* (June 1980): 46.

134 "That morning before": Bill Evans, interview.

134 "The modes used in 'Sketches'": Belden, conversation.

134 "Dizzy was the one": Amram, interview.

135 "It was as though they": Hancock, interview.

135 Bassist Frank Tate notes that in the third, B-flat Major 7 section of his solo, Evans quotes "Picnic", the popular movie theme from '55, a reworking of "Moonglow" composed by George Duning and Steve Allen.

136 "Someone should splice": Belden, conversation.

142 "When people play it": Jimmy Heath, interview, tape recording, 8 February 2000.

142 "An old traditional blues lick": Ibid.

142 "On 'All Blues', he said": Bill Evans, interview.

143 "I was fascinated with 'All Blues'": Maurice White, interview, tape recording, 26 January 2000.

143 "This ain't no blues": Davis, quoted in Amiri Baraka, "Miles Davis: One of the Great Motherfuckers," in Bill Kirchner, ed., *A Miles Davis Reader* (Washington D.C.: Smithsonian Institution Press, 1997), 67.

143 "It's essentially a blues": Fagen, interview. The introduction to Steely Dan's big hit from 1974, "Rikki Don't Lose That Number," directly copied from the propulsive, two-chord vamp that defines Horace Silver's 1964 hard bop classic "Song for My Father."

143 "It's just 'Milestones' in 3/4": Wallace Roney, interview, tape recording, 30 November 1999. The bass figure played by Chambers on "All Blues" echoes, in a slowed-down version, the characteristic syncopated horn-riff introduction to "Milestones," with both playing off intervals of thirds.

144 "On 'All blues'": Bill Evans, interview.

144 "What seems to go unnoticed": Amram, interview.

144 "Evans's technique of avoiding": Miles Davis, quoted in Ben Sidran, *Miles Davis Companion*, 190.

145 "There was a good feeling": Bill Evans, interview.

145 "Professionals have to go in": Ibid.

149 "Columbia was one of the few companies": Stanley Tonkel, interview, tape recording, 15 November 1999.

150 "Townsend handed Teo Macero *Kind of Blue* sometime early that summer": Both company records and individual memories are inexact in determining when this hand-off took place, which is of great significance since it also marked the beginning of Macero's long-running role as Davis's producer. Townsend undoubtedly produced the *Kind of Blue* sessions, while prior to *Sketches of Spain*, Macero was certainly involved with Davis's recording projects at Columbia, as he himself told *Down Beat*:

> After George [Avakian] left [Columbia Records in 1958], I worked with Irving Towsend, who was then my boss, and he was producing Miles's Kind of Blue . . . I was doing a lot of editing for Townsend at the time . . . I've been working with Miles since 1957–58, and I have been with him ever since.
> —Gregg Hall, "Teo . . . The Man Behind the Scene," *Down Beat* (July 18, 1974): 13.

150 Through the summer of 1959, Columbia's files reveal Macero's name slowly replacing Townsend's on all internal correspondence dealing with *Kind of Blue*. By mid-August, Macero appears to have been handling all matters relating to the album.

150 "I asked him specifically": Macero, interview.

151 "He wanted to connect": Quincy Troupe, interview, tape recording, 10 November 1999.

151 "He told me that many times": Ibid.

151 "Miles didn't care much about": Avakian, conversation with author, 22 February 2000.

151 "She was going around": Cobb, interview.

152 "Earlier in [Miles's] career": this quote and all following credited to S. Neil Fujita, from S. Neil Fujita, interview, tape recording, 5 November 1999.

152 "Why did you put that white bitch on there?": Davis quoted in Avakian, liner notes to Miles Davis and Gil Evans.

152 "I just got to thinking": Davis quoted in Alex Haley, "*Playboy* Interview: Miles Davis," *Playboy* (September, 1962): 61.

153 "Nobody in those days": Lampley, interview.

153 "*Suibokuga*": much of this information from Melanie Trede, Assistant Professor, Institute of Fine Arts, New York University, conversation with author, December 13, 1999.

153 "It was very much in the air": Gene Lees, interview, tape recording, 21 December 1999.

153 "There is a Japanese visual art": Bill Evans, original liner notes to *Kind of Blue*.

154 "*Jazz Track*'s "off-cycle" release": Stanley Kavan, interview, tape recording, 6 November 1999.

154 "You'd look at the expression": Lampley, interview.

155 "The French historian Andre Hodeir": Ibid.

155 "Miles was really the first cool artist": Kavan, interview.

155 "Miles was still early with us": Ibid.

156 "We had a very good list of jazz deejays": Ibid.

156 "I always had a head-start": Del Costello, interview, tape recording, 4 November 1999.

156 "I took it over to Pat Henry": Ibid.

157 "Jim Lang on KABC": Ibid.

157 "Every Sunday I devoted": Phil Elwood, interview, tape recording, 11 November 1999.

157 "I remember standing": Warren Bernhardt, interview, tape recording, 26 January 2000.

157 "Subdued stuff but nonetheless potent": Irving Kolodin, "*Miles Ahead* or Miles' Head?," *Saturday Review* (September 12, 1959): 61.

157 "Spotlight Winner": *Billboard* (August 31, 1959): 28.

157 "Fine ensemble playing": B.C., *Metronome* (October 1959): 29.

158 "This is a remarkable album": *Down Beat* (October 1, 1959): 28.

158 "This is one of Miles's great records": C. H. Garrigues, "Recapturing the Magic of Miles," *San Francisco Examiner* (October 11, 1959).

158 "The Enigma of Miles Davis": Barbara J. Gardner, "The Enigma of Miles Davis," *Down Beat* (January 7, 1960): 20.

158 "Evil Genius of Jazz": "Miles Davis: Evil Genius of Jazz," *Ebony* (January 1961): 69.

158 "Behind the cool indifference": Lionel Olay, "Miles Davis: Winner Take All," *Cavalier* (August 1964): 18.

159 "I ain't going to name": Davis, quoted in Haley, 66.

159 "He was one of the most": Lampley, interview.

159 "The greatest thing I learned": Masekela, interview.

159 "Never being involved": Bruce Lundvall, interview, tape recording, 4 November 1999.

159 "Macero even recalls imitating Miles's voice": Macero, interview.

159 "You could hear those *Kind of Blue* things": Kenny Barron, interview, tape recording, Sony Music *Kind of Blue* website, 19 December 1997.

159 "That was the one that I used to hear on the jukeboxes": Cobb, interview by Masterson and author.

160 "It affected everyone": Horn, interview.

160 "It was only much later": Cobb, interview.

160 "That is one of the striking characteristics": Quincy Jones, interview.

161 "I sit there and run over chord progressions": John Coltrane quoted in Nat Hentoff, original liner notes, John Coltrane, *Giant Steps*, Rhino 75203.

161 "The *Kind of Blue* thing": Cobb, interview by Masterson and author.

161 "When you get a group": Macero, interview.

163 "I told Miles, because he could obviously tell": Heath, interview.

163 "I heard the band": Ron Carter, interview, tape recording, Sony Music *Kind of Blue* website, 2 December 1997.

163 "I actually saw the *Kind of Blue* band": Burton, interview.

164 "Feeling on top of the world": Davis, Miles, 236.

164 "Boxers had told me": Ibid., 238.

165 "Frazzled horn": Emily Coleman, "Call it Bop or Cool, Progressive or Modern", Newsweek (February 29, 1960): 100.

166 "On the whole, Miles Davis": Martin Williams, *The Jazz Tradition*, 206. Thanks to Stanley Crouch for pulling my coattail to this astute observation by Williams at the start of the research process for this book.

166 "A friend of mine named Joe Montdragon": Davis, Miles, 241.

166 "La Nina de Los Peines": Avakian, liner notes, *Miles Davis and Gil Evans*.

166 "Everyone I knew had bullfight posters": Dan Wakefield, *New York in the 50s* (New York: St. Martin's Press, 1992), 300.

166 "I remember asking Joe Bennett": Crow, interview.

167 "After we finished working on *Sketches of Spain*": Davis, Miles, 244.

167 "I got in and there was a circular bar": Bernhardt, interview.

168 "It was the magic of hearing": Ibid.

168 "Miles, playing them every night": Cobb, interview by Masterson and author.

169 "The reason I play so many sounds": John Coltrane, interview by Carl-Erik Lindgren, tape recording, Stockholm, Sweden, 22 March 1960. Note: this interview has been reproduced on various import albums featuring live performances by the Miles Davis group from the same date.

170 "He would say": Heath, interview.

170 "So I picked up Jimmy": Davis, Miles, 249.

170 "Miles surprised me": Bob Dawbarn, "Miles Davis is a Genius," *Melody Maker* (October 1, 1960): 3.

170 "It was the very first week": Masekela, interview.

170 "I bought it": Ibid.

171 "The presence of more conventional": Bob Blumenthal, liner notes, Miles Davis, *Miles Davis at Carnegie Hall*, Columbia/Legacy, C2K 65027.

THE LEGACY OF BLUE

177 "Do you listen to records?": Davis, quoted in Stephen Davis, "My Ego Only Needs a Good Rhythm Section," in *Miles Davis Companion*, 164.

177 "'So What' or *Kind of Blue*": Davis, quoted in Sidran, Miles Davis Companion, 196.

177 "As far as I'm concerned": Orrin Keepnews, interview, tape recording, 23 December 1999.

177 "I remember musicians": Katz, interview.

177 "Attention has settled around": John Benson Brooks, "George Russell," *Jazz Review* (February 1960): 38.

178 "These three artists": Goldberg, *Jazz Masters of the Fifties*, 81.

178 "*Kind of Blue* [was] one of the most": Williams, *The Jazz Tradition*, 209.

178 "Pulling an incredible history": Quincy Jones, interview.

178 "I don't like to hear someone": Pat Harris, "Nothing But Bop? 'Stupid,' Says Miles," *Down Beat* (January 27, 1950): 18.

178 "If you like *Kind of Blue*": Sidran, interview.

179 "It wasn't just one tune": Burton, interview.

179 "By the time I came to Berklee": Ibid.

179 "It presented a doorway": Hancock, interview.

179 "Once the record came out": Macero, interview.

179 "I had mentioned a Coltrane": Fagen, interview.

179 "I was really an amateur player": Ibid.

180 "It had gotten to be where musicians": Keepnews, interview.

180 "Everybody started playing": Adderley, interview. Regarding the immediate filtering of scalar forms— such as the Lydian mode—into the jazz vanguard of the early sixties, pianist Brad Mehldau adds:

> Coltrane, Herbie, Wayne Shorter and others picked up where Kind of Blue *left off, which meant, briefly, to write in a modal fashion, but not just one or two chords—Hancock's "Little One" from [Miles Davis's 1965 album]* E.S.P., *for example, or Wayne Shorter's "Mahjong" from [his 1964 album]* JuJu. *Modal harmony finds its way into those compositions, but here's movement again. The movement from chord to chord, though, is significantly different. It's not only limited to the five-one relationships found in bebop. A functional 'one' or tonal center may wind up being in the Lydian mode. The new melodic approach is freed accordingly, thus the flowering of new blowing styles— Wayne Shorter, Herbie Hancock, Joe Henderson, Freddie Hubbard, Woody Shaw, et al.*

—Brad Mehldau, email to author, June 15, 2000

180 "Donald Byrd for a Blue Note record": Heath, interview.
180 "We wanted to experiment": Ibid.
180 "What I do recall": Keepnews, interview.
181 "I wrote many modal pieces": Zawinul, interview.
181 "We were in Detroit": Ibid.
181 "When I composed": Ibid.
181 "Let me tell you something": Zawinul, interview.
182 "[Coltrane's] "So What" solo": Lewis Porter, liner notes, *John Coltrane: The Heavyweight Champion: The Complete Atlantic Recordings*, Rhino R2 71984, 1996.
182 "This piece is built, during several measures": Francois Postif, "John Coltrane: Une Interview," *Jazz Hot*, January 1962, 12–14, quoted in Porter, 182. Much of the information regarding Coltrane's musical evolution during the sixties—including his use of modal foundations to *Impressions, A Love Supreme* and *Ascension*—is derived from Porter's comments in chapters 14–19 of his book.
182 "What John began to do": Adderley, interview.
182 "[Free players] are playing": Ibid.
183 "A lot of free players": Heath, interview.
183 "Most timelines': If Ornette signalled the breakthrough of free jazz in 1959, Lennie Tristano and Lee Konitz's 1949 recordings of "Intuition" and "Digression" (most recently reissued on the Blue Note CD *Intuition*, 52771, 1996; see Discography) mark the first breaths of experimenting with spontaneous free forms in jazz performance. Much thanks to Howard Mandel for sharing his valuable insights on free jazz in general, and Ornette in particular.
185 "*Kind of Blue* was a nice": Zawinul, interview.
185 "Cannonball, and most of the guys": Keepnews, interview.
185 "Everybody was there": Paul Bley, quoted in Francis Davis, "Out Front When Jazz Freed Itself," *New York Times* (February 13, 2000).
185 "Miles always played": Zawinul, interview.
185 "My phrasing is spontaneous": Ornette Coleman, quoted in Joe Goldberg, 243.
185 "You have some kind of form": Davis, quoted in Les Tomkins, "Miles Davis Talking," *Crescendo* (December 1969): 22.
186 "Maybe a guy wants to play out of key": Davis quoted by John Ephland, "Miles to Go," *Down Beat* (October 1988): 19.
186 "You can play sharp in tune": Coleman, quoted in Williams, *The Jazz Tradition*, 239.
186 "[I'd] rather hear a guy": Davis, quoted in Nat Hentoff, "Miles," *Down Beat* (November 2, 1955): 13.
186 "From realizing I can make mistakes": Coleman quoted by Williams, original liner notes, Ornette

Coleman, *The Shape of Jazz to Come*, Atlantic 1317–2.
186 "At first, Miles's post–*Kind of Blue* narrative": As to the respective post–*Kind of Blue* paths pursued by Miles and Bill Evans, pianist Brad Mehldau offers a perceptive overview:

I've always felt that Evans's and Miles's approach on this record [was] a one-time affair, something that was an end in itself. In a simple, reductive sense, as a soloist, there's not too much more you can do than Miles if you decide to stay within the mode, on a tune that only uses one mode in two different keys. And good luck on approaching that level of lyricism, melody, and phrasing.

Evans's case is interesting because he didn't pursue a strictly modal approach by any means after this date with his own trio. He was much more concerned with functional harmony. The melodic approach that he honed down over the years came from bebop—his own, highly personal take of bebop. His deepness and beauty (for me) is how he harmonizes those melodies with both hands, creating a rich, multidimensional texture on the piano—I'm thinking of a late record like "You Must Believe in Spring," for example. He returned to melodic voice-leading, but upped the ante.

—Mehldau, email to author

186 "It's this preoccupation": Bill Evans, interview by Len Lyons, tape recording, probably mid-seventies. Lyons's audio cassettes containing interviews with various jazz pianists—many of which were used in the writing of *The Great Jazz Pianists*, Da Capo Press, New York, 1983—are now housed at the Institute of Jazz Studies, Rutgers University, Newark, New Jersey.
187 "Most iconoclasts are contributors": Ibid.
187 "That album was really": Quincy Jones, interview.
187 "I've always felt that": Amram, interview.
187 "What I used to play": Davis, quoted in Mark Rowland, "A Life in Four Scenes," *Musician* (December 1991): 58.
187 "Name me some music": Hancock, interview.
187 "Duane Allman": Robert Palmer, liner notes, Miles Davis, *Kind of Blue*, Columbia/Legacy CK64935, 1997.
187 "Ray Manzarek": Alan Paul, "The Doors of Perception," *Revolver* (spring 2000): 73.
188 "Andy Sommers": Vic Garbarini, "60 Minutes with Andy" *Guitar World* (November 1997): 83.
188 "John Popper": Rolling Stone *Raves: What Your Rock & Roll Favorites Favor* (New York: William Morrow and Company, Inc., 1999), 98.
188 "In the early sixties": Fagen, interview.
188 "One of the things": Sidran, interview.
188 "Was hanging out": Alfred Ellis, interview, tape

recording, May 1999. Thanks to Harry Weinger of Universal Music for the tip on Ellis's creative use of "So What."

188 "The night before this one session": Ibid.

189 "I love James Brown": Davis, interview, Studio Museum of Harlem.

189 "[Miles] re-borrowed": Wallace Roney, interview, tape recording, 30 November 1999.

189 "I hear it in a whole": Crow, interview.

189 "Most of the songs": Jason Moran, interview, tape recording, 10 April 2000.

189 "Root Progression": Ibid.

189 "Some of the approaches": Mehldau, email to author.

190 *Kind of Blue* is where younger": Crow, interview.

190 "All you had to do": Adderley, interview.

190 "A big hunk of jazz": Katz, interview.

190 "I don't like guys": Davis, quoted in Ephland, 17–18.

190 "We need both simple tunes": Burton, interview.

190 "I saw those tunes": Ibid.

190 "Taking stock of the recorded interpretations": General information on recorded versions of *Kind of Blue* material came from a wide variety of sources, including: Broadcast Music Inc. (a BMI composer from the start, Davis's publishing is still represented by the performing rights organization); Sony/ATV, the music publisher that co-owns Musical Frontiers, Inc., Miles's publishing company; Shukat, Arrow, Hafer & Weber, LLP, who have represented Miles's business interests—under the rubric of Miles Davis Properties—since his passing. Further information was culled from such published and online databases as All Music Guide, CD Now and Muze.

191 "When Bill recorded": Keepnews, interview.

191 "Why don't you come": Horn, interview.

191 "Each song on that record": Carter, interview, *Kind of Blue* website.

192 "What's that supposed to be?" Davis, quoted in Leonard Feather, "Blindfold Test," *Down Beat* (June 18, 1964): 31.

193 "I was in a United Airlines plane": Oscar Brown, Jr., interview, tape recording, 11 March 2000.

193 "I had a conversation": Ibid. Brown's allusions to the two other jazz musicians refer to his lyrical versions of Nat Adderley's "Work Song" and Bobby Timmons's "Dat Dere."

194 "It averages five to seven thousand [copies sold]": Tommy LiPuma, interview, tape recording, 5 November 1999.

194 "Since 1959, the album's sales trajectory": As mentioned, current sales information on *Kind of Blue* is the result of forty years's worth of estimates gleaned from various sources, mostly from Columbia Records' own files, which often did not factor in data from important distribution channels like their own mail order branch, Columbia House. With the advent of such independent electronic tracking services as SoundScan in the '80s, accurate and complete reporting of music sales is closer to being achieved. The current keeper of information on *Kind of Blue*'s historic market performance is Tom Cording, Head Publicist, Sony Legacy, whom I thank for his diligence and for sharing the results of his research. As he pointed out, because of the many unreported sources of sales, it would seem the quoted figures are at best an underestimate of *Kind of Blue*'s aggregate sales.

196 "In the late fifties and sixties": Steve Berkowitz, interviewed by Mark Masterson and author, video-cassette, TV documentary-in-progress, 13 November 1999.

197 "So it's 1992": Ibid.

197 "Sony is a corporation": Ibid.

198 "Miles Davis's True 'Blue,'": Bradley Bambarger, "Miles Davis's True 'Blue,'" *Billboard* (August 7, 1999): 1.

EPILOGUE

200 *Shibui*": William Graves, "Keepers of Japan's Past," *National Geographic* (June, 1976): 844.

200 "When he plays": Davis, *Miles Davis Radio Project*.

Index